The
W

Dear Valued Customer,

We realize you're a busy professional with deadlines to hit. Whether your goal is to learn a new technology or solve a critical problem, we want to be there to lend you a hand. Our primary objective is to provide you with the insight and knowledge you need to stay atop the highly competitive and ever-changing technology industry.

Wiley Publishing, Inc., offers books on a wide variety of technical categories, including security, data warehousing, software development tools, and networking — everything you need to reach your peak. Regardless of your level of expertise, the Wiley family of books has you covered.

- For Dummies® – The *fun* and *easy* way™ to learn
- The Weekend Crash Course® –The *fastest* way to learn a new tool or technology
- Visual – For those who prefer to learn a new topic *visually*
- The Bible – The *100% comprehensive* tutorial and reference
- The Wiley Professional list – *Practical* and *reliable* resources for IT professionals

The book you hold now, *Streaming Media: Building and Implementing a Complete Streaming System* provides anyone who must design, develop, and implement a streaming media system with what they need to know to get started streaming content. Whether you are a software engineer, network engineer, webmaster, systems engineer, network administrator, multimedia specialist, or web programmer, this book will jumpstart your experience. It will also help you choose audio and video equipment, capture and edit, and set up a streaming site. An added bonus, the CD-ROM will include the author's streaming software package that will allow you to configure, monitor, and manage a live encoded media stream.

Our commitment to you does not end at the last page of this book. We'd want to open a dialog with you to see what other solutions we can provide. Please be sure to visit us at www.wiley.com/compbooks to review our complete title list and explore the other resources we offer. If you have a comment, suggestion, or any other inquiry, please locate the "contact us" link at www.wiley.com.

Finally, we encourage you to review the following page for a list of Wiley titles on related topics. Thank you for your support and we look forward to hearing from you and serving your needs again in the future.

Sincerely,

Richard K. Swadley

Richard K. Swadley
Vice President & Executive Group Publisher
Wiley Technology Publishing

15 HOUR WEEKEND CRASH COURSE

V™
Visual

Bible

DUMMIES

WILEY
Wiley Publishing, Inc.

more information
on related titles

Streaming Media

Building and Implementing a Complete Streaming System

Gregory C. Demetriades

Wiley Publishing, Inc.

Executive Publisher: Bob Ipsen
Executive Editor: Carol A. Long
Editorial Manager: Kathryn A. Malm
Developmental Editor: Alex Miloradovich
Managing Editor: Vincent Kunkemueller
New Media Editor: Brian Snapp
Text Design & Composition: Wiley Composition Services

This book is printed on acid-free paper. ∞

Published by Wiley Publishing, Inc., Indianapolis, Indiana

Published simultaneously in Canada

For general information on our other products and services please contact our Customer Care Department within the United States at (800) 762-2974, outside the United States at (317) 572-3993 or fax (317) 572-4002.

Wiley also publishes its books in a variety of electronic formats. Some content that appears in print may not be available in electronic books.

Library of Congress Cataloging-in-Publication Data:

ISBN: 0-471-20950-3

Printed in the United States of America

10 9 8 7 6 5 4 3 2 1

CONTENTS

ACKNOWLEDGMENTS

First, I would like to extend my gratitude to my family and friends. They have been extraordinary in sharing their individual praise of my achievements throughout my life and in supporting me in this opportunity to become an author with such a reputable publishing house as Wiley Technology Publishing.

I also would like to thank Wiley Technology Publishing for making it possible for me to become an author and to share my knowledge and experience. I want to thank Carol Long, my acquisitions editor, for introducing me to this opportunity and for allowing me latitude in the writing of this book. I would like especially to thank Alex Miloradovich, my development editor, and Kathryn Malm, the Editorial Manager at Wiley, for their ongoing support.

This book would not have been completed without the assistance of my personal assistant, Johanna Jimenez, who spent many hours helping me with the workflow.

Next, I would like to thank Fred Bonner of IBM Global Services, and Pete Hulme and Andy Norman of Sagitta Performance Systems for contributing information on asset and storage content management and distribution. I also would like to thank both Scott Labrozzi and John Bishop of ViewCast Corp for sharing their knowledge of audio and video capturing; Chuck Fuller of Virage, Inc., for assisting me with audio and video indexing, content management, and e-commerce opportunities; and Michael Gilge of VCS for contributing information on streaming for security and surveillance. In addition, I would like to thank Snell & Wilcox, Inktomi, Akamai, and Telestream for all the information they provided. A special thanks goes to all the people who have trusted and supported me throughout the years, including my employees, investors, and business associates.

Finally, I would like to thank myself for having the ability to learn and contribute knowledge to a very challenging industry, one that is becoming the mainstream of communications I believed it would be many years ago.

Recognized as one of the pioneers of streaming media, Gregory C. Demetriades has been an award-winning, serial-technology entrepreneur since 1980. He is the founder and CEO of MaxVU, Inc., a company committed to building and implementing a global, digital-communications enterprise via the video streaming marketplace. In addition to authoring this definitive guide to implementing streaming, Greg is a frequent speaker at industry events, writes numerous articles and papers on maximizing digital communications, and is helping to shape the industry by extending the application of digital communications technologies to a host of business needs.

Greg has been working with Internet technologies since 1993 and has concentrated on optimizing text, graphics, audio, and video streaming since 1997. He created a streaming broadcast to 55,000 viewers of eight live games over five days during March Madness in 1998, when the streaming industry was in its infancy. In 1999 he implemented a remote broadcast via satellite from a tiny island in the Pacific — encoded at 22 kilobits (phone line connectivity) — for a segment entitled "Live from a Shark Cage from Bikini Atoll," part of the opening show in the Discovery Channel's *Shark Week*.

In the new millennium, Greg continues to focus MaxVU on superior quality and bandwidth optimization — both dialup and broadband connectivity — with a product he calls AllBand Optimization. Recent innovations in the realm of e-commerce (with several patents pending) focus on easing digital file creation and remote conversion for streaming files (transcoding) — topics this book covers in detail.

Greg is sharing his knowledge and wide-ranging experience in the hope you will develop a successful streaming enterprise of your own.

S treaming media is the most effective and technologically advanced method of sending quality video and audio to any Web-connected site over existing data networks. With the movement away from static advertisements, more companies have been implementing streaming media systems to stay competitive, and it is estimated that close to 90 percent of all Internet sites will have some form of streaming by the time you read this. Given the present rate of technological innovation, streaming media can now be delivered effectively via 56K dialup connections as well as broadband, which makes it ripe for enterprise applications. Streaming media technology is further poised to move solidly into the growing realm of wireless delivery. In addition to advertising and entertainment, streaming content is a cost-effective solution for training, distance learning, teleconferencing, the distribution of product information, and a multitude of other innovative applications simply waiting to be implemented.

This set of circumstances provides an unprecedented opportunity for those interested in the advantages of streaming technology. Of greater importance, perhaps, is the necessity of gaining a thorough knowledge of the latest advances in design, content development, current hardware and software components, and delivery — in essence, the fundamentals of building and implementing a complete streaming media system.

Overview of the Book

As its subtitle implies, this book provides the toolkit you need to build and implement a complete streaming media system. At first glance, the topic can appear to be difficult, due to the number of divergent components and technologies one must integrate to make it all work. This book, however, simplifies the process by taking you on a journey of discovery, employing the logical step-by-step procedures currently used to build any streaming system. Along the way, you will explore and develop an understanding of the medium, learn how to choose the tools of the trade (the components of quality), process and produce content, manage and deploy streaming media, and work with advanced technologies (the worlds of wireless delivery, security, and surveillance).

As the chief executive officer of a company, I understand time constraints, deliverables, and most important, budgets and revenue generation. To ensure the practical and utilitarian nature of this book, I have filled it with detailed examples, product specifications (including URLs for further information), and a wealth of technical knowledge. This book has been written so that even those with very busy schedules can adapt the principles of streaming and integrate a streaming system within current architectures. I have asked industry leaders to assist me with their expertise to ensure the use of the most accurate information. You will find that this book, along with the accompanying resources on the CD, will help you develop a functional system so you can begin streaming immediately.

Who Should Read This Book

This book is written for software engineers, network software engineers, broadcasting engineers, media engineers, Java engineers, multimedia engineers, IS engineers, application engineers, streaming media engineers, network engineers, Webmasters, Web site developers, systems engineers, network administrators, multimedia specialists, Web programmers, and anyone with a good working knowledge of computers and networks who is eager to learn more about implementing streaming media.

How This Book Is Organized

Although many people are knowledgeable in specific areas of streaming, many others lack the overall ability to address each segment of the streaming industry. This is why I have organized the main body of this book around the natural progression of building a successful streaming enterprise system. The first four parts and 15 chapters of this book represent the logical steps in developing a streaming media enterprise. As you progress, you will not only accumulate practical knowledge of the most important aspects of streaming, but you will have followed the production process from beginning to end (concept to deployment).

Part Four is composed of three chapters on advanced technologies and a look at the future of streaming media. In keeping with the times, there's a comprehensive chapter on security and surveillance using streaming media — an exceptional section I hope you will find very helpful.

Since the broadcasting and computer industries are converging, I have also included a comprehensive glossary. And don't forget the CD-ROM attached to the inside cover of this book. It contains many valuable links and my streaming software package, which allows you to configure, monitor, and manage a live encoded media stream.

NOTE

See Appendix B "What's on the CD-ROM" for all of the details regarding the CD attached to the inside cover of this book.

Here is how the book is laid out:

Part One Exploring and Understanding the Medium

  Chapter 1 Getting Started

  Chapter 2 Understanding the Image Capture Process

  Chapter 3 Editing Movies with an iMac and a Digital Camera

Part Two Choosing the Tools of the Trade

  Chapter 4 Video Cameras and Recorders: The First Component of Quality

  Chapter 5 Audio/Video Capture Devices: The Second Component of Quality

  Chapter 6 Capture Cards Compared: Making a High-Quality Choice

Part Three Processing and Producing Content

  Chapter 7 Preprocessing Audio and Video

  Chapter 8 Building Encoders with Server Connections

  Chapter 9 Working with Compression Software

  Chapter 10 Using Cleaning, Editing, and Other Streaming Resources

  Chapter 11 Transcoding File Formats

PART ONE

Exploring and Understanding the Medium

CHAPTER 1

Getting Started

S*treaming* is simply moving complex data such as text, graphics, audio, and video at quality and speed levels acceptable to consumers across increasingly crowded communications channels without losing quality.

To *lose quality* means:

- Poor image pixelization
- Low frame rates
- Poor audio/video synchronization
- Postage-stamp-sized viewing screens

I have spent many years optimizing these four determining factors of streaming. I will share with you the knowledge I have acquired since 1993 when I first was involved with the Internet. The secret to high-quality streaming lies within these pages, and I am about to share it with you.

The Many Uses of Streaming

Streaming has several different uses—everything from entertainment to practical business applications. It can be used to broadcast a live event from a ballpark, theater, concert, boardroom, or sales meeting; provide security and surveillance for a home or business; and so on. Streaming events (such as the previous live examples) can also be saved to file for later audience viewing, as well as for product demonstrations and educational materials for distance learning.

Any event with a video and/or audio feed can be streamed over the Internet, and, as mentioned earlier, the stream file can be either real time or saved as a file to be viewed at the leisure of the audience. All you need is an encoder, a camera, and a hookup to the Internet. Send the streamed file to a server, point the Web site to the server link, and you are now streaming worldwide.

These same content providers must continually seek ways to deliver streaming text, graphics, audio, and video at quality and speed levels acceptable to their consumers, yet less than 20 percent of these consumers have broadband capability. This is the current dilemma facing those involved in streaming technology. The content of this book points the way to a solution.

The Current Dilemma of Quality Streaming

The question of how to get more and more complex data across increasingly crowded communications channels—without losing quality and in the blink of an eye—is being debated, argued, and researched by corporations across the world. The public's taste for information is becoming increasingly sophisticated, and its tolerance for poor quality and slow delivery is shrinking.

Over 80 million narrowband Internet users are currently watching bad video, if they can watch it at all. New applications that can be delivered over the Web are emerging every day but are requiring faster server processing. Personal computer (PC)/server and chip manufacturers are being driven to their technological limit to produce faster, more efficient products. Content providers and data-dependent businesses are facing spiraling costs to add the necessary muscle to meet the increasing processing and transaction demands.

The Role of Streaming in the Digital Media Revolution

Digital media components and the newest features incorporated in PCs and consumer appliances are fueling a revolution in how news, information, and entertainment are distributed and experienced. The digital media revolution, whether in the home or in the office, in the den or in the dorm, or even on the road, consists of a suite of digital, media-capable devices and services poised to deliver the promise of anywhere-anytime access to the information and entertainment you demand.

It all started with the PC and streaming media over the Internet or corporate network. This provided, for the first time, truly interactive, on-demand audio and video. Although the quality over analog modems was constrained, users were intrigued and satisfied with such capabilities as news and training on-demand, international radio, and Web-only event broadcasts.

With the maturation of many of the new streaming technologies, many people have already started to broaden the impact of streaming media, and it is having a dramatic impact on consumers and the workers, as well as the media and information technology (IT) industries.

Broadband Internet

The emergence of Digital Subscriber Line (DSL) and cable-connected homes has paved the way for the delivery of CD-quality music and near-broadcast-quality video. Streaming companies are partnering with key infrastructure players, from telephone companies (telcos) to cable television providers to Internet service providers (ISPs), to empower them to provide high-speed Internet access to the home. This, coupled with the rich interactivity and e-commerce capabilities of the Internet, is now delivering compelling pay-per-use and advertising-supported content.

Digital Music

The music industry is at the forefront of the digital media revolution. The streaming media technologies are now delivering key enabling technologies to the music industry to assist in the deployment of high-quality music promotion and secure distribution. This addresses the needs of the music industry, offering features to increase the number of listeners, protect copyrights and the distribution of content, and allow for widespread compatibility with other digital consumer devices, all the while providing CD-quality playback in crystal-clear streaming media formats.

Consumer Electronics

Consumers want media throughout their homes, in their cars, while they're exercising, or while they're just out and about. Streaming media technologies are enabling the consumer electronics industry to ensure that the digital media revolution extends beyond the PC. Digital audio players, much smaller than the traditional Walkmans of the past, are allowing consumers to create their own personal play lists and eliminate skipping and scratches. A whole suite of consumer electronics devices will soon be on the market—devices that span digital stereos, car stereos, and advanced television set-top boxes.

Business

Companies are rapidly discovering the benefits of streaming media in their organizations through virtual company meetings, just-in-time learning, and the ability to react to changing business conditions quickly, with immediate communications to employees, partners, and customers. This is becoming more evident as streaming capabilities increase and business personnel travel less. Many companies predict that they will rapidly increase their streaming initiatives by 2004.

E-Commerce

With the rapid growth in digital media and its use in both consumer and business applications, content providers are looking to move from experimentation to revenue generation as quickly as possible. Many easy-to-use and secure e-commerce solutions—enabling content providers to manage, deliver, and sell pay-per-download and pay-per-stream content—have been developed to work over the Internet. These technologies assure providers that their rights are being preserved and the rules they have established are being adhered to.

The Cost of Streaming

Streaming can be very inexpensive to set up; less than $1,000 spent on equipment gets you saying hello to the entire world. However, depending on the type of streaming enterprise you are setting up, and based on the targeted audience, I would expect your average startup cost to be between $50,000 and $150,000. This includes cameras, computers, software licensing, editing tools, personnel for a few months, and bandwidth. Of course, if you are building out an entire enterprise, the cost can be considerably more.

Your investment in streaming depends upon:

- The number of audio and video feeds you have and want to stream live at any one time
- How many stored tapes you want to transfer to a streaming format
- How many viewers you expect to stream at one time and throughout the month
- How much media storage will be necessary for your streaming content on servers
- The level of equipment and technology you desire to implement on starting up

These are the basic cost considerations as you get started. The objective is to keep growing your streaming department without management pulling the plug. An important consideration is knowing how your department is justifying this expenditure in terms of cost or what projected revenues are expected.

NOTE

By having a firm understanding of management expectations, you have a much better chance of maintaining a successful streaming department in the years to come.

Planning Your Streaming System

I have put together a checklist that will help you with your development. It is a basic exercise to get you thinking and to help you initiate the planning process for your own streaming system.

NOTE

I suggest you take an inventory of the equipment and software you already are using before considering further purchases to implement your streaming media system. What you already own may be adaptable to your streaming needs, and a wise planner takes into account issues of compatibility, where new and existing software/hardware may need to coexist and communicate.

Return on Investment (ROI)—Cost Savings
Are your cost savings based on:
- ❑ Reduced travel expenditures?
- ❑ Savings from more effective communication?

Return on Investment (ROI)—Revenue Generation
Are your revenue generation plans:
- ❑ Subscription-based?
- ❑ Event-based (pay-per-view)?

Type of Streaming
Will you be:
- ❑ Broadcasting?
- ❑ Doing security and surveillance CCTV (closed caption television)?

Streaming Target Device
Will your marketplace be:
- ❑ Desktops?
- ❑ Handheld wireless devices?

Types of Codecs
Are your preferred codecs sourced via:
- ❑ Microsoft?
- ❑ Real?
- ❑ QuickTime?
- ❑ Other third party _____?

Types of Audio/Video Equipment
Among the many ways to capture content, will you be using:
- ❑ Audio and video analog/digital cameras?
- ❑ Audio and video analog/digital recorders?

Types of Encoders (Video Compression)
Do you wish to encode via:

❑ Desktop?

❑ Rack mount with remote control?

Encoder Hardware Sourcing
Do you wish to:

❑ Build your own?

❑ Purchase?

Type of Server Distribution
Considering the expense that can ensue without proper management, will you be:

❑ Building your own server farm?

❑ Using a Content Distribution Network (CDN) service (normally recommended)?

Audio and Video Streaming Options
Among the many options to make streaming better, are you considering:

❑ Transcoding?

❑ Cleaning and editing?

❑ Audio and video preprocessing (filtering)?

❑ Audio and video indexing?

Streaming File Applications
Among delivery options (which affect file types), are you considering:

❑ Audio and video broadcasting live?

❑ Audio and video broadcasting replay?

❑ Audio and video e-mail snippets?

Types of Applications
To effectively utilize streaming technology, are you considering:

❑ Training staff and customers?

❑ Corporate communications?

❑ Distance learning?

❑ Entertainment?

❑ Product promotion?

❑ Other _____?

Taking the Next Step

The answers you give to the questions posed in this chapter point the way to a better understanding of your needs and the direction in which you may want to go. The subsequent chapters in this book are designed to review with you each of these areas and to build a firm foundation from which you can make sound decisions. In the next two chapters, I will help you build your streaming enterprise by reviewing what I believe are the next logical steps—a thorough understanding of the process of video production and editing.

CHAPTER 2

Understanding the Image Capture Process

As you perfect your techniques for streaming media, you will need to know how to use a video recorder (also known as a camcorder) correctly. This chapter covers the basic techniques for using any video recorder. These include exposure, the camera lens, focus, and depth of field (DOF). I also include several tips for making images with visual impact—such as shooting without a tripod (handheld techniques), the concept of nose room, thoughts on color, creating the illusion of dimension, the relationship between subject and camera height (point of view), backgrounds, creative manipulation of aspect ratios, and a compendium of effective composition guidelines.

Video Recorder Basics

Motion picture cameras and video recorders capture light reflected from objects and record it either chemically on film (motion picture) or with video, electronically on videotape (analog), or digitally on tape, disk, or microchips. Motion picture and video cameras differ from still cameras in that they record precise numbers of pictures per second in order to achieve the illusion of fluid movement when the pictures are projected or played back. Motion pictures are recorded at 24 frames per second (fps), whereas video is recorded at 30 fps. If either one is played back faster than its recorded rate, the result will be fast motion; slower, and you get a jerky, slow-motion effect.

In this chapter, we will be discussing video recorders—digital video being the current state of the art in image capture technology. Although you could capture your image content using a motion picture camera (or use existing motion picture footage as a source), you would have to transfer it to video before it would be suitable for streaming media production.

In the world of video, the display, or image, is made up of pixels (picture elements). When streaming video, pixel capture is very important. The larger the number of pixels, the greater are the detail and clarity of the display or image (the higher resolution). The following sections explore in detail the basics of creating high-quality video images. The last half of this chapter is devoted to the more artistic aspects of the video production process.

NOTE

Sony has developed a family of high-quality, digital video recorders that, in my experience, do a very nice job with overall digital video production. The specific features to look for are camera models that deliver higher pixel counts (image resolution), which translate into better images and detail quality. The digital recorder you choose should also allow for zooming in on subjects or pulling back for wide shots. The latest precision digital zooms use a hyperprecision-charged couple device (CCD) to maintain excellent image detail. Part Two of the book (Chapters 4, 5, and 6) addresses the topic of choosing high-quality tools of the trade in detail. For more information on the latest Sony digital video cameras, point your browser to www.sonystyle.com/ home/ and choose Digital Camcorders.

Exposure

When using a video camera for shooting for the Internet, lighting is a very important factor. The wrong camera with the wrong light can cause poor video capture, resulting in a bad bit-stream output. To get a properly recorded video image, you must control the amount of light coming into the camera through the lens. Too little light, and your picture will be dark and full of video noise (grainy with little red, blue, and green dots). Too much light, and your picture will be washed out and gray.

Whether it's automatic or manual, it is the aperture (the opening in the center of the camera lens) that controls the amount of light entering the camera. The bigger the opening, the more light that is allowed through the lens. The lens aperture (opening) is adjusted either automatically, by an electronic circuit inside the camera, or manually, by changing the exposure setting on the lens barrel.

The numbers on the exposure ring are called *f-stops*. The simplest way to understand how they work is to think of them as fractions with the *f*-number on the bottom and 1 on top. Thus $f2 = \frac{1}{2}$, $f4 = \frac{1}{4}$, and $f8 = \frac{1}{8}$. Since $\frac{1}{2}$ is bigger than $\frac{1}{8}$, it is easy to see that a lens opening of $f2$ is going to let in more light than $f8$.

Most consumer camcorders do not have manual f-stop controls. This means that you cannot get the proper exposure when there are large differences between the light and dark areas in your shot (a condition known as high contrast).

This large contrast ratio fools the camcorder's exposure setting and gives poor results. The sensing circuit cannot deal with big differences between bright and dark. It chooses one extreme or the other, depending on where you aim the light sensor. You can see this effect by viewing the scene you wish to capture through the camera's viewfinder and observing its effect on the exposure meter indicator. Moving the camera a few inches may drastically change the exposure setting for your subject.

Again, the wrong lighting can make for a poor capture. Considering that there are many cameras to choose from and that price is not always a determining factor of quality capture, I suggest that you experiment with the camera(s) you have before purchasing a new one. If you are going to be capturing many high-contrast images, a camera with manual *f*-stop controls may be a necessity.

The Camera Lens

Just as *f*-stops measure exposure level, lens length defines an image's size, apparent depth, and proportion. Every video lens has a length, which gives what we think of as a normal view—a picture closest to the size, point of view (POV), and proportion of the image our eyes see from the camera's POV.

Any lens setting shorter than normal (less than 50 mm) creates a wide-angle view and a greater sense of depth. A lens length setting longer than normal (more than 50 mm) makes an image that is narrow (magnified) in view and flattened in depth.

Table 2.1 Wide-Angle versus Telephoto Setting

WIDE ANGLE	TELEPHOTO
Broad view	Narrow view
Smaller image	Larger image
Good for close shooting	Good for distant shooting
Deep depth of field	Shallow depth of field
Increases object speed toward camera	Decreases object speed toward camera
Minimizes camera shake	Maximizes camera shake

There are two ways to change the length of a camera lens. You can use different lenses of varying lengths (wide-angle, normal, telephoto) or one zoom lens, which adjusts from short to long for an infinite range of wide-angle to telephoto views. A setting that is longer or shorter than normal affects your image in predictable ways. Table 2.1 shows the results of setting the zoom length at its extreme short or long position.

For example, to make a car look like it is moving faster than it is toward the camera, use the wide-angle setting. On the other hand, if you want to slow down the car's apparent speed, use the telephoto setting.

Let's say you need to shoot a group of people, some near the camera and some farther away. If you want them all to be in focus, you can increase the depth of field (or the depth of the area in focus) by choosing the wide-angle setting. However, if you want only the people close to the camera to be in focus (shallow depth of field), choose the telephoto position.

The range of a zoom lens is expressed as a ratio between the extreme telephoto and wide-angle settings. A 12:1 zoom ratio means that the telephoto image is 12 times larger than the wide-angle image.

Focus

Your brain is the best autofocus mechanism ever invented. Despite advertising claims, there is no electronic camera system as precise and controllable as your brain. Under unusual constraints—for example, when precise manual focus is not practical due to lack of space or when it would be too time-consuming—you can use autofocus to help ensure that your images are crisp. You can also use autofocus to create certain visual effects. Under normal shooting conditions, however, make sure that autofocus is turned off.

There are three reasons not to use autofocus:

- The constant focusing adjustment drains the battery.
- Focus can shift unpredictably if elements in your image move.
- You cannot shoot through windows, fences, trees, fabric, or do mirror shots. Focus will shift constantly between the foreground image and the background action.

Focus manually for maximum control. What you see (in the viewfinder) is what you get (WYSIWYG). If your image is out of focus during shooting, it will not look any better during playback. To focus a zoom lens, here are three tips:

1. Adjust the lens to the full telephoto position so the subject looks as big as possible in the viewfinder.
2. Turn the lens focus ring until the subject is in focus in the viewfinder.
3. Then, (without changing the focus setting you made in Step 2), zoom the lens to compose your shot and create the desired point of view.

NOTE

It's important to remember to prefocus on your subject in the full telephoto (zoomed-in) position. If you focus in the wide-angle setting, you will not be able to zoom in from wide-angle to telephoto without losing focus. Although the telephoto setting creates a short depth of field, the wide-angle setting creates a long depth of field (and is therefore always in focus).

Depth of Field

Depth of field (DOF) is the distance in front of and behind your subject that is in sharp focus. There is always less DOF in front of your subject than behind it. Certain factors (illustrated in Table 2.2) can increase or decrease DOF to enhance the visual impact of your videography.

Table 2.2 Factors Affecting DOF and the Visual Impact of Your Image

INCREASES DOF	DECREASES DOF[0]
Wide-angle setting	Telephoto setting
Bright light	Low light
High *f*-stop setting	Low *f*-stop setting
Long shots	Close-ups

Making Images with Visual Impact

When you point a camera in any direction, you put a frame around a specific part of the scene, recording some elements and not others. Put an object or a person in the viewfinder frame, and that object or that person becomes important to your audience. Leave out an item, and it will never exist for your viewers.

The way you compose a shot tells your viewer that you believe that one part of a scene is more important than other parts. Creative videographers and Webcasters consider all the visual elements in the viewfinder frame and ask how each will affect the audience's interpretation of the scene.

To begin thinking about composition, remember that while you live through the experience, camcorder in hand, you react to all the different levels of stimulation: sight, sound, smell, touch, and taste. No matter how good your technique, your video record of the event only stimulates a viewer's sight and hearing, a small part of the event.

This is your challenge as a videographer. You must learn to use the limited resources of video and audio to communicate what you feel and think about the event while you try to capture its reality electronically. How close your audience comes to sharing your vision of the reality you capture on videotape or film depends on your technical skills and your mastery of the art of visual communications.

Shooting without a Tripod

Before you begin to think about the creative content of your video, you must make sure that your images are in sharp focus and there is no possibility of accidental camera movement. Sharp focus is guaranteed by following the steps outlined earlier. Camera shake, on the other hand, can be a serious problem, even for experienced videographers when they shoot without a tripod.

All camera manuals and video textbooks insist that a tripod is essential to getting steady video images. However, a tripod's weight and bulkiness hinder the creative freedom made possible by using lightweight, portable camcorders.

- Tripods are ideal for use in controlled shooting environments: advertising productions, instructional demonstrations, speeches, or other public presentations—settings where you are not shooting spontaneously to capture unrepeatable, unpredictable action.
- Handheld videography is perfect for spontaneous, unpredictable events: news, sports, music performances, demonstrations, parades, birthday parties, and weddings, where a tripod cramps your freedom to capture the event from different points of view.

Learning to shoot without a tripod is like learning to drive a stick-shift car, even though most automobiles are equipped with automatic transmissions. Learning the art of good handheld technique will improve your tripod shooting dramatically, while increasing your shooting options greatly.

Author's Tricks for Good Handheld Techniques

To ensure steady images with a handheld camera:

1. **Set the lens at the maximum wide-angle position.**
2. **Set the lens focus at 5 to 7 feet.**

The wide-angle lens position and this focus setting give you maximum DOF with sharp focus from about 18 inches in front of the camera lens to infinity in bright sunlight. This range guarantees sharp focus no matter how close or far away your subject is.

These techniques will keep you from zooming into the action with a telephoto lens and force you to shoot from different angles and positions—a benefit you will appreciate when you edit your footage. The wide-angle setting also forces you to move the camera closer to the subject for medium and close-up shots. You will automatically end up with a greater variety of shots to use during editing.

If you must use a handheld telephoto shot, find an improvised support to keep the camera steady—lean against a wall, a chair, or a car; prop the camera on the ground, on a table, or against a bookcase. If you cannot keep the image steady in your viewfinder, you are wasting shooting and battery time.

Composing for Nose Room

A video portrait can be ruined by not leaving enough room between the person's face and the edge of the frame when he or she looks to one side or the other. Compose the image so the subject's nose is squashed against the frame edge, and he or she seems to be staring into a wall—a most uncomfortable visual situation for both the subject and the viewer.

Psychologically, viewers are more relaxed when there is empty space (nose room) between the subject's face and the frame. By framing either right or left, depending on the subject's position, your final picture will be more visually pleasing.

The nose room concept also applies to objects. If you are shooting a car, a truck, or anything with a definable front and back, make sure its nose is not slammed tight against the frame. Leaving space between the object and the frame is especially important when the subject is moving across your field of view at a right angle. For example, if a person or object moves through the frame from left to right, it looks better to leave space in front of the movement, on the right side of the frame, to give the person or object a visual destination. Nose room is not a problem when the person or object is facing directly toward or away from the camera.

Remember, you can't force viewers to look at your images. Good composition is a powerful technique that encourages them to look at your work, even if they have no interest in your chosen subject.

Thinking about Color

The most important thing to remember about color is that your viewer's attention is drawn to the most colorful areas of the scene. For example, if you shoot an interview with a talking head standing in front of a crowd of people, including a young man wearing a bright red shirt, your audience will spend more time looking at the man in the red shirt than at the speaker.

Composing with the Rule of Thirds

The rule of thirds is a concept you can learn to help you avoid compositions where all the elements are perfectly balanced (symmetrical balance). Unbalanced compositions (asymmetrical balance) create a visual sense of motion, an effect that makes the most ordinary object, such as a chair or a soda, visually exciting.

For example, if your subject's eyes are the most important part of your picture, zoom in on the eyes and focus to ensure sharpness. Then, no matter whether you choose a wide-angle or a telephoto view, tilt up or down until the subject's eyes are even with the top one-third of your viewfinder's image area (which may be outlined in a grid pattern). This gives a more pleasing, inviting composition within the frame.

An excellent way to learn the finer points of this basic rule of composition is to study TV programs, paintings, photographs, posters, and feature films to see how the rule of thirds is applied to a variety of subjects.

To avoid visual distractions, pay attention to bright or colorful objects that may divert your audience. Frame your image so the brightest colors or lights are in the area of the shot that is the focus of attention.

Bright and/or colorful objects have a dramatic effect on the composition of your shots. They must be considered as having additional visual weight compared with the darker areas of your image. If you place a dark subject next to a bright object, your viewers will look at the brighter area, even though the dark subject is the center of interest.

Creating the Illusion of Dimension

We see the world in three dimensions—height, width, and depth. However, film and video can only record and reproduce height and width. Therefore, you must use some specific visual techniques to fool your viewers into thinking that the flat image they are seeing has depth— that it resembles three-dimensional reality.

When shooting objects or people, place your camera at an angle so you see at least two sides of your subject in the viewfinder. For example, if you shoot a person head-on, so you see only his or her front, the result is a perfect driver's license portrait.

However, if you turn your subject (for example, a person or an object, such as a building) 45 degrees, so you can capture the image in profile, you create an illusion of anatomic or architectural dimension with far greater visual impact.

Adjusting the Point of View

The point of view (POV) created by the height difference between the camera lens and the subject makes a definite impression on your audience. If the camera is higher than the subject, the POV creates a feeling of inferiority, helplessness, or isolation between the viewer and the subject. On the other hand, if the camera POV is lower than the subject, the audience will see the subject as superior, strong, and overwhelming.

Keep the camera even with the subject's eye level to create a neutral POV. The audience and the subject are eye to eye—they are equals. Any camera POV above or below the subject's eye level changes how the audience interprets what it sees.

Whether you shoot a 7-foot-tall tennis player or an 18-inch-high cocker spaniel, place your camera at the subject's eye level to remain emotionally neutral and to let your viewers see reality from the subject's POV, not yours.

Choosing the Best Background

It may seem obvious, but everything behind your subject will end up in the background of your image. An effective background is one that stays where it belongs—behind the subject. A good background is either neutral or complements, enhances, or adds information about the foreground subject. A poor background overwhelms your subject by pushing forward into the shot and drawing attention away from the main part of the image.

Background objects such as telephone poles, street signs, billboards, and trees seem to grow out of your subject's head if he or she stands directly between them and the camera. You can solve most background problems by moving the subject or the camera, or changing the angle of view. Always check the distracting background details. You can't get rid of them after the shot has been recorded (see the later section on color for more insight into this critical issue).

Creating Your Own Aspect Ratios

Every TV image, regardless of picture tube size, always has a fixed 3×4 rectangular shape. And if high-definition TV (HDTV) becomes widespread, high-definition video images will have a fixed 9×116 aspect ratio.

Unlike still photographers, who can turn their camera sideways for vertical compositions, you are stuck using TV's horizontal 3×4 rectangle for every shot. However, you can create different frame shapes by proper placement of objects in your shot. Blocking out parts of your shot with doorways, windows, posts, buildings, fences, a person's shoulder, and so on changes the video 3×4 rectangle into a square, diamond, triangle, diagonal, circle, or other geometric shape.

Frame-within-a-frame composition strengthens the illusion of depth and gives your images more visual impact.

Capturing Your Audience with Images

Your major goal as a videographer is to create images that will make your audience want to continue watching your program. Since most video productions are about ordinary people doing ordinary things with ordinary objects, it is only your creative skill and talent that can make such events seem extraordinary and worth a viewer's time.

The most common mistake videographers make is to only shoot from the most convenient or accessible location and POV. Lazy videographers never get to use their full creative potential to capture images with visual impact and emotional power.

Here are a few tips on how best to capture your audience with your images:

- Look at the event from the intended audience's perspective. Choose compositions that satisfy your intended viewers' interests. For example, if I shoot an evening news feature about a new dance fad, most of my footage might be full-body shots of the dancers. However, if I were shooting a how-to-dance instructional video, most of my shots would be close-ups showing the positioning and movement of the dancers' feet.

- Whenever you shoot video, always ask, "Who are the intended viewers, and what do they want to see?" The answers will guide your choice of camera angles, lens setting, POV, and so on.

- Walk around the location. Watch the action from potential camera positions. As you move around, pick the parts of the event your audience will find the most interesting. As you experiment with different POVs, look for high and low angles, framing possibilities, annoying backgrounds, clashing colors, bright lights, and so on.

- Use your eyes, not the camera, to find your best angles. If you use the viewfinder to search out shots, you will drain your camera's battery and miss potentially exciting footage.

- You don't have to accept the location as you find it. Don't be afraid to ask permission to move furniture, objects, or people if the change gives better results. Most video production participants eagerly cooperate if you tell them that their efforts will add quality to the project.

A Quick Recap: The Rules of Effective Image Capture

- ◆ No rule is absolute. But have a good reason to break it.
- ◆ Fill the entire screen with important subject matter. Empty space is wasted space.
- ◆ Avoid tilted horizontal and vertical lines.
- ◆ Movement or bright lights in the background are distracting.
- ◆ If the background is a problem during shooting, it will be worse for your audience.
- ◆ Move the camera or the subject before taping.
- ◆ When shooting people, place the subject's eyes one-third down from the top of the frame no matter what type of shot you're taking.
- ◆ Action or line of sight toward frame right should be positioned frame left, and vice versa, for nose room.
- ◆ Avoid leaving big spaces between people or objects.
- ◆ Shoot people in full or three-quarters profile, if possible, to give viewers as clear a view of the subject as possible.
- ◆ Create the illusion of dimension by having objects in the foreground, middle ground, and background, and shooting objects and people in profile rather than head on.
- ◆ Always zoom in to full telephoto to adjust focus.
- ◆ Allow for image cutoff around frame edges. Keep the important parts of the image toward frame center.

NOTE

After your preproduction planning and arranging, take another look at your location. Remember, your brain ignores distracting backgrounds, reflections, and other visual clutter, but the camera records everything.

Taking the Next Step

As you can see, there is a real method and an art to setting up and using a video camera. Lighting, distance, background, motion, and so on can all be determining factors in the success or failure of your streaming video. Video capture is only a portion of completing your video session. You must now edit your work with editing software.

There are many good editing software packages available in the marketplace, and in Chapter 3 I will show you examples of how to edit your steaming files using a digital camera and an iMac.

3

Editing Movies with an iMac and a Digital Camera

D igital video is becoming very prevalent in today's workplace and even at home. In many of your internal applications while streaming, you may have to use standard inputs such as composite or S-Video, but now you have a chance to use higher-quality digital input, which is becoming more readily available in the latest devices. With digital video cameras and entry-level computers growing increasingly common, pretty much anyone can put video online. Because video quality is so important while we wait for broadband to arrive, I encourage you to make sure you do your homework and lay out the type of streaming system you foresee using now, as well as 12 months and 3 years from now. Although technologies will get better, actual techniques stay pretty much the same. Video editing, the subject of this chapter, is a case in point.

NOTE
■■■■ Since this book references Microsoft products frequently, I want to have at least one chapter that uses the Apple computer system. Thus, I have put together this how-to-edit chapter using Apple's iMac. For those of you who do not have an Apple iMac, the basic principles of editing still apply.

Editing with Plug and Play

For a simple turnkey, easy-to-use video-editing system, it is hard to beat Apple's iMac and iMovie. Hard-core personal computer (PC) users may scoff as they fiddle with their cards and drivers. This may work in a professional environment, but it isn't going to cut it with everyone. The iMac is a solid little computer appliance, and it is built for everyone. It is standardized and very easy to work with. Setting it up and using it for digital video is about as easy as it gets.

Video streaming is all about plugging in your camcorder, pulling your footage together, and delivering it to your audience.

Starting with FireWire

FireWire is Apple's trademarked name for a technology more commonly known as IEEE-1394. If you work with a non-Apple system, your IEEE-1394 device also may have a different name. It might be known as iLink or Lynx. Many of the latest cameras coming to market have this capability. Check to see if your camera has this capability. It will make your input source much cleaner and easier to work with when you are encoding.

FireWire allows your computer to move a lot of data in and out of another device really fast. This is where it becomes such a powerful thing for digital video. When your camcorder records a scene, it converts a huge amount of visual and audible information into a digital format that a computer can understand. However, now that the data are stored away in your camcorder, you have to find a way to get all that information into your computer. FireWire provides the solution.

Determining Your Type of Port

If you have an IEEE-1394-capable computer equipped with a FireWire, you will find a funny-shaped port on the side of the machine. This is known as a 6-pin FireWire port. Why is this important? Take a look at the side of your digital camcorder. You probably are not going to find a 6-pin FireWire port but a 4-pin port instead. This means in order to hook up your video camera into your computer, you may have to purchase a 4-pin to 6-pin FireWire (IEEE-1394) cable, depending on the type of camera you have.

Most computer stores carry such an animal, but they are not cheap. If you are shopping for such a beast from your online camera warehouse, you might do a search on 1394, if you cannot find it listed under FireWire. Look at the ends to make sure you are getting a 4-pin to 6-pin cable, as shown in Figure 3.1.

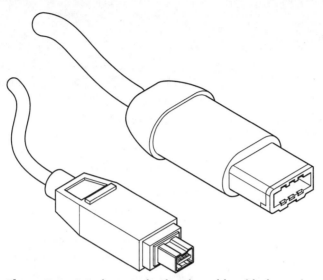

Figure 3.1 A 4-pin to 6-pin FireWire cable with the 6-pin connector on the right and the 4-pin connector on the left.

Working with iMovie

Now that you have a link between your computer and your camcorder, it's time to pull all that digital video data into your computer. This falls into the realm of your editing software. These days, nearly every machine Apple Computer ships comes with iMovie. Before you begin, it is a good idea to make sure your particular video recorder is completely compatible with iMovie (see the sidebar entitled "Getting Up to Speed" for more information on obtaining iMovie, working out compatibility issues, and purchasing FireWire conversion boxes, should such a device prove necessary).

I would suggest that you bank your money and get a newer camcorder unless you have a lot of money invested in non-FireWire gear. You might even trick iMovie into working with footage brought in with other devices. I have not tried this with the latest version of iMovie, and it is beyond the scope of this chapter, but you can read up on the technique in my earlier review on iMovie at www.smw.internet.com/video/reviews/applevid/index2.html.

Getting Up to Speed

For Macintosh users who do not have iMovie, Apple offers a $49 downloadable version for purchase on its Web site (www.apple.com/imovie). As of this writing, iMovie is not currently available for PC users, but you might find a package with the same kind of simplicity. Professionals who want control over every last nuance of the editing will find iMovie limited. However, I think that if you really sat down and looked at how people edit, you would find that iMovie covers 95 percent of the basic and professional users out there. This statement will probably bring me e-mail, but it is true. iMovie is a great quick-and-dirty video tool.

Apple lists iMovie-compatible camcorders on its Web site (www.apple.com/imovie/shoot.html). Most common camcorders are fine, but some have quirks that are documented on the site. Camcorders that are not on the list might or might not work. Digital video discussion forums are full of conflicting information about iMovie compatibility with unlisted camcorders. A little advance research can save you frustration later.

If you do not have a digital camcorder with FireWire capability, you can buy a FireWire conversion box. Sony offers a device (the affectionately titled DVMC-DA2) that is currently compatible with iMovie. In my work with the Sony conversion boxes, I have found that they are not as convenient as I would like. The conversion boxes do not give you the full control you would have with a compatible digital camcorder.

Taking the iMovie Tutorial

The first time you launch iMovie, you are given the opportunity to run the tutorial that comes with the software. You also can access the tutorial directly by pulling down the Help menu while running iMovie. In this chapter, I will cover the basics of working with iMovie. They will be enough to get you started with putting together a very simple video piece for streaming. However, I highly encourage you to spend the short amount of time that it takes to go through the iMovie tutorial before you do anything else. The software is very easy to use. Following Apple's well-written tutorial will make you that much more confident with iMovie in the long run.

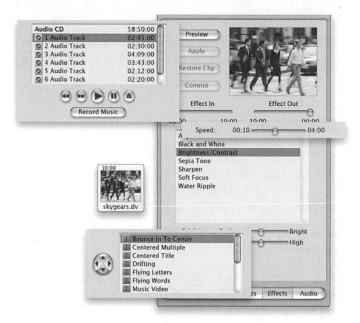

Figure 3.2 iMovie screens are very user-friendly.

You will find that the iMovie screen is broken up into three areas. Figure 3.2 shows the screen for a reference. This is where you will find the Monitor window, where you play your raw camera footage and your edited video. As I will indicate shortly, this is also where you input your camera footage into iMovie.

Starting a Project

To start a project in iMovie, pull down the File menu to New Project, tell iMovie where you want to put your files, and type in the name you want to use. Be careful here. Digital video uses up a lot of hard drive space, so make sure you have enough space available on your computer. A minute of digital video footage typically uses up about 220 MB of space.

NOTE

iMovie offers an indicator below the shelf window so you can monitor the available space on your hard drive. However, be prepared to work selectively if your system is already crammed full of games, applications, and documents.

Importing and Editing Video

With your project ready, it is time to pull in your raw video footage. To accomplish this task, use the iMovie Monitor window in the upper-left corner of your screen. As you look at the lower-left corner of the iMovie Monitor window, you will see a symbol for a film and a symbol for a digital video (DV) camera. If you get lost, use the screen shot in Figure 3.3 as a reference.

iMovie starts in the edit mode. Clicking the little digital camera symbol will—you guessed it—slide the toggle over to digital camera mode. If your camcorder is not connected properly or is not turned on, the iMovie Monitor window will turn blue and say, "Camera Disconnected." Turn on your camcorder, and slide it into its VCR mode.

NOTE

On many camcorders the VCR mode is in the opposite direction of the setting that turns the camcorder on to shoot video. On the Optura pi, for example, turning the power control to the right turns on the movie function, whereas turning the control to the left turns on the VCR function.

If you have connected the FireWire cable properly, once you turn on the VCR function, the camcorder will power up and begin to talk to the computer. Within a few seconds, the iMovie Monitor window will change from "Camera Disconnected" to "Camera Connected."

With your camcorder now connected, you can begin working on your project. iMovie offers many techniques for editing your video and audio clips. You may find that you want to remove unwanted material in a clip, make a copy of a clip, split one clip into two clips, rearrange clips, or replace or rearrange video.

Cropping a Video Clip

When you want to crop the beginning and/or end of an iMovie video clip, you first select the part of the video clip you want to keep, as illustrated in Figure 3.3. The steps for accomplishing this are as follows:

1. Click to select the clip you want to edit.

2. Click and drag below the scrubber bar. Two triangular crop markers appear, as you can see in Figure 3.3.

3. Drag the crop markers to where you want the clip to begin and end. When you release the mouse button, part of the scrubber bar has changed from blue to yellow. The portions outside the crop markers will be deleted when you crop the clip.

Adding Transitions

With iMovie, you can easily add transitions between clips or at the beginning or end of your movie. Figure 3.4 illustrates what the Transitions panel in iMovie looks like. To add a transition, use the following steps:

1. Open your iMovie project.

2. Click the Transitions button to view the Transitions panel.

3. Use the speed slider to set the speed of the transition. Slower transitions take longer to render.

4. Click to select a transition. A sample of the transition appears in the transition preview screen.

Figure 3.3 Cropping a video clip in iMovie.

Transition Button to Set Direction of some Transitions

Transition Preview Screen

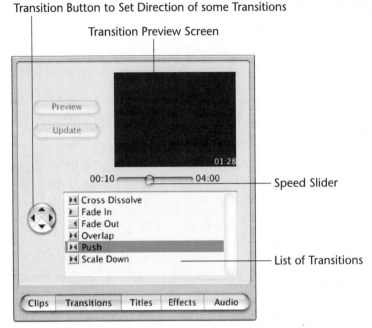

Speed Slider

List of Transitions

Figure 3.4 Adding transitions in iMovie.

An Important Note on Saving and Copying Your Project Files

It is important to make sure that you are saving your project to a reasonably fast hard drive. The built-in hard drive on your iMac usually will handle the data requirements just fine. Be careful, however, of trying to work off of external storage disks or drives. In some cases, slower external hard drives will cause data failures.

Once you have given a location and name to your project, iMovie will create a folder with that name. Inside that folder will be an iMovie file with the project name and a folder called Media. The iMovie file is what professionals would refer to as an Edit Decision List (EDL). It carries nothing more than a set of instructions for how iMovie is supposed to put your video together. The pieces of your video actually sit in the Media folder.

Adding Titles

Titles can be used at the beginning and at the end of a movie, as well as over clips throughout your iMovie project. Several title styles are included with iMovie, but you can download additional ones from the iMovie Web site at www.apple.com/imovie. The following steps demonstrate how to add titles to your project:

1. Open your iMovie project.
2. To add a title over a clip, click to select that clip in the clip viewer or the timeline viewer. A title also can appear on a black background as its own clip.
3. Click the Titles button to display the Titles panel.
4. Click to select a title style from the list in the Titles panel. A preview of the title you selected appears in the title preview monitor.

The important lesson here is that if you wish to copy your project to a backup disk or another location, make sure that you move the entire project folder, not just the project file inside the folder. Keep everything together so iMovie will know where to find it. An iMovie project file without the accompanying media files is absolutely useless.

Adding Sound and Music

Using methods similar to those previously described for adding transitions and titles (refer to Figure 3.4), you can add music and other sounds to your iMovie projects. You can record your own voice, add a sound effect from a collection that comes with iMovie, or use a clip from an audio CD.

Adding VideoEffects

Figure 3.5 illustrates how iMovie allows you to add video effects, such as soft focus and sepia tone, to your clips. You can use the effects that come with iMovie or download additional ones from the iMovie Web site at www.apple.com/imovie.

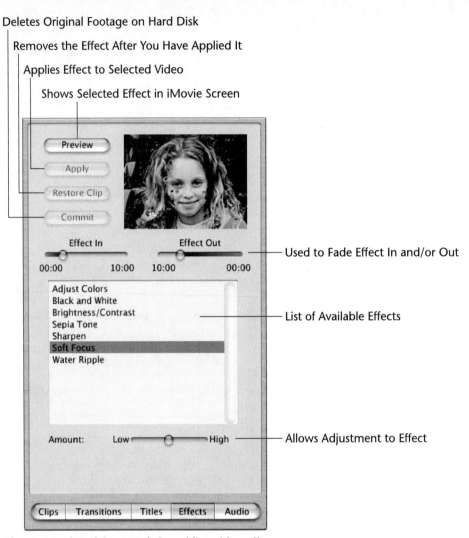

Deletes Original Footage on Hard Disk

Removes the Effect After You Have Applied It

Applies Effect to Selected Video

Shows Selected Effect in iMovie Screen

Preview

Apply

Restore Clip

Commit

Effect In   Effect Out

Used to Fade Effect In and/or Out

00:00   10:00   10:00   00:00

Adjust Colors
Black and White
Brightness/Contrast   List of Available Effects
Sepia Tone
Sharpen
Soft Focus
Water Ripple

Amount: Low   High   Allows Adjustment to Effect

Clips   Transitions   Titles   Effects   Audio

Figure 3.5   iMovie's controls for adding video effects.

Taking the Next Step

There you have it—a little more about digital cameras and more information about what Apple is doing to produce movies. Although systems like iMovie are consumer-oriented, it should be pointed out that many people are using these inexpensive tools to create streaming movies on a small scale. As you read further, you'll soon learn how to work on a much larger scale.

Part Two of the book moves on to the topic of choosing high-quality tools of the trade. Beginning with Chapter 4, we'll be exploring different types of videoconferencing cameras and video recorders. These stationary streaming devices complement the digital image capturing and editing techniques discussed in the first three chapters.

Choosing the Tools
of the Trade

Video Cameras and Recorders: The First Component of Quality

Video cameras and recorders are the real key to capturing your audio and video for streaming. This is why it is so important to choose the correct device and learn about its features. Many cameras do not produce the proper output file, such as an .avi file. They may not have the ability to do full-motion capture. Recorders may not have easy ways to show time codes or have a remote-control feature for batch transcoding.

In this chapter, I get you acquainted with the types of low-to-high-end conferencing cameras and videotape recorders capable of capturing and playing back video—the tools of the trade referred to as the first component of quality. Along the way, I also outline some of the exciting ways you can use this technology to communicate more effectively.

Video Streaming Conferencing Cameras

One of the many reasons to build and implement a streaming media system is to take full advantage of the latest videoconferencing technologies. Streaming videoconferencing can be used for distance learning in corporate and educational arenas; the diagnosis of patients using telemedicine; or just to communicate better, especially in today's marketplace, where travel is being limited.

NOTE

Many cameras are suitable for portable videoconferencing, but in the following sections I have highlighted those I can honestly recommend: cameras I have had sucessful experiences with or ones that have been recommended to me.

Portable Videoconferencing with the Intel Pro PC Camera

Videoconferencing is becoming more popular with many would-be travelers, with employees in virtual offices, and with overseas business contacts; it is even becoming popular for quick online meetings that normally are completed over the phone. Since many of us are using laptops without built-in video cameras, the portable Intel Pro PC Camera is ideal for quick setups like the ones just described. This camera also gives you the ability to record scenes and snapshots and take a video feed from a recorder or camera.

As of this writing, the software features of the Intel Pro PC Camera include:

- Intel Video Phone Software
- Intel Scene Recorder
- Intel Snapshot
- Intel Audio Recorder
- Intel Gallery
- Intel TWAINN Driver
- Intel Home Page Builder
- Intel Auto Snapshot
- Intel Movie Builder
- Bonus CD

And in the hardware category, the Pro PC features:

- A focus dial
- A tilt swivel base
- A tripod socket
- A convenient snapshot button
- A privacy shutter

- Video input from camcorder or VCR
- Option: Intel PC Camera Pro Mount

Some of its more important features include: a USB port; progressive scans; the ability to capture 640 × 480 pixels, 30 frames per second (fps) video capture, which enables full motion; and the output of .avi files—a very nice feature, especially when you need to convert over to streaming file formats such as Real and Microsoft.

NOTE

For the lastest information on the Intel Pro PC Camera and current data on other related Intel products, go to www.intel.com/pccamera/pro.htm.

Autotracking Cameras with Motion Detection

Having an autotracking camera with motion detection is a very good thing. When streaming video for live play or even replay, you cannot beat the convenience these cameras give you. I have used the Sony EVI-D30 camera, and it was a pleasure. This camera will focus in on your upper torso and stay locked while you move. Even if other people enter the room, you still have the attention of your camera and, most importantly, your audience. I would recommend this camera or others like it even to video streaming beginners.

Some of the most important features of autotracking cameras include:

AT (autotracking) mode. AT mode is a function that continually extracts a subject that the user predefines. After picking up pixels of similar color and brightness around the selected subject, the camera extracts the target by using the subject model, based on light reflection and nonlinear camera processing. There are four modes for predefining the subject.

AT pan/tilt. This function follows the moving subject automatically by controlling the pan and tilt motors without the use of special sensors.

Autozoom. This function controls the zoom lens automatically to ensure that the size of the subject remains constant on the screen.

AE (autoexposure). The camera employs the autoexposure and advanced backlight compensation systems to ensure that the subject remains bright even in harsh backlight conditions. Because the subject's position is known, a comparison can be made between its brightness and that of the background, and the camera can subsequently be adjusted to compensate for the conditions.

MD (motion-detector) mode.   MD mode basically detects the difference between the initial reference image and the current image. The conventional technique employed in MD mode uses only the brightness of the video signal. The EVI-D30 camera uses both the brightness and the color, which enables even an object of the same brightness as the background to be detected.

NOTE

The following sections cover three cameras I would recommend from Sony. For more information, go to Sony's broadcast and professional Web site at www.sony.com and navigate to electronics.

The Sony EVI-D30 Pan/Tilt/Zoom Color NTSC Camera

The Sony EVI-D30 camera is a color NTSC PTZ camera with a high-speed, wide-range, pan-tilt head; integrated 12× high-speed autofocus zoom lens; and autotracking and motion detection. It is fully controllable remotely via RS-232C/VISCA, and it has an infrared (IR) remote commander. Its features include:

- A high-speed, wide-range pan/tilter
- A 12× optical zoom, high-speed autofocus lens
- A six-position preset
- An autotracking/motion detector
- An RS232C serial control
- An IR remote commander
- A time/date generator

The Sony EVI-D30C Color PTZ Camera

The Sony EVI-D30C Color PTZ camera is a lower-cost version of the EVI-D30. This camera does not come with accessories such as the IR remote commander. It does have the ac power adaptor, Velcro strips, A/V cable, and operating instructions. Features include:

- A high-speed, wide-range pan/tilter
- A 12× optical zoom, high-speed autofocus lens
- A six-position preset
- An autotracking/motion detector
- An RS232C serial control
- A time/date generator

The Sony EVI-D30L Color PTZ Camera

The Sony EVI-D30L camera is the lowest-cost version in the Sony EVI-D30 series. It has fewer functions, but it operates like a member of the same family. Unlike the Sony EVI-D30C, this camera omits the AT and MD, A/V out, RS-232C out, and other functions. The EVI-D30L camera has these features:

- A high-speed, wide-range pan/tilter
- A 12× optical zoom, high-speed autofocus lens
- A six-position preset
- An RS232C control input terminal

Videotape Recorders and Remote Control

Now that we have discussed conferencing cameras, let's explore video-tape recorders. Although both these devices capture your raw audio and video feeds, they are used differently.

Videotape recorders are used to store captured content on high-quality tape in an analog format, which then needs to be converted to digital files for streaming. Eventually, we will eliminate analog captures and go directly to digital capture only. Until then, we must convert our current content from analog to digital. I suggest that you use the best-quality systems available for this conversion. Garbage capture ultimately results in garbage streams.

Finding a High-Quality Videotape Recorder

High-quality capture of both audio and video on tape is extraordinarily important. The old adage applies: "Garbage in, garbage out." The higher the quality of input, the better the output, especially with video streaming. There is a noticeable difference between the output of a standard VCR and that of a high-performance playback device, such as Beta SP. If at all possible, you should choose to have your video digitized using a Beta SP versus a VCR. When looking for the right videotape recorder or playback device, I suggest that you look for the following features:

- At minimum, locate a new or used VTR (videotape recorder) with a four-channel audio monitor, built-in LTC/user bit time code reader, and built-in radio frequency (RF) modulator.

- Because the industry is rapidly moving toward remote control, you should add wireless/wired remote control.

- Also look for a unit that is 19 inches wide and rack-mountable. You may want to stack this device with others and/or make it portable.

- Although there are many refurbished units in today's marketplace, look at a few new units, such as:
  - The Sony BVW22 (which is a player only)
  - The Sony BVMW55 Portable Betacam SP Editing Recorder/Player
  - The Sony BVWD75 Betacam SO Studio Recorder/Player (the system I prefer)

NOTE

Check out the Sony videotape recorders mentioned in this section at www.bpgprod .sel.sony.com/bpcnav/app/99999/16/134.99999.subcat.BPC.html. You many find that some of the features mentioned in this chapter have changed slightly and new models may have been added since this writing.

Sony BVW22 Betacam SP Player

The Betacam SP program viewer has many features and is one of the most economical systems worthy of serious consideration for streaming media. Features include a wireless/wired remote control (RM-770 supplied), time code superimposition on video, a built-in LTC/user bit time code reader (supplied), a built-in RF modulator for TV receivers (with F-cables and antenna selector), a four-channel audio monitor, and it is 19 inches wide and rack-mountable (with the optional RMM-507 rack mount kit). In addition to the features just mentioned, this player may best serve your needs with its:

- Low cost

- Easy-to-use control panel

- More than 90 minutes of playback time using L-cassettes

- Two AFM audio channels in addition to two longitudinal audio channels with the Dolby C-type NR (noise reduction) system

- Picture search capability (including a monochrome picture search at +3.5 times normal speed)

Sony BVMW55 Portable Betacam SP Editing Recorder/Player

As you progress upward with Sony, you may want to evaluate the Sony Portable Betacam SP Editing Recorder/Player with built-in LCD monitor, which, last time I checked, had a list price in excess of $24,000.

This portable editing recorder is a small, lightweight, rugged Betacam and Betacam SP recorder/player with a built-in LCD video monitor that is ideal for field editing. Two BVMW55s can be combined using a docking kit to create a portable editing solution that can perform assemble, insert, and audio-split editing. Two docked BVMW55s can also be set up to perform sequential recording from one unit to another. The unit can operate for approximately 80 minutes with a BP-L90 battery, but can be connected via an optional adaptor for ac operation. The following input and output signals are supported: SDI video and audio, analog composite video, analog audio, and time code.

An overview of BVMW55 features that may be suited to your needs include:

Record and playback.   The BVMW55 provides over 30 minutes of recording/playback time. It can be used together with existing Betacam SP or Betacam SX VTRs.

Insert/assemble editing.   The BVMW55 can be connected to various editing VTRs or controllers.

Display monitor.   It has a high-resolution LCD display with a wide viewing angle.

Shot marking.   Virtual shot marks can be recorded and stored in the BVW-55's memory. This information is retained even after the unit is turned off. Virtual shot marks can be added during playback or search.

Power requirements.   The BVMW55 has an attachment that can accommodate various batteries or an ac adapter. The unit can operate approximately 80 minutes on battery power.

Size and weight.   One BVMW55 weighs 15 pounds, 6 ounces.

Playback.   It provides dual standard (NTSC/PAL) playback for viewing purposes.

Playback confidence.   It provides simultaneous playback during recording.

Signal generation.   It has selectable video patterns and tone generator.

Input and output.   It can be connected to devices with the following input and output signals: SDI (video and audio), analog composite video, analog audio (balanced), and time code.

i.LINK input.   An interface unit that docks on the V-shoe attachment allows the BVMW55 to control an i.LINK device with LANC (Local Area Network Control) control and converts i.LINK to SDI.

Editing functions.   When combined with either another BVMW55 or the appropriate supporting device, assemble editing, insert editing, and audio-split editing can be performed, in addition to DMC (Desktop Multimedia Content) editing.

Sequential recording.   Two BVMW55s can be configured to record an event that spans two cassettes automatically. When configured for overwrite recording, the BVMW55s will record the last hour of an event continuously.

Sony BVWD75 Betacam SP Studio Recorder/Player

The Sony BVWD75 Betacam SP Studio Recorder/Player is at the high end of recorders, with a current list price nearing $40,000 when this book was written. The BVWD75 has serial digital component inputs and outputs, built-in comprehensive two-machine editing, as well as a built-in character generator. There is also a function status and shuttle tape-speed indicator, and a built-in capstan override that allows playback tape speed to be varied +/– 20 percent of normal speed in 1 percent steps. The setup menu offers operational flexibility and sophisticated, built-in self-diagnostics.

Notable features of the BVWD75 include:

Playback confidence.   The BVWD75 is equipped with video and Ch-1/2 audio confidence heads for simultaneous playback during recording.

Picture quality.   By combining the Betacam SP recording format with metal-particle tape, the BVWD75 produces very high-quality recordings, with wide luminance bandwidth, improved signal-to-noise ratio, and other key parameters.

Character display.   The BVWD75 is provided with a built-in character generator, and its output can be superimposed on the monitor out signal to display either time-code generator/reader data or CTL timer data.

Digital interface.   One-component digital video serial input and four-component digital video serial outputs are available. There are four digital audio channels, and other digital audio capabilities are available via special connections. Videocomponent analog monitor output is also provided.

Audio.   Along with its digital audio interfaces, the BVWD75 also provides conventional analog audio connections.

Dynamic tracking.   Using a dynamic tracking (DT) head and associated circuit technology, the BVWD75 reproduces low-noise, broadcast-quality video over the range (1 to +3 times normal speed).

High-speed picture.   The picture-search facility of the BVWD75 provides recognizable color pictures at up to 10 times play speed in both forward and reverse, and monochrome pictures at up to 35 times play speed.

Program play mode.   The program play mode allows video recordings to be reproduced at up to +/– 20 percent of normal play speed in 0.1 percent steps, allowing program material to be expanded or compressed to fit a particular time slot.

Remote Control of Videotape Recorders

As video streaming becomes part of our media communications, remote-control software for videotape recorders, cameras, audio and video capture cards, and other audio and video input feeds will become very useful for organization and saving time. Pipeline Digital has developed software for the Macintosh and Windows 95/NT that is used to control RS-422, RS-232, VISCA, or LANC videotape machines.

NOTE

For the latest features, prices, and specifications of Pipeline Digital remote control software, connect to www.commerce.secureinput.com/dpipe/ or AnyStream at www.anystream.com.

Taking the Next Step

This chapter covered a variety of low- to high-end video cameras and recorders (the first component of quality). The discussion included: digital cameras, conferencing cameras, and video recorders. Chapter 5 will discuss the second component of quality: audio/video capture devices and how they work.

Audio/Video Capture Devices: The Second Component of Quality

B efore one can start to stream audio/video media data, the data must be acquired, and the acquisition process is the primary role for audio/video capture devices. Since they are at the forefront of the streaming process, these devices play a critical role in the overall quality of streaming. They set the boundary conditions on the quality level throughout the rest of the streaming media experience. Moreover, since the quality level of your streaming media is a critical element in successful streaming, you must understand how a capture card works and how to choose the best capture device for your application.

Laying the Foundations of Quality

As detailed in the previous chapter, the camera, microphone, and video recorder are the first components of quality in providing audio/video media for streaming. They are the external sources used to obtain what we see and hear. The components themselves vary in quality, and they cost anywhere from a few dollars to tens of thousands of dollars (and sometimes more). While the buying decision is outside the scope of this chapter, the selection of the external device plays a critical role in the choice of a capture device (or capture card)—the second component of quality and the topic of this chapter. In addition, while external sources set the bar for the first level of audio/video quality, the choice of capture card can either sustain this quality, improve it slightly, or destroy it.

Thus a *capture card* is simply a device that acquires audio and/or video data from an external source, such as a camera or videotape recorder (VTR), and presents these data for further processing. The additional processing may be something as simple as saving the data to disk, or it may transform the format of the data into a different format, perhaps one that is more compact and thus more readily streamable.

This chapter covers the feature sets that define a video capture card and gives you a foundation of technical information that supports the significance of these features. Topics to be discussed include:

- How video devices interface with a computer
- The various external audio and video source signal formats
- Basic digital concepts, including: digitization, subsampling, frame rates, interlacing, and aspect ratios
- Capture color formats and color conversion
- Capture resolutions, frame rates, and capture bottlenecks

Capture Device Interfaces

A capture card often is first defined by its connection to the host computer. Typically, when working in conjunction with a personal computer (PC) platform, most capture cards are Peripheral Component Interconnect (PCI) add-in components that work with virtually all IBM-compatible PC platforms. Some capture cards are Universal Serial Bus (USB)–based and thus live entirely outside the host computer. In the case of digital video (DV), external sources provide audio/video data over IEEE-1394 devices, and, thus, in some simple instances, the capture device can be just an IEEE-1394 add-in card. Finally, some graphics cards, such as ATI- or Nvidia-based products, also have basic video capture capabilities.

A capture card is defined secondly by the external source signal formats from which it can acquire data. Imagine the connections between an external source, such as a camera, and a capture card as being wires. Audio/Video data flow on these wires in different formats. Tables 5.1 and 5.2 cover most source formats used today in the streaming space (in approximate levels of increasing quality).

Table 5.1 Types of Audio and Video Inputs

VIDEO SOURCE		COMMENTS
Composite	Analog	Single wire with the three video components (YCbCr) combined. Consumer grade and found on practically all sources. Connector is typically a single RCA or BNC.
S-Video	Analog	Two wires with luminance component (Y) separate from the color-difference components (CbCr). Used on Hi8, SVHS, DVD players, and so on. Connector is S-Video mini-Din.
Component	Analog	Three wires, with each video component signal separate. Found on DVD players, Betacam SPs, and so on. Connector is typically three RCA or BNC jacks.
DV DVCPro-50	Digital	4:1:1 for NTSC, 4:2:0 for PAL.5:1 DCT-based compression at 25 Mbps. Found on Digital8, MiniDV, DVCPro, and DVCam. Transmitted over IEEE-1394. Connector is typically 4- or 6-pin IEEE-1394.
Digital-S	Digital	4:2:2 for NTSC/PAL. 3.3:1 DCT-based compression at 50 Mbps. Connector is typically 4- or 6-pin IEEE-1394.
SDI	Digital	4:2:2 for NTSC/PAL stored via a 2:1 DCT-based compression but transmitted over a wire as 270 Mbps uncompressed. Transmitted over a single wire. Connector is typically via a single BNC. 10 bits/component.

Table 5.2 Various Audio Source Formats

AUDIO SOURCE		COMMENTS
Unbalanced	Analog	Single wire for each channel. Typically two channels (stereo left and right). Consumer-grade and found on practically all sources. Connector is two RCAs or a single 8-mm minijack.
Balanced	Analog	Two wires for each channel. Typically two channels (stereo left and right). Professional-grade and found on practically all professional sources. Connector is typically a three-prong XLR jack for each channel.
DV	Digital	48 kHz, 16 bits/channel, two channels or 32 kHz, 12 bits/channel, four channels. Embedded in DV signal over IEEE-1394.
AES/EBU	Digital	Typically 32, 44.1, or 48 kHz, 16 to 20 bits/channel. Two channels (left/right) are carried over a single XLR cable.
SDI	Digital	Embedded in the same signal as SDI video. Also, up to 16 channels of audio can be carried in a single SDI signal.

The external source signal formats listed in these tables play themselves out in a variety of different capture card offerings.

Basic Capture Cards

A number of capture cards are available today that are designed specifically for analog capture. Most of these devices can be purchased for less than $200. Usually, they provide inputs for composite and S-Video as well as a single stereo audio input. Examples include the Osprey-100, the Osprey-210, and Winnov Videum-AV products. A simple IEEE-1394 card that allows for capture of compressed DV by the host also can be purchased for less than $200.

Professional Capture Cards

A step up from the basic analog cards adds balanced audio to the mix of inputs. Balanced audio sources are the norm for professional end users, and thus these lines of cards sometimes are referred to as *entry-level professional capture devices.* Audio and/or video cards of this type usually cost anywhere from $300 to $800 and are available from such companies as the Osprey Video Division of the ViewCast Corporation (the Osprey-220) and Winnov (the Videum-II).

Professional broadcasters started to pick up interest in streaming around the time that broadband access for the masses appeared on the horizon. These broadcasters, already using high-end audio and video gear, needed to interface their equipment to streaming encoding solutions. The need was soon met by the release of a number of professional video capture devices targeted specifically at the streaming space.

Professional capture cards trend toward the support of media professionals by accommodating both analog and digital inputs. Some professional capture devices, such as the Osprey-500, provide for nearly all the various external source formats listed in the preceding tables. Professional cards of this type usually cost anywhere from $800 to $3,000. A few companies, such as Pinnacle, Winnov, and ViewCast, also offer some professional inputs on their encoding system products (with the ViewCast system line being based on Osprey cards).

Since most PCs today come configured with either onboard audio or an audio card already installed, the simple task of adding in a video-only capture card is all that is required to start streaming audio and video. As mentioned earlier, both Osprey and Winnov offer video-only capture devices targeted specifically at the streaming space. Streaming is not only about video, however—far from it. Most streaming today is audio-only. For audio-only streams, the standard onboard audio device often is sufficient for most users, although more professional audio devices, such as those offered by Antex, typically are used by streaming professionals for their multichannel video capture and audio preprocessing capabilities.

For the purposes of this chapter, I will be focusing mostly on the video side of capture devices, which are further defined by the video formats and video data rates they are capable of providing to the host, where further processing takes place. The term *video format* as used here is different from the external-source (video camera and recorder) *signal format*, discussed in the preceding chapter. In the context of this chapter, I will refer to the video format in terms of both *video resolution* and *video color.*

NOTE

For up-to-date information on the manufacturers and products listed in this section, browse to any of the following Web sites:

- **Osprey Video Division of the ViewCast Corporation (the Osprey-220 and Osprey-500) at: www.viewcast.com**

- **Winnov (the Videum-II) at: www.winnov.com**

- **Pinnacle at: www.pinnaclesys.com**

- **Antex at: www.antex.com**

The Advantage of Audio/Video Devices

While it is not necessary for audio and video to be on the same device, there are a few advantages to this:

- ◆ First, installing a single device with integrated audio and video capture is the easiest, most compact method for producing an encoding station that can create multiple streams with unique content.

- ◆ Second, having audio and video on the same device allows for better audio/video synchronization, because the audio sample clock can be derived from the video clock.

Digital Video Basics

Before I can expand on the topics thus far introduced in this chapter, it will be very helpful for you to have some background on the basics of digital video. This section covers a variety of digital video concepts that should give you a greater understanding of what a capture device truly does and why various features of capture devices are important.

Digitization: Sampling and Quantization

The process of creating digital video from an analog source is called *digitization*. Digitization is composed of the following two steps:

- *Sampling* is a process applied in time (one dimension, such as audio), space (two dimensions, such as still images), and space/time (three dimensions, such as moving images). An example of sampling is illustrated in Figure 5.1.

- *Quantization* defines the number of discrete levels or values that a sample can have. For example, a sample that has potential values of 0 to 255 is said to have 8-bit quantization (a reference to the amount of colors being displayed—the equivalent of 256 colors with value ranges from 0 to 255—which will become clear as you read on). While having more levels improves the accuracy or precision of the sample, there is a point at which additional levels become inefficient and no longer yield information that human beings are able to perceive.

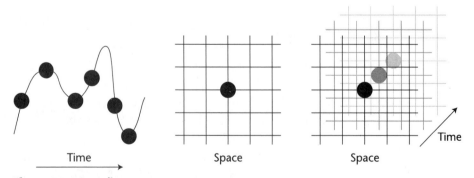

Figure 5.1 Sampling.
Credit: Osprey Video Division for the ViewCast Corporation.

Human Vision and Subsampling

The human vision system has three input sensors that represent nearly all colors a human being can perceive. Studies of human color perception have further discovered that:

- Human vision has an extremely high acuity for brightness, or *luma*.
- Human beings have a poor visual response to color.

To give you a better understanding of how we see colors, direct light coming from the sun or from any other light-emitting source, has properties. White light is a combination of all the other "colors" of light. Note that this is different (the opposite) from mixing pigments (of paint), where a mixture of all colors results in black. When white light strikes a blue shirt, all the colors (wavelengths) of light are absorbed except the (B) blue wavelength, which is reflected back into the eye. The reason that a black shirt is hot in the summer is that all the wavelengths of colored light are changed into heat; none of the colors are reflected into the eye.

Therefore, within every light source is a combination of wavelengths of light. These wavelengths correspond to what we perceive to be colors. The short wavelengths are the (B) blue, (U) indigo, and (V) violet end of the spectrum. The long wavelengths are the (R) red, (O) orange, and (Y) yellow ends. The human eye (central vision) is most sensitive to the wavelength corresponding to yellow. That is why we see black letters best against a yellow background. Yellow is the most "seeable" wavelength.

For these reasons, video samples are coded by a luminance component of yellow (Y) and two color-difference signals, blue and yellow (B-Y) and red and yellow (R-Y), and the three input sensors of the human eye are yellow and indigo or ultraviolet (Y, U) and violet (V). The two color-difference signals have a few scaling variations that are used frequently. UV scaling is properly used only as an intermediate step in the formation of composite NTSC or PAL video signals.

All the hue information (chroma) is held by the Cb and Cr values. Roughly, Cb corresponds to chroma (Y) yellow and (B) blue, and Cr corresponds to chroma (Y) yellow and (R) red. Another frequently used color component is PbPr, which comes from SMPTE (Society of Motion Picture and Television Engineers) 240M, and specifies RGB (the basic color palette of video, composed of the colors red, green, and blue) or YPbPr. The terms UV, CbCr, and PbPr are common.

Crucial Little Facts

In standard computer graphics RGB (8-bit per channel) encoding, each value ranges from 0 to 255. (0,0,0) is black and (255,255,255) is white. In YCbCr (always 8-bit per channel) encoding:

- ◆ Y ranges from 16 to 235 (16 darkest and 235 brightest).
- ◆ Cb and Cr range from 16 to 240 (with 128 as the zero point).
- ◆ Thus, (16, 128, 128) is pure black, and (235, 128, 128) is pure white. (A lot of sloppy software gets the scaling right, but misses the 16 offset!)

Note that there are combinations of individually *legal* Y, Cb, and Cr values that do not specify *valid* RGB colors! For example, (235, 240, 240).

Pixel Component Values

A single video sample picture element, or *pixel,* is thus composed of three component values. For this discussion, I will refer to these as Y, U, and V. If each component has an 8-bit quantization, then this video sample is represented by 24 bits. This is where the phrase *24 bits per pixel* comes from. However, by taking into account the poor color acuity of human beings, one can actually *subsample* the color components without reducing the human response, a topic explained in the next section.

The Technology and Types of Subsampling

We start off with each pixel being represented by three unique component values. Since each component is equally represented, this could be called *1:1:1 sampling.* However, this is typically referred to as *4:4:4 sampling.* You will see why in a moment. Subsampling the color components horizontally by 2 yields 4:2:2 sampling. With 4:2:2 sampling, each pixel has its own unique luminance component but shares its two color, or *chrominance,* components with a horizontally adjacent pixel. In Figure 5.2, the illustration of 4:2:2 subsampling shows that pixel 0 and pixel 1 in a row share the same U and V component values, while they have unique Y values. This format has an effective bandwidth of 16 bits per pixel (assuming 8 bits per component).

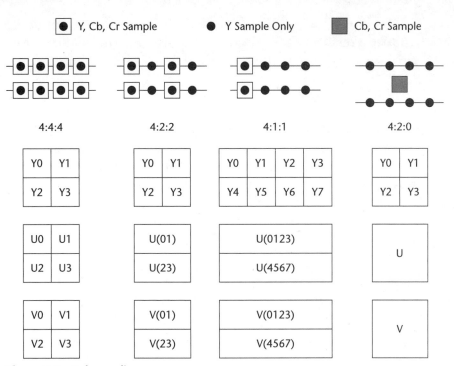

Figure 5.2 Subsampling.

Credit: Osprey Video Division for the ViewCast Corporation.

Subsampling the color components horizontally by 4 yields 4:1:1 sampling. With 4:1:1 sampling, each pixel has its own unique luminance component value but shares its two chrominance component values with three other horizontally adjacent pixels. In other words, pixels 0, 1, 2, and 3 in a row share the same U and V component values, while they have unique Y values. This format has an effective bandwidth of 12 bits per pixel.

A final form of subsampling involves subsampling the color components by a factor of 2 in both the horizontal and vertical directions. Thus, in a quad of four pixels, each pixel has its own unique luminance component value but shares its two chrominance component values with the other pixels in the quad. This type of subsampling is called *4:2:0 sampling*. Like 4:1:1 sampling, the 4:2:0 format also has an effective bandwidth of 12 bits per pixel.

The standard for television video (CCIR-601) requires 4:2:2 sampling. Thus, practically all capture cards that perform an analog-to-digital

(A/D) conversion on their composite, S-Video, or component inputs produce a resulting 4:2:2 digital video stream. They also typically quantize each component into 8 bits, although some solutions do generate 10 bits per component.

NOTE

As mentioned under external source formats earlier, SDI (serial digital interface) video is also a 4:2:2 digital stream, but it has a quantization of 10 bits per component. Thus SDI has an effective bandwidth of 20 bits per pixel. While DV is a compressed format, the sampling before compression is 4:2:0 for Phase Alternate Line (PAL) DV and 4:1:1 for National Television Standards Committee (NTSC) DV.

Temporal Frame Rate and Interlacing

Sampling an image in space produces a still image. When you also sample it in time, motion video is produced. Yet motion video is composed of still images. When displaying these still images to a viewer, the rate at which the images are displayed in order to avoid flicker and the rate necessary for good motion perception by human beings depend on the ambient light levels. This is one reason why film is composed of 24 frames per second (displayed at a rate of 48 Hz in a movie theater) as compared with NTSC television, which typically is watched in a home living room and has an approximate rate of 30 frames per second (displayed in interlaced form at 60 Hz). Another factor is that television systems originated with field rates based on local ac power-line frequencies, for example, 60 Hz in North America and 50 Hz in Europe.

Most video is viewed in an interlaced format. For simplicity, the NTSC standard is used in the following explanation of an interlaced format. NTSC video is composed of images taken approximately 60 times a second. Each image is called a *field,* and there are odd and even fields. Although these odd and even fields are temporarily adjacent to each other in time, the horizontal lines that make up these fields are spatially different.

Figure 5.3 is a simplified view of interlaced video and fields. The two fields are taken $\frac{1}{60}$th of a second apart, and the lines of each field are not aligned but rather are staggered. Most televisions are interlace-display devices, where the 60 fields are displayed individually, and the viewer perceives only one field at a time. Each field has a size of 720×240 pixels. There are actually more horizontal active lines, but they, for the most part, contain nonvideo information. For simplicity, this discussion will assume 240 active lines per field.

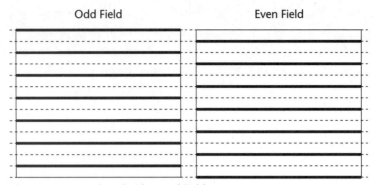

Figure 5.3 Interlaced video and fields.

Credit: Osprey Video Division for the ViewCast Corporation.

Typically, the notion of a video *frame* implies two fields of video. Thus a full-resolution video frame is 720 × 480 pixels. However, most computer monitors are progressive and not interlaced display devices. Progressive displays do not split video into fields and draw them one after the other. On a progressive display, when video is viewed at its full resolution, viewers see both the odd and even fields at the same time (Figure 5.4).

There are various issues with combining temporally different fields into a single frame, and these will be discussed later in this chapter. However, it is sufficient to say at this point that if a user desires a video image less than or equal to the field height, most capture cards can return only video from one of the two fields that make up a frame. Thus a request for a video capture size of 240 lines or less typically results in the capture of a single field.

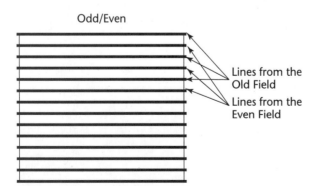

Figure 5.4 Combining both odd and even fields into a single frame in a progressive display.

Credit: Osprey Video Division for the ViewCast Corporation.

A final point to cover here is that some video sources are not interlaced. These are called *progressive sources*. A frame of a progressive source is composed of a full-resolution image in which each pixel is sampled at the same instant in time. Various cameras have progressive capture modes. Film is also progressive in nature. The 24 frames per second of film is composed of 24 progressive images.

Square versus CCIR-601 Aspect Ratios

The width-height ratio for the *physical* pixels on a TV does not have a 1:1 relationship. TVs are said to have a *CCIR-601* aspect ratio. Computer monitors do have a 1:1 width-height ratio for pixels and are said to have a *square* aspect ratio. Do not confuse this with the concept of the display resolution. The latter is the ratio of the *number* of horizontal pixels compared with the *number* of vertical pixels. This resolution is commonly 4:3 (640 × 480, for example).

The reason that this concept is important to capture devices is that these devices often capture CCIR-601 video signals to be further processed and eventually displayed on a square aspect ratio display, such as a computer monitor. The following example illustrates these issues: An image of circles is drawn on a piece of paper. A video camera is then pointed at this paper, and a video capture device is used to capture the image and display the result on a computer monitor.

If the image is captured using a CCIR-601 aspect ratio by the capture device and then displayed on the square aspect ratio computer monitor, the image will appear stretched.

The correct procedure is to rescale the image if the video source provided a CCIR-601 digital signal. In the case of analog video signals, sample the analog video using a square aspect ratio sampling procedure. This results in a proper capture and display of the image.

Capture Formats

As stated previously, a capture card is further defined by the video formats (video resolution and video color) it is able to provide to the host for further processing. Pixels of uncompressed, or raw, video formats usually are based on a YUV color space, as discussed earlier in the digital video basics section. If a capture can provide RGB (the basic color palette of video, composed of the colors red, green, and blue) video formats, then it is said to have the feature called *color-space conversion.*

Typical video formats are given in Table 5.3. Note that Four-Character Codes (FOURCC) are a set of codes that are four characters in length and were introduced by Microsoft to clearly identify video data stream formats.

NOTE

There are many variants of FOURCC codes for a given format, and Table 5.3 includes only one variant. Refer to www.microsoft.com/hwdev/devdes/fourcc.html for a complete list.

Table 5.3 Capture Color Formats/FOURCC Codes

FORMAT	FOURCC	COMMENTS
YUV 4:4:4	IYU2	4:4:4 sampling, 24 bits/pixel, packed format ($U_0Y_0V_0U_1Y_1V_1$)
YUV 4:2:2	YUY2	4:2:2 sampling 16 bits/pixel, packed format (Y_0UY_1V)
YUV 4:2:0	I420	4:2:0 sampling, 12 bits/pixel, planar format
YUV 4:1:1	Y41P	4:1:1 sampling, 12 bits/pixel, planar format
YUV 9	YVU9	9 bits/pixel, planar, subsample of CbCr by 4 vertically and horizontally
Grayscale	Y800	8-bit Y only
RGB 32	RGBA	4:4:4 sampling, 32 bits/pixel, packed, RGB plus alpha channel
RGB 24	BI_RGB	4:4:4 sampling, 24 bits/pixel, packed, RGB
RGB 16	BI_RGB	4:4:4 sampling, 16 bits/pixel, 5 bits for R and B and 6 bits for G
RGB 15	BI_RGB	4:4:4 sampling, 16 bits/pixel, 5 bits for R, G, and B, 1 unused bit
RGB 8	BI_RGB	8 bits/pixel yielding 256 colors

A key feature for a capture device is the card's ability to provide various color formats via hardware processing. Host processing tasks often have preferred formats. For example, the Windows media codec internally uses the IYUV format (this is the same as I420 in Table 5.3). If a user were using this codec and chose to capture images in an RGB format, then the capture device would first color-convert YUV 4:2:2 to RGB, and then the host encoder would have to convert these RGB data back to YUV as well as subsample the images down to YUV 4:2:0.

If the user plans on editing capture footage before encoding, in this example it would be best to capture the video in YUV 4:2:2 because this is probably the native pixel format of the source video signal. Editing could be done in YUV 4:2:2 space, and then later this material could be subsampled down to YUV 4:2:0 and used by the encoder.

Resolution and Capture Rates

Another core feature used to define a capture device is the video data rate and resolutions at which the device can provide video to the host for further processing (Figure 5.5). While this is truly a *key* measurement, it is probably the most difficult to nail down because there are a number of system components that affect this measurement.

An analog or digital video signal enters a video capture device that *captures* these data to memory. The locations into which video frames are typically captured are memory buffers provided by a host application. Once the data are captured into a memory buffer, the video device returns the memory buffer to the host application, where the buffer is processed further (perhaps saved to disk or encoded for streaming purposes).

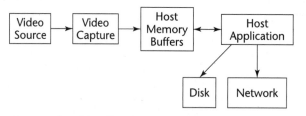

Figure 5.5 Video flow into a capture device.

Credit: Osprey Video Division for the ViewCast Corporation.

The First Bottleneck: Device-to-Host Memory Capture Speed

The speed at which video can be captured from the device to host memory is the first potential bottleneck. For example, due to the limited bandwidth associated with USB 1.0, many USB video capture devices can only transfer 320 × 240–sized images to the host and perhaps only at 15 frames per second (fps). Some USB video capture devices may attempt to get around the bandwidth issue by compressing video in the device itself and then decompressing the resulting data stream on the host. While this may allow for larger resolutions at faster rates, the quality of the resulting video suffers. (It had to be compressed and then decompressed.) In addition, precious central processing unit (CPU) cycles are used on the host for the decompression in order to provide the application with its requested color format.

PCI-based devices are not as limited in bandwidth as are USB devices, but even some PCI-based capture cards do some form of compression in hardware and decompression in software in order to capture full-resolution images. Some video capture cards even may provide to the host application what appears to be full-resolution video but is, in fact, a line-doubled or scaled single field of video. Even PCI capture devices that can capture full resolution and full rates to the host can be at the mercy of other devices on the PCI bus because all devices on the bus roughly share the bus's bandwidth. It is critical that a PCI capture device is able to direct memory access (DMA) video it is capturing into memory. DMA uses little, if any, CPU resources to move video from the device into memory.

DV over an IEEE-1394 device normally does not have bottleneck issues in terms of the transfer to host memory. Thus every DV frame, at full resolution and full frame rates, can be captured to host memory. However, DV is a compressed format and is not readily usable by most streaming encoders without some additional CPU processing on the DV data, as follows:

- First, the DV data stream will need to be decompressed, producing a 4:2:0 or 4:1:1 YUV format.
- DV is also in a CCIR-601 aspect ratio (720 × 480) format. Thus, the host will need to resize the nonsquare DV pixels into square aspect ratio pixels (640 × 480).

- Finally, the streaming audience profile may not be full resolution, and, therefore, the full-resolution decoded DV may need to be scaled down further.

All these tasks can be very CPU heavy and thus leave little CPU power for encoding, especially when the encoding is performed in real time.

However, there are video capture devices that accelerate these tasks entirely with hardware, such as the Osprey-500 and Osprey-2000 products, thus enabling real-time encoding and streaming from a DV source. These devices decode DV in the hardware and resample the video stream back to YUV 4:2:2. This stream can then be rescaled to a square aspect ratio and further scaled to smaller resolutions. It can also be color-converted or subsampled.

The Second Bottleneck: Buffer Availability Speed

Once video is captured into a memory buffer, the next bottleneck is the speed at which another buffer is made available to the device for the next frame capture. For example, if a host application uses five buffers for video capture, then these buffers will be filled in approximately ⅙ second. If the host application takes too long to process the buffers, perhaps due to its workload and high CPU use or due to latency writing the buffers to disk, then the capture device may not have a place into which to capture video data when the sixth frame is ready to be captured. A *dropped* frame will result. Typically, most capture devices can capture at full frame rates if:

- There is a buffer available to capture into
- There is not a bus bottleneck getting the video data from the device into the memory buffer

Too often dropped frames are blamed on the capture device when, in truth, another system resource is the cause of the bottleneck.

Moving toward Quality Performance

Since it is difficult to quantify the expected capture frame rate with a given application because of various potential system bottlenecks, documentation for a capture device should give performance numbers for pure capture to memory. These numbers should include the *true* video resolution being captured, the rate at which this resolution can be captured, and the amount of CPU or host processing needed to capture the video to memory.

While performance numbers often are given for the largest resolution a device can transfer, it is typical that host applications will desire much smaller resolutions. To accommodate this, it is important that capture devices have *hardware-based scaling*. This allows a capture device to sample video in full resolution and then scale it down to 320 × 240—for example, for broadband streaming or even 160 × 120 for dialup streaming. Although it does make a difference when such hardware-based scaling occurs during the capture process (for example, does it occur before or after subsampling of 4:2:2 video to 4:2:0), capture device vendors often do not explicitly document this level of detail. Finally, it is true that software-based scalers frequently provide better results than many hardware-based scalers, although at the expense of various system resources such as the CPU cycles needed for the software scaling and the extra memory and bus bandwidth required for the initial higher-resolution capture. Usually this is too high a price to pay, and it is best and reasonable to leave the scaling to the hardware device.

Another capture device performance measure is how fast the device can display what it is capturing into the graphics/VGA (video graphics array) card on the host machine. There are a number of ways a capture card can move video into the display device. The most optimal method is via a dedicated connection between the capture card and the VGA card. Cards that have physical VIP (video interlaced protocol) headers can support this ability (Figure 5.6).

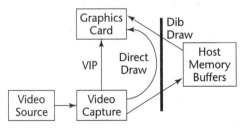

Figure 5.6 Capture device performance measurement.

Credit: Osprey Video Division for the ViewCast Corporation.

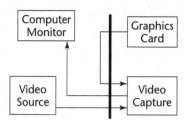

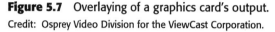

Figure 5.7 Overlaying of a graphics card's output.
Credit: Osprey Video Division for the ViewCast Corporation.

A second method has the capture card moving video directly into the memory of the display card, usually via DMA. This is called *DirectDraw* (refer to Figure 5.6). Another method is to go through system memory. Here, the capture card copies video to memory on the host machine, where it is later copied into the graphics card for display. This method uses the most CPU processing and is called *DibDraw* (refer to Figure 5.6). Osprey products, for example, support both DirectDraw and DibDraw.

Yet another option is to have the capture card and display card be one and the same, such as the ATI All-in-Wonder products. Here, the video being captured already exists on the display card.

A final option is called *Overlay* and is shown in Figure 5.7. Here, the graphic card's output to the computer monitor is redirected to the video capture card. The video capture card first overlays the video it is capturing onto the graphic card's output and then sends this to the computer monitor.

Other Capture Device Features

In addition to the base capabilities described so far, there is an assortment of other capture device features that enhance the overall capture quality and encoding workflow. These include:

- Multiple devices per system
- Cropping
- Bitmap overlays
- Closed-caption processing
- Deinterlacing
- Video and audio controls
- Noise reduction
- Inverse telecine
- Multiple audio/video data streams

Multiple Devices per System

For those who require streams of different video content, it is important to make sure that the capture card vendor supports having multiple devices in a single system. Typically, other system resources gate the number of devices. For example, a PCI machine with only three PCI slots is going to allow only three PCI cards. Moreover, a machine may run out of CPU power needed to encode more unique streams even though there is space available to add more cards. Bottlenecks in capture bandwidth, due either to the memory subsystem or to the underlying bus architecture, also can limit the number of devices per system.

Cropping

Cropping is a method for specifying a region of interest within a video source and discarding video data outside this region. A typical use of cropping is to capture video that is in a letterbox format. Letterbox material usually contains what appear to be black bars at the top and bottom of the video content.

As seen in Figure 5.8, the video source normally would be captured at 640×480 in size. However, the video material of interest is letterboxed and, thus, is actually 640×360 in size. Cropping removes the black bars so that only 640×360 is captured.

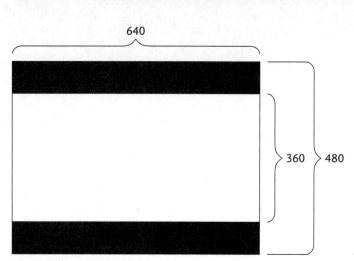

Figure 5.8 Video capture source of 640 × 480.
Credit: Osprey Video Division for the ViewCast Corporation.

Why would you want to do this? In the case of letterboxed material, the answer is fairly simple. By removing unwanted material from what is captured, the amount of captured data is significantly reduced. If you are saving your video to disk, this means:

- *Less disk space* is required for saving the material of interest.
- The *throughput,* both on capture and in saving to disk, *is smaller,* and thus capture is *less demanding* on the host machine.
- When encoding for streaming, either live or from a previously saved .avi file, the amount of *CPU processing* necessary to encode the video *is less* because there is less data to encode.
- Finally, because there is less data to encode, more valuable encoding bits can be applied to the material of interest, and, thus, *quality improves.*

Other reasons for cropping include:

- The removal of noise that is sometimes found on the horizontal or vertical edges of video content.
- You are just interested in a particular area of what a camera is pointing at.
- You need to have an unscaled image of a size less than that of a full-resolution image.

NOTE
In this latter case, without cropping, the only way to capture, say, a 256 (256-sized image, would be to scale the full-resolution image down to this size. This may have an adverse effect on the aspect ratio of the content, and the resulting video may appear stretched or squashed. With cropping, you can capture a 256 (256-sized video stream without scaling.

Bitmap Overlays

Some capture devices allow a bitmap to be superimposed over video as it is being captured. These bitmaps can be anything. Overlaying a company logo is a typical use. These bitmaps can take the place of video data in the area in which the bitmap is placed or they can be embossed. If they are embossed, frequently each pixel color value displayed is the average of the pixel value of the bitmap and the pixel value of the underlying video. Color-keying so that a specific color in the bitmap is not overlaid onto the captured video is also sometimes an option.

Closed-Caption Processing

Closed Captioning (CC) is a method of encoding text within a video signal. CC is included widely in broadcast video, cable, videotapes, DVDs, and so on. CC data are embedded on a video line before the first line of active video. In order to extract CC data from a video stream, a capture device either needs to provide a method for passing this data line to the host for decoding or must decode the CC data line in hardware itself. In either case, the decoded CC text data can be passed to applications out of band from the video stream or even overlaid in the video itself—thus having the appearance of movie subtitles.

RealNetworks' RealText is a method for streaming text. Some capture devices, such as the Osprey products, provide methods for interfacing their drivers directly with the RealText engine. They can easily stream CC data along with streaming audio/video data. CC is also often used for logging and searching purposes in conjunction with the creation of streaming content. Such companies as Convera and Virage are well known for this type of work.

Deinterlacing

The problem with progressive display devices is that if an object is moving, its position is not the same in both the odd and even fields. When odd and even fields are merged together, interlacing artifacts occur. This merging of the odd and even fields is required when the requested capture size is greater than a field size. In NTSC video, for example, this would occur when capturing greater than 240 lines. The artifacts are seen and commonly described as *streaking* or *feathering.*

The screen pictured in Figure 5.9 illustrates the streaking or feathering problem that occurred when the interlaced odd and even fields in this video were captured. Only a slight amount of motion took place, yet streaking is obvious in the overall result. Note the prominent horizontal lines outlining all the objects on this screen. Although the artifacts are most notable on the edges of moving objects, the interlace *noise* is present throughout objects in motion.

When encoding interlaced images, the encoder has a *significantly* harder time processing and compressing such interlaced video. The result is a *loss of overall quality* and perhaps a *loss of frame rate* as well. The reason frame rate can suffer is twofold. First, the encoder will be expending many valuable bits on encoding the interlace noise. In order to stay within a given encoding bit rate, the encode may have to drop frames so as not to exceed the available target rate. Second, encoding the extra noise wastes significant CPU cycles. If the CPU load becomes too high, the encoding session may start to drop frames for various reasons. Although the encoding process will smooth out some of the interlace artifacts/noise, the resulting compressed video still may appear somewhat streaked or feathered on playback and may not play back smoothly due to frame drops on the encoder.

Figure 5.9 Streaking of interlaced captured video.
Credit: Osprey Video Division for the ViewCast Corporation.

Some capture devices can apply a deinterlacing motion filter to any video source processing to eliminate interlace streaking or feathering while maintaining motion content. Some devices such as the Osprey-500 do this in hardware, whereas others, such as the Osprey-100 and Osprey-2x0 products, allow for this in software. For the Osprey-500, the deinterlace operation occurs prior to the optional scale and color-convert phases and thus produces an optimal-quality deinterlaced image.

In the screen snapshot shown in Figure 5.10, where a deinterlace motion filter has been turned on, note that the strong horizontal streaking or feathering around the subject's head has been smoothed to a slight blur. While the blur is noticeable in a single screen snapshot, the human eye perceives only natural motion when the video is played back at normal frame rates. Encoding the deinterlaced image significantly improves the output of the encoder in terms of overall quality and smoothness. The encoder has an easier time compressing the deinterlaced video and, thus, can expend saved bits and CPU cycles to produce higher-quality streams.

Video and Audio Controls

The ability to tweak various audio and video parameters is a plus for capture cards. Most video capture cards allow for adjustments to brightness, contrast, hue, and saturation. These typically can be done on the fly during encoding, and many vendors offer remote control interfaces for these parameters and/or SDKs (software development kits) that allow developers to customize their own control look and feel.

Figure 5.10   Effects of a deinterlacing motion filter.
Credit: Osprey Video Division for the ViewCast Corporation.

Audio-only devices, such as those from Antex, tend to have the most flexible control over audio-specific parameters, such as offering a wide range of hardware sample rates, hardware gain and attenuation control, hardware mixing, noise gating, and digital equalization. Most audio/video capture cards offer only a subset of these features but are still viable solutions.

Noise Reduction

Video noise reduction is just starting to be introduced into some video capture devices; for example, there is some level of noise reduction in Pinnacle's HiQ product. To date, most noise reduction has been either in the domain of very high-end video preprocessing devices, such as those available from Teranex and Snell & Wilcox, or accomplished as a postprocessing software task, perhaps with some hardware assistance, from such companies as Anystream and Media-100. A description of the various filters is beyond the scope of this chapter. However, it is sufficient to state that capture card vendors are focused on improving the quality of video, and we should start to see some forms of video preprocessing migrating to this class of devices.

Inverse Telecine

In the section covering frame rate and interlacing it was mentioned that film is actually progressive in nature and has a frame rate of 24 Hz. When film is converted to video, it undergoes a telecine process that converts the 24-fps source to an approximate 30-fps rate. The extra fields inserted during this process are not only redundant but also can introduce seemingly interlace-like artifacts if the resulting video is captured and treated as if the original material were 30 fps. A process called *inverse telecine* removes the extra fields and generates a 24-fps video stream. While the streaming encoders of today include software options for performing this action, it is actually best handled by hardware. Unfortunately, few capture cards provide this function today, although it is available with some of the high-end video preprocessing units mentioned in the noise-reduction section.

Multiple Audio/Video Data Streams

Traditionally, only a single application could acquire uncompressed audio and video data streams from a single capture device. This is certainly true of nearly all traditional capture cards (that is, cards used primarily for nonlinear editing). Yet it is often the case in the streaming space that producers of streaming content need to create streams at an assortment of data rates and various resolutions in order to optimally cover the diverse set of connection speeds. The customary methods for doing this are as follows:

Performing multiple encode sessions, one for each target profile. This option consumes time and does not provide for an efficient workflow, especially for users encoding lots of content at various profiles.

Externally splitting the video signal and sending it to multiple capture cards and having each card capturing for a specific encoding profile. This requires larger encoding machines due to the space requirement for each card. In addition, slight variations in each card or card settings can result in slightly different video being sent to each encoding session.

Using the single-stream/multirate encoding methods of the encoding platform (Real or WindowsMedia). This has the current drawback that settings for each profile within the single stream cannot be individually optimized. In addition, this does not solve the workflow problem if a streaming producer needs to generate Real, Windows-Media, and/or QuickTime format streams.

However, capture card companies who have a streaming focus have seen the need to improve the deficiencies mentioned in these scenarios. They do this by allowing the capture of multiple audio/video streams from a single device. These companies are Pinnacle Systems, Winnov, and the Osprey Video Division of the ViewCast Corporation. The basic multistreaming concept these companies offer is fairly similar: The goal is to allow a single device to feed more than one encoder. To see how and why this is advantageous, let's do a quick case study of Osprey's SimulStream technology.

SimulStreaming is the ability to simultaneously provide uncompressed audio and video streams to multiple applications. Other than some minor caveats, each application is unaware that there may be other applications also requesting audio and video data from the device it is using. Thus each application *thinks* it owns the device. This allows multiple applications to access a single device at the same time, and each application can independently control capture in the manner that it wants.

There is practically *no* limit to the number of applications from the Osprey product perspective (this differs from other companies' offerings that today limit the number of streams to four). Limitations on the number of applications are solely in the domain of other system resources. For example, if 8 applications using a single device consume 100 percent of the CPU bandwidth on a given machine, then the limit is eight applications. If these same 8 applications consume only 50 percent of the CPU bandwidth, then perhaps the user may be able to run 16 applications.

The same analogy is true for other system resources, such as network bandwidth, disk bandwidth, system memory, and so on. The concept to focus on here, however, is that these system resources are all scalable. You can add more or faster CPUs. And CPUs *will* get faster. You can add more memory. You can increase your network bandwidth. The Simul-Stream capability of the Osprey products has been designed for scalability. The following are some examples of what you can do with SimulStreaming:

- Run three copies of a WindowsMedia encoder and three copies of a RealProducer encoder, each streaming the exact same content at different sizes and rates. This is six different encode sessions. Perhaps this is a 320 × 240 WindowsMedia stream at 300 and 100 kb, a 320 × 240 RealMedia stream at 300 and 100 kb, a 160 × 120 WindowsMedia stream at 56 kb, and finally, a 160 × 120 RealMedia stream at 56 kb. The result of this is six completely independent streams that can be completely optimized for their individual target profiles. Although the WindowsMedia and RealProducer encoders internally support multiple streams with different encoding rates (the concept of multiple-bit-rate encoding), at present they do not support different input sizes for each stream. Nor is there refined control over optimizing each of the multiple streams with the single encoding session. The Osprey SimulStream approach is superior in this respect.

- The preceding example generated two CIF (common intermediate format) streams and one QCIF (quarter common intermediate format) stream in both the RealMedia and WindowsMedia formats. With a fast enough machine, one also could do one high-quality, high-bandwidth video stream of 640×480 at 30 fps for users with high-speed connections, a stream of 320×240 at 15 or 30 fps for midspeed users, and finally a stream of 160×120 at perhaps 7.5 fps for modem connections. Audio sample rates for each of these streams also can vary from 48-kHz/16-bit stereo down to 8-kHz mono.

- Encode one or more streams in multiple streaming formats while running another application that grabs individual frames at longer intervals for archival or logging purposes or even captures, and achieves an .avi uncompressed master stream to disk. At the same time, another application runs and acquires CC data for logging or streaming text purposes. All this occurs on a single machine from a single device.

In summary, the ability to provide multiple-application audio and video data streams from a single device:

- Provides *optimized* streaming for all audiences
- Addresses the broadest reach of users
- Maximizes streaming media production density
- Maximizes scalability
- Increases streaming production workflow efficiency

The ability to provide multiple streams from a single device is yet another way that capture cards targeted at the streaming space differentiate themselves from traditional capture cards—often marketed at the editing and authoring space as well as those who want to watch TV on their computers.

Table of Various Capture Cards

The following table summarizes the features of a number of the most popular video capture cards used in streaming today. Note that the information gathered for this table came from product literature and does not represent a complete list of the feature sets of these devices.

	OSPREY VIDEO DIVISION, VIEWCAST CORP						WINNOV					
	100	210	220	500 DV	500 DV PRO	2000D DV PRO	VO	AV	1000	1010	1020	VIDEUM II
NTSC	X	X	X	X	X	X	X	X	X	X	X	X
PAL	X	X	X	X	X	X	X	X	X	X	X	X
Composite (RCA or BNC)	X	X	X	X	X	X	X	X	X	X	X	X
S-Video	X	X	X	X	X	X	X	X	X	X	X	X
DV via IEEE-1394 (audio and video)				X	X	X						
SDI video					X	X						
Unbalanced audio	X	X	X	X	X	X		X	X	X	X	
Balanced audio		X	X	X	X	X						X
Digital audio: AES/EBU					X	X						
Embedded SDI audio						X						
720 × 480, 30 fps capture	X	X	X	X	X	X						
640 × 480, 30 fps capture	X	X	X	X	X	X			X	X	X	X
640 × 480, 15fps capture							X	X				
CCIR-601 video capture	X	X	X	X	X	X						

(continues)

	OSPREY VIDEO DIVISION, VIEWCAST CORP						WINNOV					
	100	210	220	500 DV	500 DV PRO	2000D DV PRO	VO	AV	1000	1010	1020	VIDEUM II
Square aspect ratio capture	X	X	X	X	X	X	X	X	X	X	X	X
Hardware scaling	X	X	X	X	X	X	X	X	X	X	X	X
Hardware color conversion	X	X	X	X	X	X	X	X	X	X	X	X
Hardware cropping	X	X	X	X	X	X						
DMA capable	X	X	X	X	X	X	X	X	X	X	X	X
Bitmap overlays	X	X	X	X	X	X	X	X	X	X	X	X
Closed Caption	X	X	X	X	X	X						
Deinterlacing HW				X	X							
Deinterlacing SW	X	X	X			X						
Audio monitoring output	X	X	X	X	X	X		X	X	X	X	X
Hardware gain and attenuation controls		X	X	X	X	X		X	X	X	X	X
Breakout input box				X	X	X			X	X	X	X
Rack-mounted input box				X	X	X			X	X	X	X
Windows API/SDK	X	X	X	X	X	X	X	X	X	X	X	X

Taking the Next Step

In conclusion, while a capture device is simply an acquisition tool used to move audio and video data from external sources into a host computer for further processing, it is an essential component of streaming. Because they are at one of the initial stages of the streaming content process, the quality and feature sets of these devices play a critical role in defining the overall quality of the content encoded. As mentioned in the previous chapter, "Garbage in, garbage out"—so the saying goes. This chapter has reviewed the following highlights of audio/video capture devices:

- Bus interface type (USB, PCI, IEEE-1394)
- External signal/source formats (composite, DV, SDI, balanced/unbalanced audio, AES/EBU audio)
- Color formats, color/format conversion, and subsampling (YUV, RGB, YUV 4:2:0)
- Capture resolutions and frame rates (for example, 640 × 480 at 30 fps)
- Bus mastering (DMA) for efficient transfer of video data to the host
- Hardware scaling
- Multiple devices per system
  - Cropping
  - Bitmap overlays
  - Closed-caption processing
  - Deinterlacing
  - Video/audio controls
  - Noise reduction
  - Inverse telecine
  - Multiple audio/video data streams

Hopefully, this chapter has given you a foundation of technical information and insights that supports the significance of these features. Perhaps some of what you have read here may aid you in improving your future capture needs. To help you to make those decisions, Chapter 6 will review some of the most popular types of audio and video capture cards available on the market today.

Capture Cards Compared: Making a High-Quality Choice

I have worked in the streaming video industry for many years, and I have found that the best way to provide a high-quality stream is to use high-quality products. A number of the products I describe in this chapter are capable of both audio and video capture, although a few are capable of only one type of capture. Some of the most popular, high-quality capture cards available will be reviewed, starting with Osprey.

Establishing a High-Quality Feature Set

Finding the proper audio/video capture card is very important. There are many manufacturers to pick from, but it is important to look for these features:

- Does the capture card work with Microsoft Windows 2000 or Windows XP?
- Does the capture card have the ability to capture at least S-Video?
- Is it compatible with the hardware components you already have installed?

Concerning the nature of your input (analog or digital), I suggest your video capture card have these feature sets:

- If you want to input analog only, the card must work with Windows 2000 and Windows XP, and, if possible, have balanced audio.

- If you want to capture a digital feed, I suggest either a serial digital interface (SDI) card, referred to as an *SDI card,* or FireWire IEEE-1394, developed by Apple.

Osprey

Osprey makes high-quality products from low-end audio and audio/video capture cards to much more robust capture cards such as those in the Osprey-500 and Osprey-2000 product lines. Osprey also has supporting software called *SimulStream* that enables you to use multiple formats and streams simultaneously.

The following subsections describe Osprey's current product line.

NOTE

Osprey is a subdivision of ViewCast Corporation; to find the latest information on the Osprey products mentioned in this chapter, access the Internet in one of the following ways:

- www.viewcast.com

- www.viewcast.com/products/osprey

- info@ospreyvideo.com

- You can also call 1-800-250-6622.

Osprey-100 Series: Video Only

An Osprey-100 board is included with every copy of RealNetworks' Streaming Media Starter Kit and also is bundled as part of the RealMedia Creation Kit. The Osprey-100 also allows for Windows Media encoding, along with capture into other popular software packages.

Benefits

- Multiple cards can be used simultaneously in a single system.

- They capture full-frame video at 30 frames per second (fps).

- They are recommended by Microsoft and RealNetworks.
- Windows 95/98/Me, 2000, and NT support is available.

Features

- Closed captioning (CC)
- Phase alternate line (PAL) and National Television Standards Committee (NTSC)–supported video formats
- Image overlay
- Supports video for Windows application programming interfaces (APIs) and OPI (Osprey Programming Interface)

Osprey-200 Series: Video and Audio

The Osprey-200 family combines the ability to capture professional-quality stereo audio with the industry-standard video capture capabilities of the Osprey-100. From the entry-level Osprey-200 to the midrange Osprey-210 and professional-level Osprey-220, this family of streaming capture products addresses many of the needs for analog audio and video capture.

Osprey-500: Video and Audio

The Osprey-500, hailed as the "Rolls-Royce of the industry" by *Streaming Media World,* is a professional-level digital capture card designed to provide streaming video from an analog or digital source. This professional streaming capture card provides end-to-end digital encoding and advanced preprocessing features. With these new features, the Osprey-500 provides high-quality video for streaming audio and video. It is available in two models, each offering professional audio and video input types.

The Osprey-500 DV. This is a professional digital streaming capture card with DV and analog inputs. It provides an IEEE-1394 port for DV input coupled with professional analog audio capabilities. The inputs include:

- DV
- Analog composite
- S-Video
- Unbalanced and balanced audio

The Osprey 500 DV Pro. This is a professional digital streaming capture card with SDI, AES/EBU, DV, and analog inputs. It provides SDI inputs as well as DV inputs like the Osprey-500 DV. It also includes digital audio as well as unbalanced and balanced analog audio. Its audio and video inputs include:

- External AES/EBU audio
- Unbalanced and balanced audio
- Consumer SP/DIF
- DV
- SDI video (SMPTE-259M)
- Embedded audio via SDI video input

The Osprey-500 ships with a breakout cable for video and audio inputs and a special audio and video output cable. Several other breakout options are available for the Osprey-500 to meet your specific work environment requirements, such as:

- A breakout box for the Osprey-500 has inputs for composite video, S-Video, balanced and unbalanced audio, and digital audio. It also features unbalanced (RCA) and balanced (XLR) audio connectors. Additionally, the right XLR balanced input is used as the digital AES/EBU audio input.

- A rack-mountable version of the breakout box is also available. The 1U rack input box has the same type of inputs as the breakout box but provides an additional set of inputs. This provides rack-saving benefits when you use multiple Osprey-500 streaming capture cards.

- In addition, a rack-mountable breakout panel is available that is ideal for systems using remote-control encoding. This provides rack-saving benefits when you use multiple Osprey-500 streaming capture cards.

Benefits

- Digital end-to-end capture
- Enhanced scalability with digital audio and video on one card
- Hardware decode and repacking of all sources for optimal real-time encoding

- Multiple card support
- Hassle-free XLR and BNC connectors for trouble-free use

Features

- Video inputs available: Digital SDI and IEEE-1394, analog composite, and S-Video
- Audio inputs available: Digital AES/EBU and S/P DIF, analog balanced and unbalanced stereo
- Hardware deinterlacing, scaling, and color conversion
- Software gain control
- Multiple hardware audio sampling rates

Osprey-2000: Video and Audio

The Osprey-2000 series of streaming capture cards provides transcoding from MPEG into streaming media format on the fly. This ability allows a myriad of VOD (video on demand) applications, where content can be repurposed and streamed from a central archive, eliminating the need to retain multiple resolutions of the same content. The Osprey-2000 family also provides professional-quality digital and analog video and audio inputs. Osprey-2000 bridges the gap between the streaming and professional video markets and is a multifaceted product with four distinct modes of operation:

- MPEG encoding
- MPEG decoding
- Streaming capture and preview
- File format transcoding

There are four versions of the Osprey-2000 product family, which are categorized in two groups:

Codec. These Osprey-2000 cards provide MPEG encoding and decoding as well as capture, preview, and file format transcoding. They vary by offering different audio and video input types, depending on your input needs.

Decoder. These Osprey-2000 cards provide MPEG decoding as well as capture, preview, and file format transcoding. Each card provides different audio and video input types. These cards are distinguished by the letter D after Osprey-2000.

The Osprey Programming Interface

OPI is an application programming interface (API) for cross-platform multimedia programming using Osprey streaming capture cards. The OPI API provides a mechanism for accessing card-specific capabilities in a platform-independent way and serves as the framework for producing platform- and hardware-independent applications.

OPI is not the only interface for programming Osprey multimedia cards under a single operating system (OS) platform. Developers who are implementing applications under a single OS platform are strongly encouraged to use the supported video and audio standard interfaces, such as Video for Windows on the Windows platform. OPI may be the solution for cross-platform multimedia development or the solution for dealing with any card functionality that is not supported by industry-standard video capture or standards-based interfaces suited to MPEG, such as DirectShow.

The OPI API is a collection of C++ classes. OPI represents a device as an instance of a generic class, with derived classes providing for specific capabilities of specific devices. OPI provides the ability to query devices about the capabilities they provide. Through OPI, programmers conceptually define how to process audio and video data. OPI will map the conceptual view to actual hardware and software modules. A "C" interface to OPI has been added into the current release. Future releases of OPI may include interfaces for other programming software and platform-specific languages.

The DirectShow Software Development Kit

Osprey Video has developed a DirectShow Software Development Kit (ODSDK) that can be used for DirectShow-based application development. The ODSDK provides DirectShow filters for both the MPEG encoding and MPEG decoding functionality, as well as for the Osprey-2000's audio/video capture functionality. Using the information provided in the

ODSDK developer's manual, OEMs and system integrators can write custom software applications that can fully use the Osprey-2000 hardware MPEG encoder and MPEG decoder, with software and applications developed specifically for Microsoft's DirectShow Filter Graph Interface Model.

Working with Video for Windows

Video capture source filters are installed with the Microsoft DirectShow at runtime. If you have video capture hardware that uses Video for Windows such as the Osprey-2000, special category filters are available in the Filter Graph Editor when you choose Insert Filters from the Graph menu under the Video Capture Sources.

Unlike ordinary DirectShow filters, special category filters, such as Video capture source filters, can work with more than one device. When DirectShow is installed, it will look for devices installed on your computer that work with the special category filter and list the options in that category. For example, in the Video capture source filter category, DirectShow will list all the video capture cards installed on the system. You then need to choose which device to use.

Winnov

Winnov is another leader when it comes to audio and video capture cards. Like Osprey, Winnov is recommended by OEM leaders, such as Microsoft, Intel, AVID, Adobe, and any other company that wants to support video streaming.

NOTE
The most up-to-date specifications on the Winnov products covered in this chapter, can be found at: www.winnov.com.

Winnov 1000 Series: Video and Audio

Videum 1000 series capture cards are high-performance video and audio capture devices designed for corporate video communications and collaborations, video streaming, and video surveillance markets. The devices in this series are:

The Videum 1000. This is Winnov's second generation of the award-winning Videum AV PCI card. Based on Winnov's proprietary ASIC technology with its unique high-performance frame-buffer architecture, the Videum 1000 digitizes and encodes audio and video of unmatched quality. The Videum 1000 supports only Windows 2000, NT4.0, and Windows XP.

The Videum 1010 capture card. This is a high-performance video and audio capture card designed for all-in-one computers. The Videum 1010 is a low-profile version of the Videum 1000, designed for desktop PCs and ideal for OEM and integrators. Like the Videum 1000, the Videum 1010 is based on Winnov's proprietary ASIC technology with its unique high-performance frame-buffer architecture, and digitizes and encodes audio and video of unmatched quality. The Videum 1010 supports Windows 2000, NT4.0, and Windows XP.

The Videum 1020 capture card. As the high-performance member of the Videum 1000 family, Winnov's Videum 1020 digitizes video of unmatched quality at various size and frame rates. Featuring four locking BNC connectors, the Videum 1020 allows you to connect up to four switchable video sources. Furthermore, it enables you to populate a system with multiple cards to provide scalable solutions. A bundled application called Videum Source Switch automatically switches between the four video sources on the fly. Winnov's Videum 1020 is a perfect solution for any video-surveillance application, and it's compatible with Windows 2000, NT4.0, and XP.

Winnov's Frame-Buffer Architecture

Most decode chips implement inline buffer architecture, which cannot reliably capture 640 × 480 video to disk. Depending on the PCI bus traffic, it will skip pixels in a frame when the buffer overflows. These artifacts are more likely in a system with multiple capture cards and high-performance PCI add-in cards. In order to guarantee audio and video synchronization, in even the most demanding PCI load situations, Winnov's research and development (R&D) team opted to design its own PCI interface and frame-buffer architecture.

The Videum 1000 implements a high-performance frame-buffer architecture that reliably captures 640 × 480 video to memory or disk. Its large buffer can bridge any extended latencies on the PCI bus, which makes it ideal for high-performance and multiple-card systems.

Audio Capture Cards

Although many capture cards include both audio and video, some only have audio. Some applications of streaming do not require video capture. You will find thousands of examples of this when you log on to the Internet and listen to music. If you are planning on having an audio-only stream, I recommend a cost-effective product such as the Sound Blaster product line. Although some Sound Blaster products, such as the Sound Blaster Live! Platinum 5.1, may be considered overkill, they all have the necessary technology, including drivers, to work with most types of configurations.

NOTE
To get the full picture (and maybe an earfull) of all the Sound Blaster product line has to offer, go to: http://www.soundblaster.com.

Taking the Next Step

You can see that there are a few decisions to make when choosing the right capture card for your needs. It comes down to the following requirements:

- Do you need audio only or both audio and video?
- If both, then which manufacturer do you feel comfortable with?

In my experience, both Osprey and Winnov have pretty much the same technical specifications, and both are recommended by the majority of OEMs. Check out the Web sites noted in this chapter to get the latest specifications before you make a decision.

Part Two of this book moves on to the topic of processing and producing content. Chapter 7 will discuss audio and video preprocessing. Although audio and video preprocessing are not absolutely necessary to provide audio and video streams, it does enhance your streaming quality output and should be examined thoroughly, especially when you are developing your enterprise system.

PART THREE

Processing and Producing Content

Preprocessing Audio and Video

They may be hard to find, but there are solutions that provide links between different worlds: the analog and the digital, the baseband and the compressed. As increasing amounts of time and money are spent to add value to the entire range of streaming video and the services it offers, so preservation (or improvement) of the technical quality of the video becomes even more important. The fundamental technology that defines digital compression—that is, MPEG (the standard of the Motion Picture Experts Group)—is now well established.

Over the last few years, vast expertise has been applied to the continual improvement of this core technology. As a result, a number of key techniques are now available that address two vital areas: channel bandwidth and viewer picture quality. Since both the size of the data pipe and the ability of servers to deliver bandwidth are limited, there is a need to compress video channels down to ever fewer bits, while retaining high-quality images. Achieving high quality with fewer bits enables the delivery of more channels, data, and any other services to more customers.

The most popular technique for achieving this is preprocessing. In this chapter, we will explore the impact that preprocessing has on both video quality and the number of bits required for a given sequence. Then, an examination of the proven technologies specifically applicable to the broadband industry is addressed in the following chapters.

Exploring MPEG Technology

It is the nature of MPEG compression itself that produces the need for effective preprocessing of the video signal. This involves modifying certain of the signal's characteristics to ensure optimal results from the encoder (a subject fully covered in Chapter 8).

The Battle for Bit-Rate Reduction

One of the principal techniques by which MPEG achieves bit-rate reduction is to eliminate from the signal any information repeated from previous pictures. Eliminating this redundant information—generally areas of the picture that are unchanged from frame to frame—means that only the active, changing information needs to be transmitted. In deciding which parts of the picture to send and which to discard, MPEG compressors look for changes between successive pictures. Changes in pixel values between pictures are usually a sign of movement—usually, but by no means always.

Noise and other picture imperfections also cause changes in successive pixel values. Not knowing any better, an MPEG encoder will interpret these as indications of movement and, therefore, will encode them. The result spells double trouble. It is a lose-lose situation. Any imperfections in the source video not only can be encoded into the video stream, with a resulting loss of visual quality, but can also result in a significantly higher bit rate than necessary.

Here is where the case for high-quality preprocessing is made—the problem of noise, which can be summed up as follows:

- Noise can have consequences for static pictures. Highly compressed MPEG-2 video typically codes a whole static reference frame (I-frame)—independent of other frames—every half-second. The frames between are sent as the difference (that is, data *between* the I-frames). The I-frames are encoded using very JPEG-like algorithms. Here, the compressor has to make a decision between allotted bandwidth and the amount of picture detail it can include (controlled by the quantizer). High-frequency noise looks like added picture detail and will rapidly cause the quantizer to ramp up the compression in the noisy areas. This can result in detailed areas, such as the textures of skin and grass, becoming flat—like poster paint.

- The most common enemy of efficient compression is the high-frequency (HF) noise that creeps in at every production stage—from cameras, recorders, compressors/encoders, decompressors/decoders, and transmission/delivery systems. The common practice of image enhancement or sharpening tends to multiply the HF noise, which looks like rapid movement and more picture detail—information the encoder thinks is important. There are other causes of extra movement, such as film grain, film weave, and unsteady cameras. Again, all these sources of movement represent more information for the encoder. Not all preprocessing functions, however, are designed to minimize losses due to picture impairments.

What is needed here is a preprocessor that reduces noise while keeping the detail, and, clearly, feeding impaired signals into an MPEG compressor is simply bad news. It produces poor-quality results, and wastes bandwidth, *and* money.

The Search for High-Quality Compression

In theory, the input stage of any compression engine features a preprocessor. However, a closer examination of such onboard preprocessors is worthwhile. In most cases, the two main operations performed are straightforward 4:2:2 to 4:2:0 color-sampling conversion and bandwidth reduction. Compared with the real-world enemies of efficient encoding, these accomplish little and actually manage to discard potentially useful HF picture detail. By simply trusting the MPEG encoder's input preprocessor, you ignore the many potential problem areas of video sources. Close attention should be paid to the quality of the preprocessor filters.

There are, in fact, far more advanced and much more effective sets of preprocessing filters available. A no-holds-barred road test of their characteristics, and especially their automated features, is well worth the trouble. Ideally, preprocessing filters should feature an intelligent decision engine capable of switching filters dynamically, based on picture content coupled with the user's guidelines. In short, the filters should do the whole job automatically in accordance with the user's wishes.

NOTE

My personal experiences have shown that preprocessing is a necessity for a streaming media enterprise. Good preprocessing can make a big difference in solving the bit-rate/picture-quality conundrum.

Optimizing Preprocessor Performance

Arguably the most cost-effective approach is a preprocessor specifically designed to optimize the input signal to a video compression system. At the heart of a high-level preprocessing device (such as Prefix from Snell & Wilcox—see the section in this chapter on making a high-quality choice for details on their full product line) is a suite of advanced digital filters, each designed to counter the many different impairments found in video signals. These include dropouts, impulse noise, scratches in film-originated material, over enhancement, and so on. All filter parameters should be fully user-defined and capable of being applied in combination to allow exactly the right degree and type of preprocessing for the material.

Such a preprocessor should provide:

- A range of brick-wall filters with adjustable cut-off frequencies at the peak, enabling the user to save bit rate while maintaining quality.

- A series of enhancers/deenhancers as a standard feature.

- A motion-adaptive recursive filter to remove analog noise or, in the case of film-originated material, unwanted grain.

- A semitransversal recursive filter available for use in conjunction with the recursive filter. This improves results in the more difficult cases where there are significant levels of motion.

- A set of filters (spatial and median) for basic work such as impulse noise reduction. While popular block-matching-based motion estimation systems often produce too many motion vectors, a high-quality preprocessor, such as the one described, makes the job easier for the encoder's motion estimator. Fewer motion vectors are produced, and this significantly increases the amount of data available to encode—the wanted video material.

- Finally, when encoding back (catalog material taken from an NTSC analog composite video, for example), high-quality composite decoding before compression is crucial. Top-quality composite decoding is also vital if picture quality and bit rate are to be optimized. This is so because decoder artifacts, such as cross-color, are as wasteful of bit rate as noise.

NOTE
■■■■■ **A number of interesting articles on the subject of high-quality composite decoding are available at www.snellwilcox.com.**

Measuring MPEG Picture Quality

It should be no surprise to anyone who has read up to this point that what you feed into the MPEG encoder is not necessarily what the viewer finally gets out of the final video stream. There is a long and complex process between video encoding and the customer-received result. It is therefore useful to check the MPEG-encoded video assets before they are delivered to the streaming server.

To realize this goal, the collective experience gained in MPEG transmission has resulted in the development of an offline MPEG analyzer—capable of providing all the information needed to assess the encoding characteristics. Because bit-rate management is key to quality in video streaming, it is extremely important to compare encoders and analyze the effectiveness of both their encoding and their onboard preprocessing engines. To this end, Snell & Wilcox has developed an objective measurement technique that provides a rapid, automatic, and easily interpreted indication of picture quality within the MPEG data stream.

Initial considerations determined that this had to be a single-ended algorithm, where the source is not required for comparison (because this is too costly and impractical). The company's research and development labs took peak signal-to-noise ratio (PSNR) as a reference-model indication of noise. This proved to be an accurate reference according to the recent report by the International Telecommunications Union's (ITU) Video Quality Experts Group (VQEG). The idea was to estimate the PSNR measure for MPEG pictures with a process called *picture appraisal rating* (PAR). This measure, calculated on a scale of 48 dB (48 representing a theoretically lossless 8-bit compression), proved accurate.

PAR and Preprocessing

During initial testing, the most exciting challenge was to find out whether the preprocessing had any impact on the PAR measure. To make sure things worked properly, a number of reference streams were chosen specifically for their complexity. It was interesting to watch such parameters as the quantizer scale code (QSC) of the MPEG encoder because it acts directly as the bit-rate saver. Any indication in the 1 to 5 range of QSC confirms transparent encoding. Anything registering above 5 (QSC ranges up to 32) means lossy encoding. The bit-rate measurement is fundamental to determining the effect of a certain type of filter and to calculate exactly how much bit rate was saved.

The results of the analysis differed from one stream to another. However, PAR clearly showed improvements when noisy material was preprocessed or when bandwidth had to be restricted for space-saving reasons. I encourage you to perform your own tests with the PAR algorithm (see the note on the following page on how to contact Snell & Wilcox via the Web).

Offline PAR Analysis for Quality Control

The beauty of offline analysis is the ability to provide quality guarantees. For PAR, the analysis report is simply numbers, the PAR rating for the video sequences. Since the PAR rating has a close correlation with subjective human-eye measures, it can operate unmanned as an effective automatic eye to monitor MPEG video quality. It can be carried out automatically overnight, and any out-of-limits material can be flagged for corrective action the next day. One fundamental advantage of this is the ability to check picture quality and consistency.

PAR alone is a great step forward, but for deeper analysis, the ability to see encoding parameters on a picture-by-picture basis helps enormously. Mosalina, a personal computer (PC) software application for MPEG offline analysis, has been developed by Snell & Wilcox as a monitoring tool for just this purpose.

Good downconversion is very demanding on processing power. For example, going from a 1,080 lines standard (now used in most HD production systems) down to 480 lines requires extremely complex filters. Very, very few PCs are capable of running any such conversion in real time, certainly not while retaining much of the original quality. A dedicated HD downconverter that renders as much detail of the HD original into the standard-definition (SD) result is a valuable asset. This can enable the opening of new businesses in the expanding areas where HD masters are used. Since the images have little noise, they compress easily and provide the double benefit of good pictures and low bit rates.

What of HDTV?

As production and postproduction businesses head toward end-to-end digital video and, ultimately, high-definition (HD) video solutions, it increasingly makes sense to be able to accept work originated in an HD format. The easiest way to get the best standard-definition MPEG encoding is to downconvert the HD material. A few Hollywood postproduction houses already use this technique and produce amazing results. An HD source works like good 35-mm film material; both are effectively oversampled, and high quality shows all the way through to the standard TV-definition, MPEG-compressed results. However downconverting should never be applied simply to drastically reduce the definition of the HD footage. Do not consider it as a cut-down-the-definition process.

Preprocessing Equipment: Making a High-Quality Choice

As made quite clear in the preceding sections of this chapter, the performance of digital video compression systems, such as MPEG, can be improved significantly by high-quality preprocessing—removing unwanted components of the signal, including: video noise, cross-color artifacts from decoders, satellite impulse noise, and so on. Using the best preprocessing equipment available is crucial to the streaming media process. That is why the following sections are devoted entirely to the Prefix product line of Snell & Wilcox, which in my opinion offers the level of excellence required.

NOTE

Check out Snell & Wilcox at www.snellwilcox.com for up-to-the-minute specifications on their products (such as Mosalina, Prefix, and IQM) and information on the latest advances in broadcast television, video, satellite, cable, film, and image communications technologies.

Prefix CPP100

The Prefix CPP100 is a one-box solution to MPEG preprocessing. The 10-bit CPP100 offers dramatically reduced bit rates, while visually improving image quality. The Prefix CPP100's proprietary design incorporates no less than seven filters, giving Prefix a uniquely powerful ability to remove unwanted signal elements. Prefix also allows the enhancement or reduction of HF signal content. Sophisticated video analysis circuits not only provide optimal noise reduction but also generate signals embedded in the auxiliary data of the SDI output for use as early-warning signals by the compression encoder (shot change, 3:2 sequence, film/video identification, and so on).

Prefix CPP200

The Prefix CPP200 is a digital processor designed to optimize input signal to video compression. Like the CPP100, the CPP200 incorporates no less than seven filters, allows enhancement or reduction of HF signal content, and utilizes sophisticated video analysis circuits for optimal preprocessing and the generation of early-warning signals. Added to this is the ability to provide the conditioning and conversion of analog audio channels into a digital format.

HDPrefix CPP1000: HD Compression Preprocessor

HDPrefix, a new version of the SDPrefix, is a digital preprocessor designed to optimize the input signal to HD video compression systems. As SD versions of Prefix have successfully demonstrated, the bit rates produced by digital video compression systems can be reduced significantly by removing noise and other unwanted components of the signal. In a compact 2RU enclosure, HDPrefix extends its uniquely powerful capability to HD transmissions. HDPrefix also allows the enhancement or reduction of HF signal content and has a number of other features, including: test pattern generation, automatic gamut limiting, down-converted SD (SMPTE-259M-C) monitoring output, AES-3/AC-3 audio embedding with audio monitoring output, SMPTE-292/9M loop output, and an integral synchronizer capable of genlocking to either an analog studio reference or the currently selected input. The unit also has a number of unique picture-splitting facilities to enable effective comparisons between input and processed output.

The IQ Modular Family

In addition to Prefix, Snell & Wilcox offers a number of products from its IQ Modular (IQM) family suitable for signal preprocessing and related requirements. With over 300 audio and video modules to choose from, IQM intelligent modules can be configured for any exacting requirement. Specifically:

- The IQMDANR module incorporates the semitransversal, recursive, median, and spatial filters of Prefix.

- The IQMSDP, a module especially useful for video streaming, provides high-quality adaptive decoding and adaptive recursive noise reduction. The multiaperture adaptive comb filter gives excellent results for all types of images with frame synchronization for non-stable sources such as VHS.

Taking the Next Step

This chapter has covered many aspects of preprocessing and the importance of integrating these types of devices in your streaming enterprise system. Chapter 8 will guide you in actually building an encoder. You will need to refer to Chapter 6 to understand which capture board best fits your streaming plans.

Building Encoders with Server Connections

B uilding an encoder can be very challenging if you are not familiar with the industry. I have been building encoding systems since 1997 and have yet to find an easy way to keep up with the ever-changing technology. In general, however, the steps for building an encoder will include identifying the components, assembling them, connecting your encoder to your local area network (LAN), and installing and initializing the software, including server updates. All these topics, and a listing of recommendations for the purchase of bundled encoding systems, are the subject of this chapter

Developing a Plan of Action

The encoder is one of the most important pieces of equipment you will be working with. It has a profound effect on your streaming quality. Many components are unique to an encoder, from the types of RAM, hard drives, and processors, to the kinds of motherboards and capture cards (see Chapters 5 and 6). In developing a plan for building a device adequate to the task at hand, I have found that the best encoders provide efficient solutions to the following questions:

- Are all the components designed to work together? For example, if you are working with an Intel Pentium 4 (P4) processor, it is best to use an Intel motherboard. In the example developed in this chapter, I follow this advice and use both the Intel P4 processor and the Intel 850MV motherboard.

- Are you using a Small Computer System Interface (SCSI) or a Integrated Digital Environment (IDE) controller?

- What is the best way to load your software? If you do not install the software in the proper sequence, the system will underperform, not boot properly, freeze, or just hang at times when shutting down.

The main content of this chapter provides a step-by-step procedure to assist you in building an encoder and developing suitable answers to the questions just posed, but before we begin, let's take a closer look at the components.

Hardware Chassis

Your first step is to determine if the chassis for your encoding system will be rack-mounted or used as a desktop device. The decision you make here sets the standard for determining future choices. The type of chassis you pick may depend on the following:

- If you plan to control your encoding with remote-control software and have no need for it to be on a desktop, choose a rack-mounted chassis. Rack-mounted systems usually are found in larger network operations where many feeds from tape decks or live feeds are present—such as in broadcasting facilities, postproduction houses, and larger in-house production facilities.

- If you plan on using your encoder for smaller applications, choose a desktop chassis.

General Hardware Components

It is very important to choose the proper components. I suggest you use:

- A processor configuration running at a minimum of 800 MHz with a minimum of 256 MB of RAM.

- A hard drive that can be standard IDE or SCSI, running at least 40 GHz.

- A recommended motherboard by Intel or AMD, if you are building your own system.

NOTE
The motherboard is one of your most important components, and price, although important, should not necessarily make or break this decision. The motherboard is not the component to skimp on.

Video Capture and Audio Cards

Video capture and audio sound cards are other key components for video streaming.

- Video capture is very important, as is the speed at which the card accomplishes this task. Chapters 5 and 6 cover the technology of video capture and the ins and outs of making a high-quality choice.

- Audio sound cards are relatively inexpensive, but audio quality is important too. Some video capture cards include audio capture, but if your video device of choice does not have this capability, I suggest you take a look at the SoundBlaster line of cards (detailed in Chapter 6). Although they may seem to be overkill, they have served me very nicely.

Building an Encoder

Building your own encoder can be challenging, and this is why I have spent considerable time making sure you have plenty of photographs and instructions to reference.

Installing Your Codec

Once you have built a running encoding system, you need to install a software codec. In Chapter 9 I give you an opportunity to review the latest codecs at the time of this writing.

Simple installation instructions for these currently free codecs are available on the Web. To make sure you are also using the latest codec versions, visit the following Web sites:

- www.real.com
- www.microsoft.com
- www.apple.com

Gathering the Parts

Before you can build the encoder described in this chapter, you need to collect the parts from the appropriate vendors. The following parts list includes the manufacturer's part numbers (P/Ns) for your convenience:

- Boom 2U Rack-Mount Chassis 300W PS—BOOM 2U300XB (order it with the 2-in PCI bridge used for Osprey capture card)
- Intel P4, 1.8 GHz, 256-kB L2 cache, PGA478, 400 MHz—BX80531NK180G
- Intel 850MV motherboard—BOXD850MVL
- 256-MB 800-MHz Non-ECC RDRAM RIMM—KVR800X16/256
- EIDE ULTRA-ATA/100, as follows:
  - Choice 1: 40-GB 7200 RPM—WD400BB
  - Choice 2: 80-GB 7200 RPM—WD800BB
  - Choice 3: 120-GB 7200 RPM—WD1200BB
- Pick one of the following:
  - Choice 1: Osprey-220 video capture card with audio—95-00149-01
  - Choice 2: Osprey-500 DV Pro professional digital streaming capture card with audio—95-00148-02
  - Choice 3: Osprey-2000 DV Pro MPEG-2 codec and streaming capture card with audio—95-00160-01
- Visontek Graphics Card, 5564 GForce 2 64-mg video card—72402.0
- AGP-FLEX-01-1.5V-3, AGP flexible extender with 3-in cable (used with AGP video card; contact ADEX Electronics at 949-597-1772)

NOTE

If you find it more convenient and would like technical support, MaxVU can provide some limited technical support. You can contact the company at info@maxvu.com. Please feel free to include a note stating that you have purchased this book and are in need of additional assistance.

Putting It All Together

Once you have received the parts, you can build your new encoder. Start out with the empty case (the chassis you decided upon in the action plan earlier in the chapter), and after making sure it has the proper power supply for the P4, follow these steps:

1. Take the Intel 850MV motherboard out of the box and place it on an antistatic bag.

2. Before you insert the P4 central processing unit (CPU), notice the pin-grid array on the CPU. Look closely (see Figure 8.1) and you will notice the rounded corners on both the CPU and the array connected to the motherboard.

NOTE

Take precautions not to touch the pin-grid array on the bottom of the CPU. This may cause damage to the components, resulting in malfunctions during startup.

Offset Corner Aligns with CPU

Figure 8.1 Aligning the offset corner in the CPU mount with the CPU.

3. Raise the arm of the ZIF (Zero Insertion Force) socket, and making sure the offset corners mentioned in the previous step are aligned, insert the P4 CPU in the ZIF slot. When the CPU is in position, lower the arm of the ZIF socket and lock the CPU into place.

4. Insert the CPU heatsink mount into position on the motherboard, as shown in Figure 8.2.

5. Install the heatsink fan over the CPU, and clamp it down securely.

NOTE This can be a little tricky, and you may need a needle-nose pliers and a screwdriver. Be very careful not to break or bend the clamps.

6. Once you have completed locking down the heatsink fan, attach the fan power connection to the motherboard. You will notice the plug inches away (Figure 8.3).

Heatsink Mount   12-Volt Power

Figure 8.2 The CPU inserted with the heatsink mount in place.

Heatsink Fan Power Connection

Figure 8.3   Heat-sink fan power connection.

7. The next step is to install the Rambus RAM bank. Memory slots are numbered from 1 to 4, starting at the CPU and moving away from it. You should place the Rambus memory in slots 1 (the slot closest to the CPU) and 2.

8. Next, it is necessary to install Crimms, which are nonmemory products, in the empty Rambus slots. Gently push the Crimms into remaining slots 3 and 4. The Crimms are properly installed when you hear a click (see Figure 8.4).

NOTE

If you decide to double your memory, remove the Crimms and replace them with Rambus memory.

Figure 8.4 Rambus memory in slots 1 and 2, with Crimms inserted in slots 3 and 4.

9. Now that the memory is installed, raise the motherboard by its edges and insert it into the chassis. Line up the holes in the mother-board with the risers in the chassis. Secure the motherboard tightly with screws, but do not overtighten them.

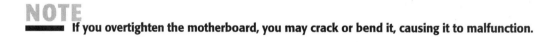

NOTE If you overtighten the motherboard, you may crack or bend it, causing it to malfunction.

Future Position of CD-Drive   CD-Drive Housing

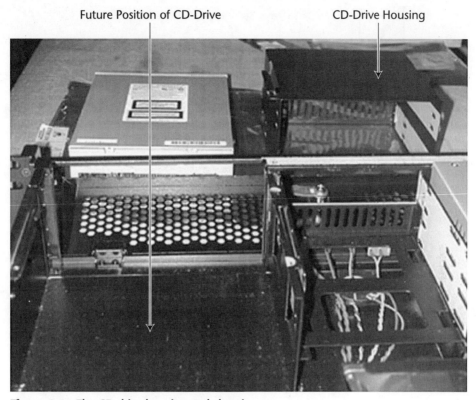

Figure 8.5 The CD drive housing and chassis.

10. Next, install the CD drive. To do this, remove the CD drive cage from the chassis (see Figure 8.5), and insert the CD drive unit into the drive cage. Tighten the screws.

11. Now install the floppy drive unit into the chassis. Once both the CD drive and the floppy drive units have been placed in the chassis, secure both units with three screws. You should now have something that looks like Figure 8.6.

CD-Drive Secured in Position

Floppy Drive Secured in Position

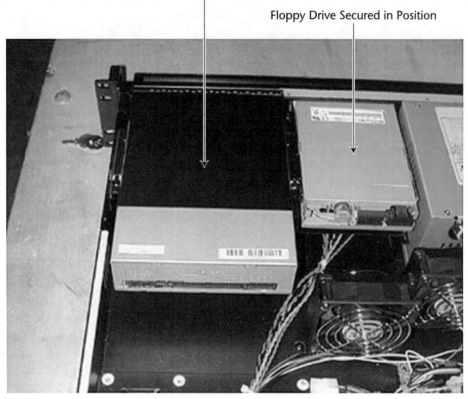

Figure 8.6 CD drive and floppy drive secured in chassis.

12. Insert the hard drive into the top front position on the chassis, and secure it tightly with two screws.

13. Now that the components installed in the previous steps are in place, it's time to plug everything into the power supply. Figure 8.7 provides an overview of the motherboard, showing the main connection points. The connection sequence is as follows:

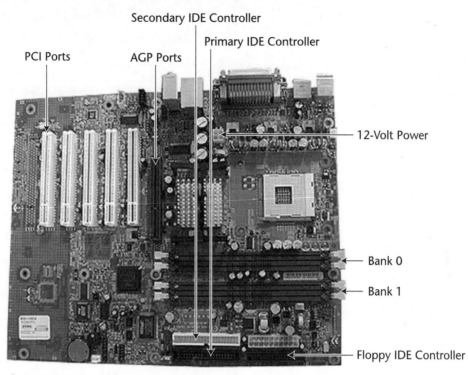

Secondary IDE Controller

Primary IDE Controller

PCI Ports   AGP Ports

12-Volt Power

Bank 0

Bank 1

Floppy IDE Controller

Figure 8.7   Connecting the power to the drives and fan.

NOTE

There is a small arrow painted onto the motherboard that designates the location of pin 1 on the floppy and the primary and secondary IDE controllers. This red arrow designates where the red stripe on the ribbon cable should go.

- Connect the power supply connectors to the motherboard power switches and light-emitting diode (LED) lights. Although the connections are very small, they are labeled.

- Insert one end of the floppy ribbon into the motherboard (red stripe facing toward the top of the chassis) and the other end of the floppy ribbon into the floppy drive (Figure 8.8).

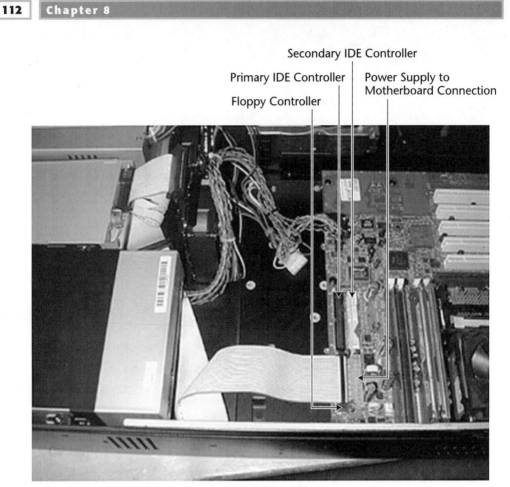

Secondary IDE Controller

Primary IDE Controller | Power Supply to
Motherboard Connection

Floppy Controller

Figure 8.8 Connecting the floppy drive ribbon cables.

- Insert the CD drive ribbon cable into motherboard (primary IDE) and the other end (master) into the CD drive (Figure 8.9). The primary IDE controller is black (refer to Figure 8.8). This cable is the one with fewer wires running through it. Do not use the middle connection (slave) on the ribbon.

CD Power Connection

Notice Red Stripe on
Ribbon Corresponds to
Red Stripe on Power
Connection

Floppy Power Connection

Fan Power Connection

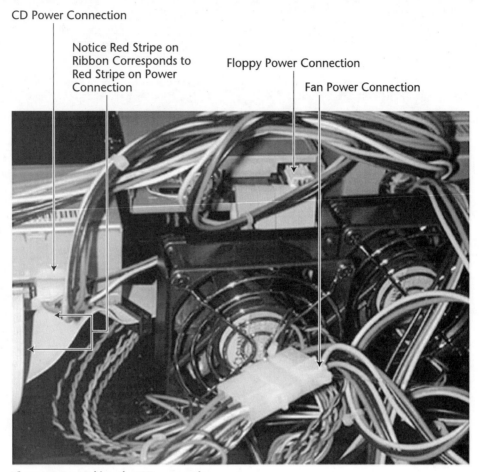

Figure 8.9   Making the CD connection.

- Insert the hard drive ribbon into the motherboard (secondary
  IDE controller) and the other end of the ribbon (master) into
  the hard drive (see Figure 8.10). The secondary IDE controller
  is white (refer to Figure 8.8). Again, do not use the middle
  connection (slave) on the ribbon cable identified by the greater
  number of wires running through it.

Hard-Drive Ribbon Cable.
Notice That Red Stripe Will
Be Nearest to Red Stripe
on Power Connection.

Figure 8.10 Hooking up the hard drive.

- Referring again to Figure 8.8, make the power connection from the fan to the power supply.
- Insert the AGP extension into the AGP slot, which is brown (see Figure 8.11).

AGP Extension

AGP Port

Video Card Insertion End

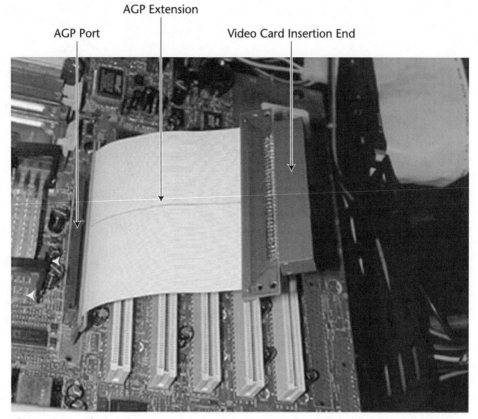

Figure 8.11 Placing the AGP extension into the AGP slot (labeled "port" on the figure).

NOTE

Please be very careful to install the correct 1. 5 V AGP cable and not the 3.3-V floppy cable into the AGP port. If you put the incorrect AGP extender cable into the slot and power up the computer, many of your components will be destroyed. This cable is not necessary if you are building in a 4U chassis.

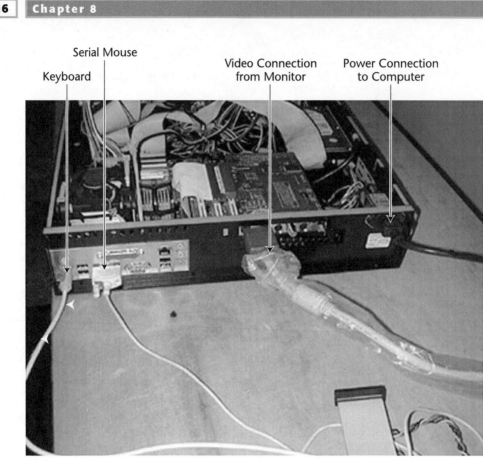

Serial Mouse

Keyboard

Video Connection
from Monitor

Power Connection
to Computer

Figure 8.12 Making peripheral connections and connecting the external power cord.

- Hook up the keyboard and mouse connectors, securely fasten the video cable from the monitor to the video card, and then plug the power cord into the back of the case. (see Figure 8.12).

14. For the PCI Osprey card, first insert the PCI bridge that came with the BOOM chassis. Attach the Osprey video card and fasten the screw (refer to Figure 8.11 to view the card's insertion end and Figure 8.13 to see the card in position).

Video Card Secured in Position

Figure 8.13 Securing the Osprey video card.

Not shown is the connection of your Osprey video card into your video capture device. If you are using either an analog or a digital video camera, the connectors are self-explanatory. The same holds true with the recording device, such as a Sony Beta SP deck. The Osprey video card that you decide on will determine what inputs you will use. In general, the Osprey-220 supports both composite and S-Video for analog input; whereas the larger models, such as the Osprey-500 and Osprey-2000, support SDI and IEEE-1394 (FireWire) for digital input. All these cards support both audio and video capture.

Verifying Your Work

Please use the following checklist to verify that you have completed all of the steps. I suggest you copy these pages and then make your check marks.

Encoder Assembly Checklist

❑ Motherboard, CD-ROM, hard-drive, floppy, and AGP card are all secured to the chassis.

❑ CPU fan is secure.

❑ CPU heatsink fan is attached to the motherboard-located proper fan number.

❑ Rambus memory is inserted into memory slots 1 and 2.

❑ Crimms are inserted into memory slots 3 and 4.

❑ All memory is placed securely into the proper memory banks and is locked down.

❑ All fans are plugged into the power supply and the motherboard.

❑ The chassis LED wires and power switches are connected properly to the motherboard.

❑ The power supply is connected to the motherboard.

❑ The CD-ROM drive is installed to the primary IDE controller.

❑ The hard drive is installed to the secondary IDE controller.

❑ The floppy drive is connected and secured to the motherboard.

❑ The CD-ROM drive, hard drive, and floppy drive all have power connections.

❑ The PCI Osprey capture card is installed properly and completely inserted into PCI slot.

❑ The AGP video card is installed properly and completely inserted into AGP slot.

❑ Turn on the machine.

❑ The CPU fan is running.

❑ All case fans operate.

❑ Check the front of the case to make certain that the hard drive light and power light function.

❑ Make certain that the floppy light does not remain on.

Implementing an Internet Connection

Because there are different desktop settings, I have included two different ways to implement an Internet connection. The first shows you how to implement an Internet connection through a LAN by using the Internet Connection Setup icon, and the second shows you how to implement the connection through a LAN using the Internet Explorer icon.

Connecting through a LAN Using the Internet Connection Setup Icon

This portion of the installation is very tricky when using Windows 2000 because each of the following steps must be carefully taken in the exact order:

1. Start the connection process by right-clicking with the mouse on the Internet Connection Setup icon.

2. First, you have to select what you want to do. Of the three options, choose the third, "I want to set up my Internet connection manually, or I want to connect through a LAN," and then click Next.

   - Choose to sign up for a new account using a modem.

   - Transfer an existing account to this computer using a modem.

   - Set up a connection manually for a LAN.

3. The second screen of the wizard asks you to indicate how you connect to the Internet—by phone line and modem, or by LAN. You should choose the second option, "I connect through a local-area network (LAN)." Then click Next.

4. The next screen allows you to configure proxy settings. In selecting the LAN Internet configuration, usually the default configuration is adequate. Continue by clicking Next.

5. The next screen asks you to set up an e-mail account. For the purposes of this demonstration, you do not need to go through the process of setting up an e-mail account. Choose No, and continue the process by clicking Next.

6. You are now ready to connect to the Internet. Proceed by clicking Finish. The wizard confirms your connection by launching Internet Explorer to access the Internet. The default home page is MSN.com.

Connecting through a LAN Using the Internet Explorer Icon

In some cases, you may not have access to the wizard or simply may choose to connect through a LAN using the Internet Explorer icon. For this reason, I have provided these steps:

1. Start the process by right-clicking with the mouse on the Internet Explorer icon, and then selecting Properties on the drop-down menu.

2. The Internet Properties window contains six tabs. Click the Connections tab, and then click the Setup button, as shown in Figure 8.14.

3. The steps in the setup dialog are similar to the steps you followed using the wizard. Again, choose the third option, "I want to set up my Internet connection manually, or I want to connect through a LAN." Then click Next.

4. On the second screen, choose the second option, "I connect through a local-area network (LAN)."

5. Usually the default configuration is adequate. Continue by clicking Next.

6. As we did when we used the wizard, choose No for setting up an e-mail account, and continue the process by clicking Next.

7. You are now ready to connect to the Internet. Proceed by clicking Finish.

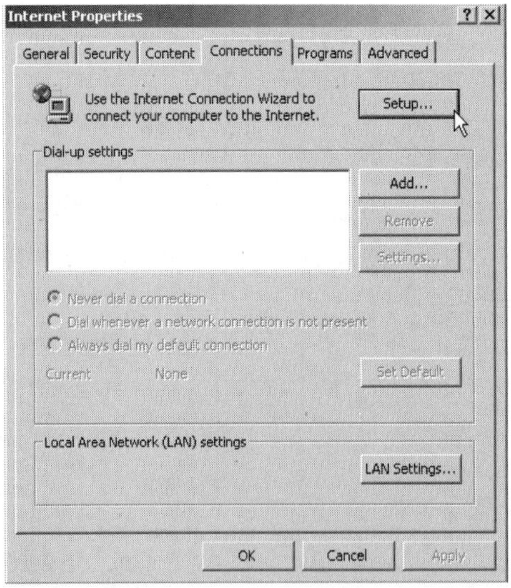

Figure 8.14   Internet Properties connection setup.

8. If the default settings apply to your environment, then you should receive an opening screen when an Internet connection is established. If not, you may need to see your network administrator for further assistance. More than likely, the administrator has put a restriction on the network and needs to give you access to certain ports.

Setting up the Software

Now that you have built the encoder and made an Internet connection, you will need to update the server on your encoder. Using a Windows 2000 server or an advanced server makes this installation a snap.

Install the Windows 2000 server or advanced server first. You must then follow the steps in this section carefully because, if you do not, the Intel P4 architecture modifies its performance to work with your configuration.

NOTE

If the software is not installed correctly, the computer could be running at much lower speeds than the capabilities of the processor you purchased.

Once you have installed Windows 2000 server or advanced server, use the following steps to complete the installation:

1. Install Service Pack 2.

2. Install Direct X 8.1 (automatic in Windows XP).

3. Install Windows Media 7.1 Update (automatic in Windows XP).

4. Go to Add/Remove Windows Components, and let the system do its search for new components.

5. Install Windows Media Services.

6. Install File Transfer Protocol (FTP) server located within Internet Information Services (IIS).

7. Open Windows Media on the server and perform the URL LAN connection setup, via the Properties/Options/Connect commands, according to the following example:

   ■ URL Internet

   ■ URL LAN: http://encoder:8080

You should now have put together an encoder, and it should be working. You will now be able to move to the next step, setting up a separate server for your encoder.

Setting up a Separate Server for Your Encoder

You will need to set up a separate server to complete the system. The reason you need to have a server connection is basic. The encoder receives the audio and video media from the capture device, converts it to selected bit rates, and then must send these files to a server. The encoder is not meant to encode and serve the streams to your audience. Therefore, you must set up a server. Using a Windows 2000 server or advanced server makes this installation a snap. The following is a brief overview of this procedure:

1. Assuming that your network administrator does not have a computer server for you to use, you will need to acquire one, preferably a dual-processor system.

2. You will also need to have a Windows 2000 server or advanced server and install it on your dedicated computer system.

3. Once you have completed this installation, you will need to add any updates (see the sidebar on accessing Windows Updates for details).

The Windows 2000 server has preloaded the media services necessary for you to start streaming.

NOTE

If you wish to use RealNetworks or Apple QuickTime, you will need to acquire their software and follow their installation instructions (the subject of Chapter 9, the next step in the process).

Windows Updates is located at the top of the Start menu. Simply press the Start button on the toolbar. This link will bring you to the Windows Update page of the Microsoft site at http://windowsupdate.microsoft.com. Here you will find the updates you may need for your system.

Accessing Windows Updates

Every few weeks or during installation of any new software updates, you should be running Windows Updates. The procedures in this chapter only show the installation of Windows software packages, such as Service Pack 2, as of this writing. Your environment may require more current updates to be viable. When performing normal Windows Updates, you are prompted to review what other updates may be useful for your system, including Critical Updates, which are very important.

Regular updates of your system can easily be accomplished at the same time you maintain your encoder through scheduled uses of system tools, such as the disk defragmentor. You will have the option of choosing which files to download, and you will be walked through all the options.

Bundled Encoding Systems: Making a High-Quality Choice

I have experienced some very high-quality encoding at low bit rates. MaxVU is unveiling its new Plug-n-Stream streaming media system using the Intel P4 processor running at a minimum of 2.2 GHz with the proprietary AllBand technology, which enhances current codecs and makes the bit rates better by at least 40 percent. MaxVU expects this architecture to scale to 10 GHz and beyond.

What is nice about these systems (described in the following sections) is that MaxVU's objective is good style, form factor, security, power consumption, reliability, communications functions, and price. Underwriters' Laboratories (UL) approval is also included on all its server lines.

NOTE

For full details on all the MaxVU products (specifically the Plug-n-Stream Nighthawk with AllBand Optimization product line covered in this chapter) point your browser to info@maxvu.com.

Plug-n-Stream Nighthawk 220 with AllBand Optimization

The Nighthawk 220 is ideal for light encoding but durable enough to be on all the time. This system has the power to capture and encode any composite or S-Video stream input and handle any files to be transcoded into popular video formats for Real, Microsoft, QuickTime, or third-party codecs.

The encoding device features:

- P4 processor with 400-MHz system bus
- 1.4-GHz CPU clock speed
- 128-MB, 800-MHz RDRAM memory
- 40-GB, 7200-rpm system disk
- 4 USB ports, AC97, LAN, dual Ultra ATA/100
- Dual RDRAM channels
- Intel hub architecture
- CD-ROM drive
- 3.5-inch floppy drive

The Intel P4 processor and Intel 850 chipset provide the latest techno-logical enhancements to maximize the power of the Intel P4 processor with Intel NetBurst microarchitecture. This ensures the highest perfor-mance for video, graphics, and multimedia. With the Osprey-220 video capture card, you can be assured that you are using leading-edge ana-log video and audio capture technology. All of this is brought together with the superior operating system of Microsoft Windows 2000. Microsoft Windows Media encoder and RealSystem Producer Plus 8.5 also are included.

The encoding capabilities include:

- Multiple Osprey-220s per chassis (NT and Windows 2000)
- Advanced DMA for ultrahigh performance (full 30 fps)
- DirectDraw for 30-fps overlays to a video screen with minimal CPU utilization
- BNC composite video input
- XLR balanced audio input
- Audio loopback

- Hardware audio gain control
- Closed captions

Plug-n-Stream Nighthawk 500 DV Pro with AllBand Optimization

The Nighthawk 500 DV Pro is ideal for industrial encoding. This system has the power to capture and encode any digital SDI and IEEE-1394, S-Video, and analog composite stream input, and to handle any files to be transcoded into popular video formats for Real, Microsoft, Quick-Time, or third-party codecs.

The encoding device features:

- P4 processor with a 400-MHz system bus
- 1.6-GHz CPU clock speed
- 256-MB, 800-MHz RDRAM memory
- 60-GB, 7200-rpm system disk
- 4 USB ports, AC97, LAN, dual Ultra ATA/100
- Dual RDRAM channels
- Intel hub architecture
- CD-ROM drive
- 3.5-inch floppy drive

The Intel P4 processor is the latest generation of Intel processors and is designed to deliver advanced performance for emerging Web and personal computer (PC) technologies. Based on Intel NetBurst micro-architecture, the P4 processor provides superior performance for users who demand the latest technology. The Osprey-500 DV Pro, hailed as the "Rolls-Royce of the industry" by *Streaming Media World,* is a professional-level digital capture card designed to provide streaming video from an analog or digital source. The advanced Microsoft Windows 2000 operating system drives the whole package. Microsoft Windows Media encoder and RealSystem Producer Plus 8.5 also are included.

The encoding capabilities include:

- Video inputs available: digital SDI and IEEE-1394, analog composite, and S-Video
- Audio inputs available: digital AES/EBU and S/P DIF, analog balanced and unbalanced stereo

- Hardware deinterlacing, scaling, and color conversion
- Software gain control
- Multiple hardware audio sampling rates

Plug-n-Stream Nighthawk 2000 DV Pro with AllBand Optimization

The Nighthawk 2000 DV Pro is the Mercedes of encoders. This system has the power to capture and encode any digital SDI and IEEE-1394, S-Video, and analog composite streaming input, and handle any files to be transcoded into popular video formats for Real, Microsoft, QuickTime, or third-party codecs. Nighthawk 2000 DV Pro provides transcoding from MPEG into streaming media format on the fly. This ability allows a myriad of VOD applications where content can be repurposed and streamed from a central archive, eliminating the need to retain multiple resolutions of the same content.

The encoding device features:

- P4 processor with a 400-MHz system bus
- 1.8-GHz CPU clock speed
- 512-MB, 800-MHz RDRAM memory
- 80-GB, 7200-rpm system disk
- 4 USB ports, AC97, LAN, dual Ultra ATA/100
- Dual RDRAM channels
- Intel hub architecture
- CD-ROM drive
- 3.5-inch floppy drive

Modes of operation include:

- MPEG encoding
- MPEG decoding
- Streaming capture and preview
- File format transcoding

The Intel Desktop Board D850GB harnesses the advanced computing power of the Intel P4 processor. Designed with the new Intel 850 chipset, the Desktop Board D850GB uses the Intel P4 processor's full bandwidth and performance with dual Rambus channels and support for Intel NetBurst microarchitecture. The Osprey-2000 DV Pro provides transcoding from MPEG into the streaming media format on the fly. This ability allows a myriad of VOD applications where content can be repurposed and streamed from a central archive, eliminating the need to retain multiple resolutions of the same content. The Osprey-2000 DV Pro bridges the gap between the streaming and professional video markets. It all uses the Microsoft Windows 2000 operating system, of course. Microsoft Windows Media encoder and RealSystem Producer Plus 8.5 also are included.

The encoding capabilities are:

- MPEG encoding (codec card) and MPEG decoding
- Analog composite, S-Video, unbalanced and balanced audio
- DV IEEE-1394 input (audio and video)
- SDI video, SDI embedded audio, external AES/EBU
- Outputs: composite, S-Video, unbalanced audio

Taking the Next Step

You now should have a very good idea of what it takes to start assembling your components to stream—from what types of cameras and video devices are available to how to capture video through audio and video capture cards in an actual encoder. Chapter 9 discusses which types of compression software to use with your encoder, referencing Real, Microsoft, and Apple QuickTime.

Working with Compression Software

The crux of the Real, Microsoft, and/or Apple QuickTime codec issue is the need to make a choice. Over the years, I have heard many opinions on the codecs most used by video streaming companies and on the numbers of players really being downloaded and used regularly. Because Microsoft, Real Networks, and Apple have free players and servers, it comes down to what the end user is most comfortable with. Of course, there are some costs associated with both Real and Apple QuickTime codecs as you expand your audiences, but you can make that choice yourself. This chapter begins with some helpful hints to assist you in making an informed decision, and then moves on to the details of working with RealProducer Plus 8.5, Windows Media Encoder 7.1, and the latest version of Apple's QuickTime.

Making an Informed Decision

Most Web sites cater to at least two codec platforms. The reasoning is that those who use Macintosh computers may prefer to use a Quicktime or Real player whereas others who use a Microsoft-based computer may prefer to use a Microsoft or Real player. Recent advancements in all three players allow their files to work on all the platforms (Windows Media Encoder, QuickTime, and Real), but there is still, in my mind, a quality issue when porting over from Microsoft to Apple or the reverse.

It all comes down to preference. There are also some good third-party codecs that you may want to experiment with, such as ON2, Ligos, DivX, and others.

As a result of what you learn about converting file formats (transcoding) in Chapter 11, you may want to batch your original high-quality capture, and then transcode the file into many formats and bit rates. It is up to you.

I also suggest that you visit the following Web sites for the latest releases and information:

- Real: www.realnetworks.com/products/producer/index.html
- QuickTime (Sorenson Video codec): www.sorenson.com/products/video.asp
- Microsoft: www.microsoft.com/windows/windowsmedia/en/wm7/Encoder/default.asp
- ON2: http://www.on2.com
- Ligos: www.ligos.com
- DivX: at www.divx.com

NOTE
Microsoft has an excellent online training program. In the Windows Media encoder you can find the most current instructional link under the Help menu.

RealProducer Plus 8.5

Figure 9.1 illustrates the main working area of the RealProducer Plus 8.5 encoder and shows how you can change any number of settings. I describe all the new features later in this section.

NOTE
For RealProducer Plus software, go to www.realnetworks.com/products/producer/index.html, where it is available for a fee. Although you may also find a free version, it does not support a lot of the features I am about to share with you.

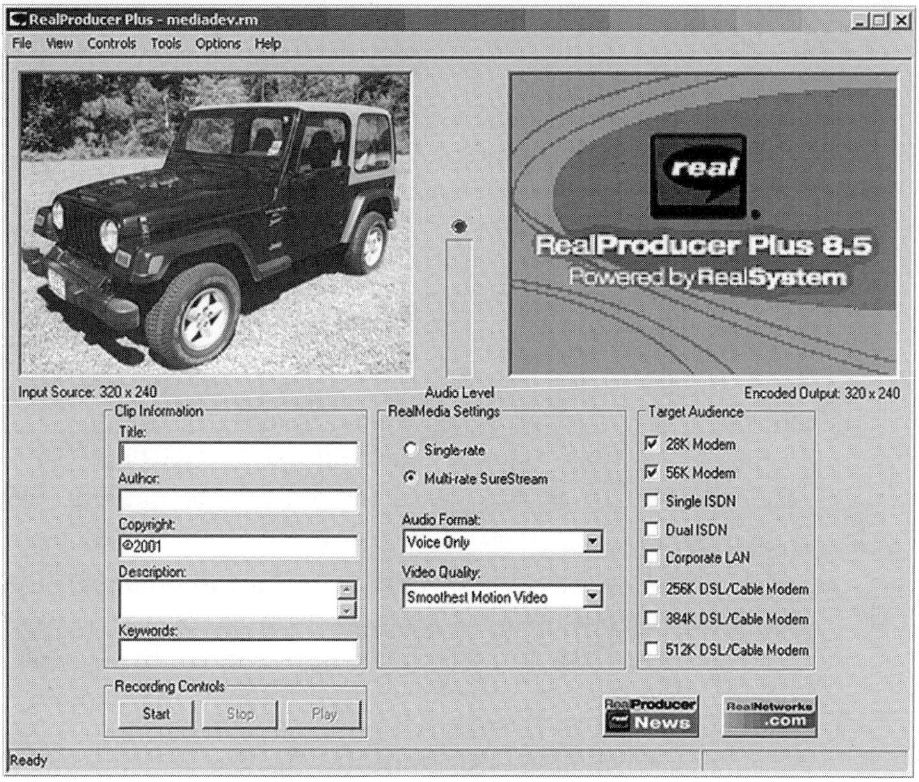

Figure 9.1 Main working area for RealProducer Plus 8.5.

I have found the RealProducer Plus 8.5 to be very easy to use, and with over 200 million RealPlayer users currently online, this is a streaming software package you really should consider using. Once you have developed your encoder, and installed this software (which recognizes the capture card), you press a few control buttons to determine your output. You are then encoding your files for replay. Of course, you will need to purchase Real server software, which supports up to 25 simultaneous users before additional licensing fees are incurred.

NOTE

Over and above the CD entitled, "How to Use RealProducers," there are many online instructional sessions and books on how to use RealProducer Plus. I also suggest you use the resources on the Internet and the many books available for purchase at your local bookstore or online.

I am including some screen captures of Real to show how basic it really is. In addition, you can target up to eight audiences. Some of the most notable features of this product, I believe, are:

- A deinterlace filter that removes artifacts introduced when encoding National Television Standards Committee (NTSC)– or Phase Alternate Line (PAL)–formatted video to clean up specific types of source content for broadband RealVideo.

- The introduction of Neuralcast Live Redundancy software, which ensures that your media reaches your audience. It sends redundant-encoded streams to Real system servers to provide a failover feed in the event of a network or equipment issue. You now have full codec control, giving you the option to optimize the particular codec or the bandwidth assigned to each audience, or to configure how the system responds under duress.

- RealAudio 8 that lets you hear the natural and broadest range (12 to 352 kbps) of your music. With the integration of two new codecs—RealNetworks Low Bit Rate Stereo Music and Sony ATRAC3—RealAudio 8 delivers a vastly improved music listening experience in the range of 12 to 352 kbps, from dialup connections to broadband. Most people cannot tell RealAudio 8 at 64 kbps from the original CD. Encoding RealAudio 8 is easy, requiring no changes to your production process. It is as simple as checking a dialog box in RealProducer Plus 8.5.

NOTE To hear samples of the RealAudio codec, visit the RealAudio showcase at www .realnetworks.com/solutions/ecosystem/realaudio.html.

- A better opportunity to achieve superior video quality by using Real's full power and control of variable-bit-rate and two-pass encoding.

- Real now runs on four operating systems: Windows, Linux, Solaris, and Macintosh. Encoding from files or live sources is available on all four platforms.

- SureStream is a unique RealSystem feature that allows the Real server to dynamically adjust the stream for each of its unique listeners, depending on the dynamic network conditions of the user's connection. If the network path becomes congested, RealSystem shifts down, like an automatic transmission on a hill. Once the congestion is gone, the connection will shift back up.

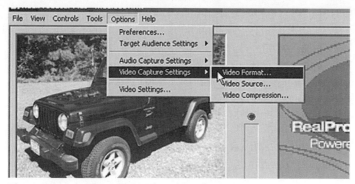

Figure 9.2 RealProducer Plus video format screen.

Figure 9.2 is a screen shot of some pull-down menu choices as well as the options to choose single or multirate SureStreams, audio and video formats, and the target audience, and those enabling you to change previously decided-on settings when setting up a session. I find this feature very helpful when testing output and creating nonbatch or transcoded sessions.

Figure 9.3 illustrates setting your source. A nice aspect of the software is that this screen is also available during the session. There are times when you will need to make adjustments to the video, and having the capture card settings readily available to you without changing screens or sessions is very helpful. You also can change the type of input you are using, another must when you do a variety of encoding from a live camera, videotape recorder (VTR), or another audio and input device.

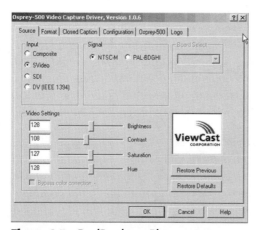

Figure 9.3 RealProducer Plus source screen.

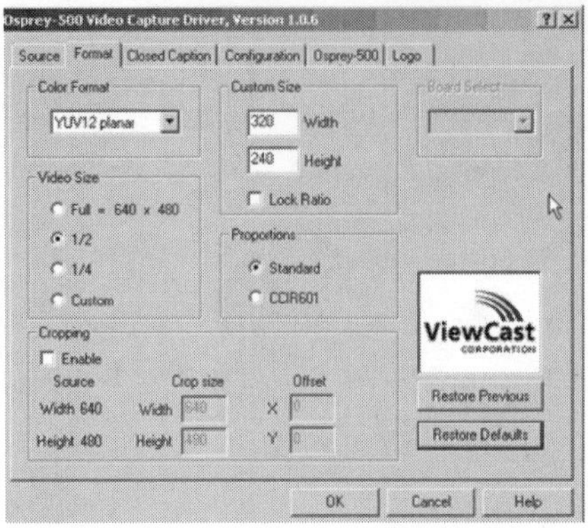

Figure 9.4 RealProducer Plus format screen.

Figure 9.4 shows how you set the format. When capturing video, you must have the ability to adjust your capture video size, and Real gives you this opportunity on the fly. When encoding low-bandwidth video sizes, typically you are capturing at 160×120 or 176×144 pixels. Now that DVD is becoming more popular, you may even desire to customize your capture. Real gives you the ability to make these adjustments on the same screen and within the same session.

Figure 9.5 is a screen shot of other helpful choices for closed caption encoding.

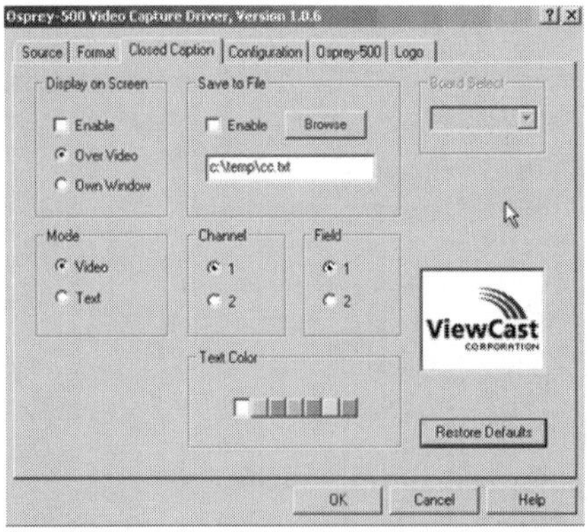

Figure 9.5 RealProducer Plus Closed Caption screen.

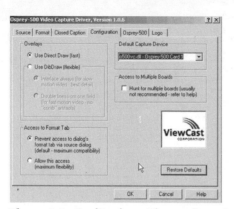

Figure 9.6 RealProducer Plus configuration screen.

Figure 9.6 demonstrates the configuration settings. It gives you the ability to use overlays, to access format tabs and your capture device, and provides access to multiple boards (capture).

The Osprey-500 screen is shown in Figure 9.7.

The Logo tab (see Figure 9.8) gives you the ability to use graphic inserts while the video is streaming. This is quite a tool for company promotion or even possibly generating revenue. This feature is very nice if you are looking for impact.

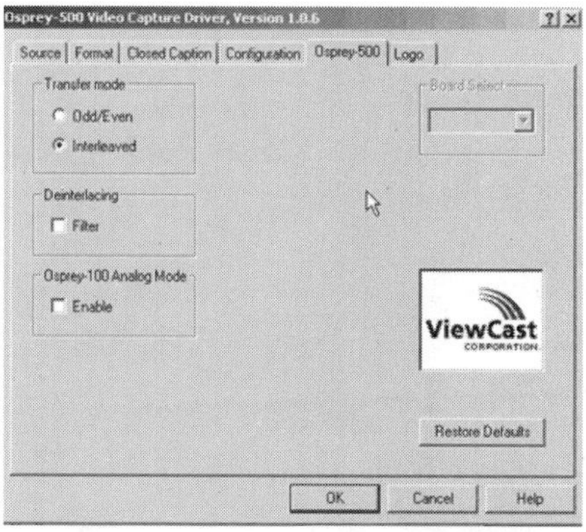

Figure 9.7 RealProducer Plus Osprey-500 screen.

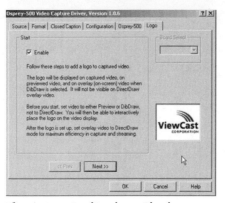

Figure 9.8 RealProducer Plus logo screen.

Windows Media Encoder 7.1

Although there are many decisions you must make in choosing between Microsoft Media Encoder 7.1 and RealProducer Plus 8.5, the quality of the output with Microsoft Media Encoder 7.1 is worth the extra steps.

NOTE
Go to www.microsoft.com/windows/windowsmedia/en/wm7/Encoder/default.asp to view the Windows Media Encoder 7.1.

The choices for setting up your capture cards for a particular session are shown in Figure 9.9. If you have installed your video and audio capture cards incorrectly, it will be evident at this step.

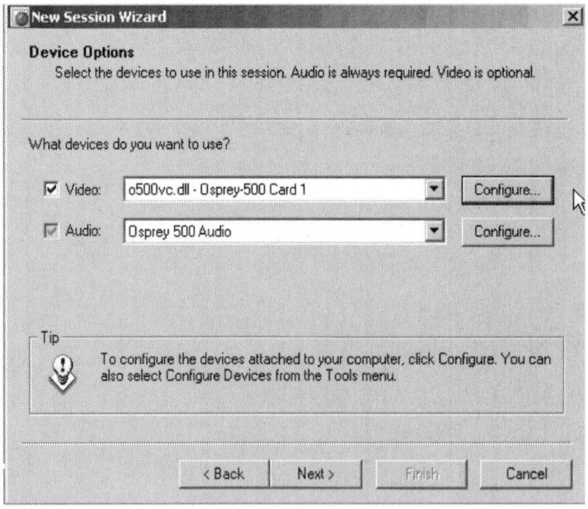

Figure 9.9 New Session Wizard.

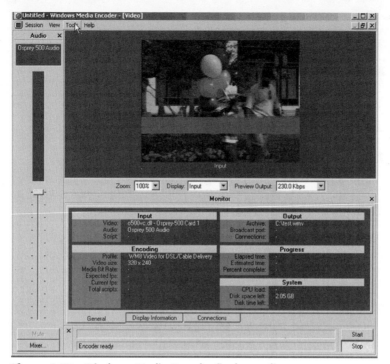

Figure 9.10   Windows Media Encoder final encoding screen.

Figure 9.10 illustrates the final encoding screen used for your session.

NOTE I have skipped several screens because I feel that you will download the latest version of Windows Media Encoder and go through the accompanying online tutorials.

Among the better features of this session screen is the ability to view your encoded material as a split screen: You can view only encoded output, preview original input, or both. I find this very helpful when doing comparisons, especially at lower bandwidths.

Figure 9.11 shows the pull-down choices you have under Tools. You can make adjustments to your profile directly from this session screen. I frequently use Generate Stream Format File and Manage Profiles.

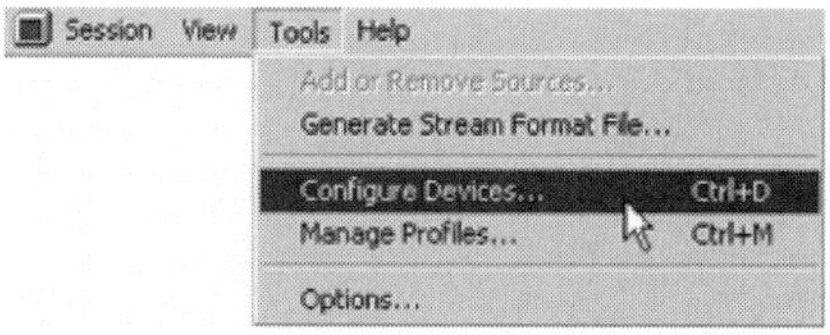

Figure 9.11   Windows Media Encoder tools.

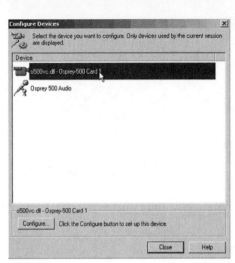

Figure 9.12 Windows Media Encoder Configure Devices screen.

The Configure Devices command, previously referred to (see Figure 9.12), allows you to adjust your video card capture settings. This is a tool I use frequently, especially when adjustments to the video source are required.

Frequently the video is too dark, and quick modifications to the input source are very important. Figure 9.13 shows the screen where you can adjust your video capture card settings. In addition, when you are working with many audio and video devices, being able to change your input source with a quick click is a must.

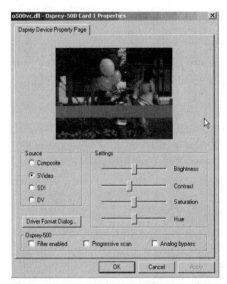

Figure 9.13 Windows Media Encoder Osprey-500 device settings screen.

Apple's QuickTime

At the time of writing, I have not had the opportunity to actually spend time with the latest version of the Sorenson Video 3 codec for Apple QuickTime. I have, however, researched the capabilities of this codec and studied its installation procedures. Since the majority of those reading this book will be using Microsoft products, I feel it's important to build a very good understanding of the latest Apple-compatible codecs that run on the Microsoft platform.

The Sorenson Video 3 codec is the result of over 10 years of intensive research and development. The evidence of this investment is seen in the unparalleled combination of compression and quality. As an integral part of Apple's QuickTime technology—beginning with Quick-Time 3—Sorenson Video has delivered high-quality compressed video across multiple computer platforms and the Internet.

NOTE

To purchase the Sorenson Video 3 codec software, or the upgrade, go to www .sorenson.com/products/video.asp.

Standard versus Professional

Two versions of the Sorenson Video 3 codec are available:

Standard Edition.   The Sorenson Video 3 Standard Edition codec is included as part of Apple's QuickTime 5. The Standard Edition has the basic compression controls for data rate, frame rate, and fixed-keyframe intervals. Unfortunately, some of the advanced compression features are applied with default settings, which you cannot modify. The Standard Edition codec produces good results for average video content at moderate data rates (50 KB or above).

Professional Edition.   The Sorenson Video 3 Professional Edition codec adds additional control to the compression process for serious multimedia content producers. Using the Professional Edition features, you can produce high-quality video even at very low data rates. The Professional Edition has the fine control necessary to handle all types of video from interviews to sports footage. The features include:

- Data-rate tracking for superior quality at low bit rates
- Automatic keyframe sensitivity control

- Bidirectional prediction
- Video watermarks
- QuickTime streaming support
- Video masking

NOTE For a complete list and explanation of all features, see the Sorenson Video 3 Feature Reference at www.sorenson.com.

Sorenson Video 3 Codec Features

Sorenson Video 3 codecs contain a number of exciting features and improvements, including the following:

- Optimized for Macintosh G4, MMX, and SSE
- Image smoothing
- Fixed quality option
- Full-color video watermarking
- QuickTime 5 streaming support
- Bidirectional frames
- Video masking
- Media key encryption
- Variable bit rate (two-pass and one-pass)
- Multiple-processor support

Installation

The Sorenson Video 3 Professional Edition codec is available for the Apple Power Macintosh and for the Windows 9*x*, 2000, and NT systems. Prior to installing your codec, be sure the installation CD is the correct one for your operating system.

NOTE If you have the wrong CD, contact your software supplier or the technical support department at support@sorenson.com.

System Requirements

Make sure that your computer meets or exceeds the following system requirements:

Compressor. The Sorenson Video compressor on this CD requires a QuickTime 4.0 or later development environment. Current development platforms include:

- Power Macintosh (OS 8.6 or later, including OS X)
- Microsoft Windows 9*x*, 2000, XP, and NT

Playback. Current playback platforms include:

- Power Macintosh
- Macintosh G3 and G4
- Microsoft Windows 9*x*, 2000, and NT

NOTE
All playback platforms must have QuickTime 5 or later installed.

Macintosh Installation

To install the Sorenson Video 3 codec on a Macintosh, do the following:

1. Insert the Sorenson Video 3 CD in your CD-ROM drive.
2. Double-click the Sorenson Video CD icon.
3. Double-click the Install Sorenson Video icon to start the installer.
4. Follow the steps of the Install Wizard to complete the installation.

Windows 9x/2000/NT Installation

To install the Sorenson Video 3 codec on a Windows 9*x*/2000/NT platform, do the following:

1. Insert the Sorenson Video 3 CD in your CD-ROM drive.
2. From the Start menu, select Run.
3. In the Run dialog box, enter the following command (where D: is the drive letter for your CD-ROM drive):

```
D:\Setup
```

4. Follow the steps of the Install Wizard to complete the installation.

Validating Your Installation

A quick way to validate a successful installation is to use Apple's QuickTime Player Pro. Using QuickTime Player, load a movie file, and then set the export video options to Sorenson Video 3. If the installation was successful, the Sorenson Video 3 Options button displays the full advanced features dialog box.

NOTE
This procedure requires QuickTime Player Pro in order to use the movie export features.

Use the following steps to test your installation:

1. Open an uncompressed movie file in Apple's QuickTime Player Pro.

2. From the file menu, select Export. The Export dialog box appears. At the bottom left of the Export dialog box is a drop-down list of output formats.

3. In the Export dialog box, set the output format to Movie to Quick-Time Movie.

4. Click Options to display the Movie Settings dialog box.

5. From the Video section, click Settings to display the Compression Settings dialog box. The top selection list of the Compression Settings dialog box contains a list of video compression codecs.

6. From the codec drop-down list, select Sorenson Video 3. When you select Sorenson Video 3, an Options button appears at the bottom-left corner of the Compression Settings dialog box.

7. Click the Options button to display the Sorenson Video 3 Settings dialog box. If you have installed the Sorenson Video 3 Professional Edition successfully, the Sorenson Video 3 Professional Edition Settings dialog box appears. If you still have the Standard Edition of the Sorenson Video Settings dialog box, try the installation again.

NOTE
If installation problems persist, contact Sorenson Media technical support at: support@sorenson.com or at the Web site: www.sorenson.com.

Now that the Sorenson Video 3 codec is installed, you are ready to compress video.

Taking the Next Step

There are other types of codecs currently on the market. Some require player downloads and some do not. Real, Microsoft, and Apple Quick-Time are the three most popular codecs available today and are viewed by millions daily.

Chapter 10 will discuss cleaning and editing the captured stream once it has been encoded and other streaming resources. If you remember the basic image capture and editing processes covered in Chapters 2 and 3, you already know that the topics covered in Chapters 10 and 11 are the next logical steps.

Using Cleaning, Editing, and Other Streaming Resources

There are many ways to clean and edit streaming video. Many of us have been using these types of tools for years with video broadcasting footage. Traditional companies such as AVID and Adobe have enhanced their software so that it now includes video streaming capabilities. Other companies have also emerged in this fast-growing industry.

This chapter provides an overview of the most popular and most reasonably priced software in these categories, and it contains an extensive resource section, including contact information, for some of the other players in the game. This chapter also sets the stage for further discussion of topics such as: advanced encoding, project setup, and media management (issues covered in greater detail in Part Four of this book).

Using Adobe Premiere

Adobe Premiere has made great strides in the last few years. Improvements in Premiere 6.0 are grand and exceptional, with functionalities far exceeding those of previous versions, such as:

- IEEE-1394 (FireWire/i.Link) capability.
- DV presets for National Television Standards Committee (NTSC) and Phase Alternate Line (PAL) video for your equipment.

- DV device control, which allows you to use batch capture of video or to capture in-points to an out-point and immediately record from tape.

- Support for nonsquare pixels, which include DV's wide-screen (cinema) pixel aspect ratio of 16:9 (1.2) and the anamorphic pixel aspect ratio of 2:1 (2.0).

- DV editing mode, where the program sends captured/rendered video through the IEEE-1394 connection to the DV device with full-quality previewing.

- Import/export in a variety of formats, including QuickTime, type 1/type 2 .avi files, and DV stream files.

- An upgraded Capture window.

- Export to the Web with three different methods in only one step.

- The ability to set timeline markers that include links to HTML pages or to chapters in a QuickTime movie/DVD.

- Enhanced monitor and timeline windows.

- An audio feature, including an audio mixer, that allows you to mix your audio with professional results directly in Premiere.

- A Project window for managing all your media.

- Visualization tools that increase productivity, including storyboard windows, with the Automate to Timeline command plus a Commands palette.

- An Effects Control palette, which allows you to control all effects in one area, and a Keyframe track for the Timeline window, which gives better visualization for effect keyframes.

- The ability to customize and save a workspace setup: The A/B Editing workspace allows you to simplify the area and use the Single-Track Editing workspace for a more professional environment.

- Integration tools, which includes the Edit Original command for editing clips in their source program while still working in Premiere.

NOTE
■■■■■ **For more information on Adobe Premiere 6.0 and other Adobe products, go to www.Adobe.com.**

Working with Discreet Cleaner

Another very popular capturing, authoring, encoding, and editing software program—a pretty good way to put streaming audio and video on your Web site—is Cleaner version 5 (a product of Discreet, a division of Autodesk, Inc.). Cleaner 5 features of merit include the following:

- A complete camera-to-Web solution, allowing you to easily capture, author, encode, and publish your streams from one streamlined workflow.

- Support for all streaming formats—QuickTime, RealSystem, Windows Media, and MP3, as well as MPEG-1 and MPEG-2—and easily deliverable content in your clients' preferred formats.

- EventStream authoring that allows you to add stream navigation, synchronize HTML to streaming media, embed buy-me links and interactive hotspots, insert advertising, and more.

- Advanced video and audio processing combined with its intuitive Settings Wizard, making it easy to put the highest-quality streaming media on your site.

- The capability to work with all your favorite Web design tools— Dreamweaver, GoLive, Flash, and Shockwave.

- Built-in StreamPublisher technology, which lets you publish your finished projects directly to a streaming server.

- Batch processing, an intelecine feature for 2:3 pull-down removal, powerful A/V filters, and Windows and Mac scripting XML-based settings that take you to the next level.

Learning More about Discreet

Discreet, a division of Autodesk, Inc., is a leader in digital content creation, management, and distribution tools. Discreet develops systems and software for visual effects, three-dimensional (3-D) animation, editing, and production (used in the creation of digital moving pictures for feature films, video, high-definition TV (HDTV), broadcast graphics, interactive games, and the Web).

In addition to streaming media, Discreet products are used extensively in:

- ◆ Film and video postproduction
- ◆ Games and multimedia
- ◆ Broadcast graphics
- ◆ Programming
- ◆ On-air event coverage

For the latest information on Discreet Cleaner (covered in this chapter) and other Discreet products, contact any authorized Discreet reseller, call Discreet at 800-869-3504, or visit www.discreet.com.

Exploring Other Resources

The alphabetical listings in this final part of the chapter can be a valuable resource in building the right streaming media system to suit your needs. Each entry contains a description of the services offered plus complete contact information for making your concept a reality.

Agents-Everywhere

Agents-Everywhere is an integrated strategic design and publishing firm that develops and markets original content and intellectual properties. The company specializes in music and video. Agents-Everywhere provides clients with solutions for all their dynamic media development and production needs through a process known as *accelerated convergence.* The company is also a virtual agent, working with independent artists, writers, designers, and producers.

Contact Information

3633 248th Avenue SE
Issaquah, WA 98029
Phone: 427-837-3642
www.agents-e.com

AIST, Inc.

AIST offers a comprehensive production suite for all aspects of video and TV production—video editing, compositing, graphics, titles, effects, audio, and much more—all seamlessly integrated into one user-friendly package with database and back-office integration as well as full support for all digital formats, including streaming video.

Contact Information

Mobil-Oil-Str. 31
Ampfing, Germany 84539
Phone: 877-380-9877
www.aist.com

AVID Communications

AVID Communications, a business unit of Rockwell International, is a full-service video and multimedia production studio specializing in business-to-business communications in marketing, sales, and training programming. The company has been serving local and national accounts such as KeyCorp, The Cleveland Clinic Foundation, Rubbermaid, Marconi, Lincoln Electric, and more for over 20 years.

Contact Information

33433 Curtis Boulevard
Eastlake, OH 44095
Phone: 216-266-7551
www.avidcom.com

Be Here Corporation

Be Here iVideo, the next generation of interactive content for the Internet, combines the interactivity of 360-degree panoramic immersive imaging with full-motion video. Immersive video removes the limitations of fixed-frame video by putting the viewer in control of where to look within a live or recorded immersive environment. The iVideo experience is enabled by the iVideo 360lens. This revolutionary patented optical system captures the full 360-degree environment surrounding the camera in a single frame. Be Here also provides a family of iVideo software products for on-demand and live Webcasting.

Contact Information

20300 Sevens Creek Boulevard
Suite 100B
Cupertino, CA 95014
Phone: 408-873-4918
www.behere.com

InterMedia Solutions

InterMedia Solutions was founded in Vaterstetten, near Munich, Germany, in March 1999. With offices in Munich and Boston, the company focuses on rich media-authoring software and enterprise streaming solutions. The innovative authoring tools of the company have successfully established themselves in the growing market for streaming media software and rich media applications. The company is one of the world's leading enterprises in these technologies and has a number of development and sales cooperations. Using streaming media, single frames, graphics, and text information can be posted automatically on a single Web page at the same time as video. Rich media Web sites are more attractive, provide more information, and are more entertaining. Visitors spend more time at the site, which indirectly increases not only online sales but also advertising revenue. The i-CONTROL, LiVE-CONTROL, and DESiGN-CONTROL software packages let TV broadcasters, organizations, and agencies publish their news, production information, and entertainment offerings as rich media on the Internet without visitors to the Web site needing to have sophisticated hardware or software.

Contact Information

101 Federal Street
Suite 1900
Boston, MA 02110
Phone: 800-689-6001
www.intermedia-solutions.net

Ligos Technology

Headquartered in San Francisco, Ligos Technology is a leading world-wide provider of real-time, software-only media stream management technology. Founded in 1997, Ligos developed the GoMotion codec, which has the ability to compress high-quality MPEG-2 video in real time using only software on a Pentium-based PC. GoMotion offers Ligos customers the distinct advantages of speed and affordability when compared with more expensive hardware-based MPEG solutions.

Contact Information

55 Stockton Street
San Francisco, CA 94108
Phone: 415-249-0100
www.ligos.com

Macromedia

Flash is Macromedia's solution for producing and delivering high-impact Web sites—pulsing musical tracks, sound effects, gorgeous animations, and innovative interfaces. Developers can create an array of dazzling effects by using the drawing tools in Flash or by importing artwork from favorite vector illustration tools, such as Macromedia Free-Hand. Easy to learn for developers of any skill level, Flash puts the flash in Web sites and other Web-enabled devices (such as WebTV).

Contact Information

www.macromedia.com

MAGIX Entertainment Corp.

MAGIX Entertainment is the leading entertainment software publisher of music, video, and Internet streaming solutions for consumers. MAGIX pioneered the technology of producing music and video on a home PC and created a line of intuitive and affordable applications that allow consumers to capture, record, create, edit, deliver, and manage multimedia content. In the streaming product category MAGIX offers @Audio & Video Office—software to capture, record, edit, and encode both audio and video content.

Contact Information

Michael Niermann
11400 W. Olympic Boulevard, No. 450
Los Angeles, CA 90064
Phone: 310-656-0644, ext.104
michael@magix.net
www.magix.com

MaxVU, Inc.

MaxVU delivers the highest-quality streaming video content using the least amount of bandwidth on the Internet. MaxVU specializes in enabling watchable video over dialup access and the best-quality video over any bandwidth connection. MaxVU technology is transparent to viewers, requiring neither additional hardware nor software downloads. The MaxVU solution is anchored by the MaxVU Plug-n-Stream Encoding System, a digital video encoder appliance that accepts all NTSC- and PAL-based image sources, including CD, DVD, TV, VHS/Beta S, satellite, and so on, and then streams out the encoded images to the Internet or local networks. MaxVU stands ready to help you open the vast narrowband Internet market to your video-rich applications, while also delivering best video quality at any narrowband or broadband connection with their AllBand optimization technology.

Contact Information

MaxVU, Inc.
Chase Bank Building
25025 I-45 North
The Woodlands, TX 77380
281-364-6926
291-364-6909 fax
www.maxvu.com

Media 100 Inc.

Media 100 develops software and systems that simplify the creation and delivery of video on the Internet, DVDs, and CD-ROMs. Media 100 also provides the most comprehensive suite of streaming media services to its customers by offering encoding (audio and video compression) and hosting (delivery) services for Internet broadcasters, Web designers, and digital media content creators.

Contact Information

290 Donald Lynch Boulevard
Marlboro, MA 01752
Phone: 508-460-1600
www.media100.com

Pinnacle Systems, Inc.

Pinnacle Systems is the leading supplier of cutting-edge tools for performing live Webcasts. Known for its innovative digital video solutions, Pinnacle Systems focuses on quality to ensure that customers receive high-performance audio and video encoding combined with integrated production value. Pinnacle Systems' Webcasting solutions are recognized for their value, quality, and ease of use. From rich media corporate training to mission-critical broadband streaming deployments, Pinnacle Systems has the streaming solution that works.

Contact Information

280 North Bernardo Avenue
Mountain View, CA 94043
Phone: 650-526-1600
www.pinnaclesys.com

Point Cloud, Inc.

Point Cloud provides 3-D imaging services to e-commerce companies. The company's 3-D technology does not require a plug-in, like that of many other 3-D companies.

Contact Information

13220 County Road 6
Plymouth, MN 55441
Phone: 763-551-1950
www.pointcloud.com

Sonic Foundry

Sonic Foundry Media Services, a division of Sonic Foundry, Inc., is a comprehensive service offering the highest-quality encoding of audio and video, in any format, to the music, film, broadcast, and corporate markets. Sonic Foundry is a pioneer and leader in the digital media management and tools industries. The company has created what may be the world's most advanced collection of digital media processing algorithms—in other words, the fundamental code behind encoding technology. The company's filtering processes are the most sophisticated in the world and provide video output with sharper images, higher frame rates, and overall superior fidelity to the original. Only Sonic Foundry CODE delivers true-to-the-original, 24-frames-per-second encoded output. Sonic Foundry Media Services is the only business of its kind to use its own fully proprietary, end-to-end production systems to encode, verify, and move high volumes of media over the Internet.

Contact Information

754 Williamson Street
Madison, WI 53703
Phone: 608-256-3133, ext. 2468
www.sonicfoundry.com

Sync4Media

This is a browser-based studio for synchronized multimedia authoring. It is used to create rich Webcasts and presentations that integrate audio, video, graphics, text, flash, and Web pages. It allows you to add interactivity, search, and navigation capabilities to clips. You may use Sync4Media to customize an embedded player for your Web site and much more.

Contact Information

182 East 95th Street, Suite 16E
New York, NY 10128
Phone: 212-426-7458
www.sync4media.com

TV Builder

TV Builder represents a comprehensive, end-to-end suite of à la carte rich media streaming services: production, editing, encoding, hosting (live or VOD), satellite, design and integration, and multifunctional and fully personalized viewer interfacing. At the heart of this company's range lies the turnkey TV Builder platform, both an authoring and rich content management tool that enables you to have complete control over the profile of your content, its management, and automatic uploading to the company's global content delivery network partner, AKAMAI.

Contact Information

Wilberforce House
Station Road
London, UK NW4 4QE
Phone: +44-20-8457-4344
www.tv-builder.com

Taking the Next Step

In this chapter, you have taken another step in the process of providing high-quality encoding streams to your audience. Anytime you can save time and resources while streaming, you are freer to concentrate on other areas to perfect your streaming output.

Chapter 11 takes this concept further into the realm of transcoding, a more effective way to take in one input and send it out in many formats and sizes.

CHAPTER 1

Transcoding File Formats

The optimization of video formats for either compression or editing is known as transcoding—that is, the conversion of files from one format to another (from large file sizes to smaller ones, or vice versa). Transcoding may be needed to convert a file from an acquisition to an editing format, or from a high-bit-rate format to a low-bit-rate distribution format. In practical streaming terms, transcoding can be used in automatic batch output to convert initial video and audio capture files to much smaller Real, Microsoft, or QuickTime formats.

This chapter explores the technology and practical applications of transcoding in the context of streaming media. In presenting some real-world examples, I chose Telestream and its product line to best illustrate how transcoding is used. This company has been in business for some time, and I consider it to be a leader in streaming media.

Revisiting the Compression Process

For distribution to the home, MPEG-2 compression coding is universally used. Video compression is also being applied increasingly to parts of the broadcast chain. Compression techniques are not limited to the example just given, however. They can also be extended to generic transcoding methods suitable for other common standards, such as

JPEG, H.263, MPEG-1, and the like. For other parts of the broadcast chain (acquisition, postproduction, and archiving), there can be a multitude of different compression formats.

In the current broadcast environment, it is common for transcoding to consist of decoding the input bit stream and then recoding it with a standalone coder to the desired output format and bit rate. This is also the approach proposed in MPEG-2 verification tests for coding multiple generations. The experimental results of these tests confirm that high picture quality can be maintained.

NOTE

Transcoding, however, can have a price: It can introduce significant impairments if performed without due care. Each subsequent generation of transcoding can introduce additional coding impairments—even for the special case where there is no change of bit rate.

Meeting the Demand for Streaming Media

Streaming media is growing on the Internet at exceptional rates and should continue to accelerate as last-mile bandwidth improves. Streaming media is not only popular for entertainment sites but is also becoming an important tool for businesses. Based on my experience in the industry, the number of U.S. companies that use streaming media on their Web sites and intranets are increasing on a daily basis. More and more websites are integrating streaming media to communicate their messages.

Unlike MP3 for music, video over the Internet is not converging on a single standard. Because of the large data rates required, a number of video formats for the Internet will continue to be used to address the wide range of platforms, pipe speeds, and user preferences. Today, Web sites that offer streaming media typically offer multiple formats at multiple bit rates in order to address a reasonably broad audience of viewers.

While building your encoder (refer to Chapter 8), it is important to note that if you can capture audio and video once and then convert it into multiple formats, you can save time and money. It behooves you to deliver media seamlessly in any format, optimized for specific applications.

The goal is to transcode source media into virtually any number of streaming formats and to deliver the encoded media to the desired content distribution network servers. These types of transcodings can be done both live and on replay.

As mentioned at the beginning of this chapter, I've asked Telestream to help me with this subject, and they have shared with me several examples of transcoding methods along with their particular solutions to transcoding problems.

NOTE

For more information on the products and solutions mentioned in the following examples, contact Telestream at www.telestream.net.

Application Example 1: Publishing Multiple Formats

A broadcaster is creating 8 hours of content per day, which it wants repurposed into streaming media for video on demand (VOD) from its Web site. While a program is airing, a Telestream ClipMail Pro captures the program and encodes it into a high-quality MPEG format. At the completion of the program, ClipMail Pro delivers the MPEG file to the FlipFactory running on a local server. FlipFactory, which has been configured previously to produce 2 bit rates each for WindowsMedia, RealVideo, and QuickTime, flips the source file into the specified formats and automatically forwards them via FTP to the three streaming servers at the broadcaster's hosting partner. The operator then receives links to the media locations via an e-mail message.

Application Example 2: Flipping on Demand

A cable channel wants to simplify storage of its media archive while providing universal access for purchasing and downloading. Media are stored in a high-quality MPEG format in a digital archive. A request to browse a particular clip comes in through the Web site. The asset-management system identifies the archived clip and tells the Flip-Factory where to get it. FlipFactory localizes the file, flips it into the proper format, inserts a watermark to ensure that the owner's rights are protected, and delivers the file to the streaming server for immediate playout. Then, when the customer chooses to purchase the clip, FlipFactory is called on again to deliver the clip in the specified high-quality format.

Application Example 3: Collaboration Distribution

A content distribution service provider has signed up a large corporate client to facilitate collaboration when working on all its marketing materials. Over 100 people need copies at the client and its agencies, production houses, and consultants. A rough cut on a new commercial has just been completed and must be distributed to everyone in the group. The postproduction facility uses ClipMail Pro to deliver the commercial in MPEG format to the service provider, where a Flip-Factory server flips the media into the format specified for each recipient, holding some for streaming and delivering high-quality MPEG to the desktops of those who want it. The system administrator has performed most of the account setups, although some of the power users have optimized their settings at FlipFactory to ensure that they receive the media just as they want it. Recipients are notified by e-mail with a link to the media or an attached file when flipping is complete. The asset-management system handles the follow-on feedback and approval process.

Application Example 4: Live Flipping

A Fortune 500 company wants to broadcast its chief executive officer's quarterly address to its internal and external shareholders. The Flip-Factory server takes a live digital feed and flips it into the specified formats for real-time delivery to the ingress server for the distribution network. The operator has reserved the proper number of output channels previously when setting up the live feed.

Application Example 5: Broadcast Transcoding

In the broadcast world, all major video server manufacturers have proprietary methods of storing video and audio data for playback. File schemes are different, as are file systems, transfer methods, metadata and frame-table parameters, and format types (MPEG-2, M-JPEG, and DV). FlipFactory Pro solves the incompatibility problem by acting as a universal format translator that allows broadcasters to move media directly to and from different servers.

In addition, FlipFactory Pro can acquire media assets directly from the broadcast server for transcoding to streaming formats. Telestream's

ClipMail appliances can be used to digitize, encode, and move media from tape or MPEG file formats to the broadcast server from any location in the world. An example would be a commercial produced in Los Angeles that can be moved directly onto the playout server via the Internet Protocol (IP) without resorting to tape.

Working at the FlipFactory

Virtually any format source media file may be submitted to FlipFactory, which decodes, enhances, and then reencodes the media into the desired formats before delivering it to the destination servers. Based on industry standards, including Extensible Markup Language (XML) and TCP/IP, FlipFactory can be controlled by an easy-to-use Java application or may be integrated seamlessly with the customer's own database or asset-management system.

Of equal importance, the FlipFactory technology can be extended in a number of directions. In the broadcast space, for instance, FlipFactory has optional modules that allow direct file transfer between proprietary video servers and the rest of the broadcast center.

Flipware

FlipFactory is one application in Telestream's strategic Flipware architecture. I believe that the best way to distribute media will not be based on a single format or hot new protocol. Given the diversity of media-viewing requirements and the constraints of network topology, viewing platforms, and user preferences, the best platform for media distribution is a flexible one that adapts to the requirements of each application. Flipware is Telestream's family of solutions for versatile media distribution and optimizes media delivery based on the capabilities of each network and the preferences of the users.

Flipware incorporates patent-pending technology from Telestream that provides a platform for building powerful media distribution applications now and in the future. It has three main components:

MDML.   An XML-based language that describes media, messages, network capabilities, and events

MDP. A protocol that controls, negotiates, and monitors media delivery

Flip Engine. The core licensable media reformatting software

The protocol negotiates delivery of media prior to any transmission, ensuring compatibility with playback platforms and guaranteeing that optimal-quality media reaches the destination(s) via the most efficient path(s). These three elements form the foundation not only for Flip-Factory but also for other powerful applications such as Gigaflip mail.

NOTE
Gigaflip mail is available at the Telestream video services Web site (www.gigaflip.com).

Modularity and Flexibility

The versatile XML-based Flipware architecture that supports Flip-Factory facilitates modular product configurations that can be combined in a number of ways to meet a wide range of customer needs. For example, service providers who have their own media distribution systems in place may not require the complete messaging and database transactions of Flip Engine. They can use the core Flip server to handle their transcoding needs in the context of their own systems for moving media around the nodes in a network.

Media Delivery Appliances

Telestream's first products employ an early form of the Flipware architecture. The ClipMail Pro and, more recently, ClipExpress media encoding and delivery appliances provide peer-to-peer delivery of high-quality MPEG media files over standard data networks. They offer solutions to the broadcast and content-creation markets—the markets that care the most about high quality and are willing to pay for it. The early mantra was, "Never ship a tape again!"

Introduced in April 1999, ClipMail Pro was, and still is, a breakthrough solution that simplifies a previously cumbersome process of encoding, and then sending media files. By creating an extremely intuitive interface and integrating all the functions in a single space-efficient unit, sending video is as easy as sending an e-mail or a fax. The ease of use, high media quality, and robustness of the products have won sales at major broadcast and content-creation companies around the world, including: CNN, Time Warner, NBC Studios, Bloomberg, Fox Sports, APTN, Discovery, Disney, and AT&T Media, to name a few. Telestream appliances are the standard for high-quality media delivery in the broadcast, postproduction/ad agency, and production dailies markets.

These appliances now fit into the greater Flipware picture, providing critical leading-edge devices for submitting and/or receiving and playing high-quality media. The lineup of network-savvy media appliances will continue to grow to complement software solutions for large-scale media distribution networks.

Whether you are starting from a tape, live camera source, archive, or editing system, Telestream's Flipware solution provides smart, simple media encoding and delivery tools that efficiently get your media onto a network and/or to your colleagues.

NOTE

For more information, please visit the Telestream Web site at www.telestream.net.

Transcode on demand also solves another problem: format obsolescence. You only need to worry about the master copy (typically MPEG), while the transcoding engines keep up with the latest versions and trends in the streaming technology space.

Transcoding on Demand

A new trend in content distribution, transcoding on demand, is gaining a foothold. Companies such as Generic Media, Telestream, and Vingage argue that you do not need to encode and maintain multiple copies of each video asset (in different formats and bit rates) and that you especially do not need to distribute those multiple copies to the edge of the network.

Instead, they argue that you should encode a single high-quality master and perform on-demand transcoding at the edge of the network. The end user then gets optimal access to his or her preferred format at a bit rate that works best for his or her connection speed at that moment. And you save on storage and distribution fees. Hence: the Content Distribution Network (CDN) alternative, otherwise known as transcoding on demand.

Taking the Next Step

You can see how transcoding can be very effective when you are encoding files and can also be a highly effective first step in managing the streaming process, especially when you start using this technology on a daily basis. Why spend time on each individual bit rate and format when you can let a server automatically do it for you?

Part Four of this book deals with managing and deploying your streaming media. Chapter 12 starts off with a discussion of content management and e-commerce solutions, the next step in building a streaming media enterprise.

Managing and Deploying the Media

Developing Content Management and E-Commerce Solutions

T his chapter addresses the ever-growing need for viable content management solutions in today's streaming media environment—the
real-world requirement for audio and video indexing and streaming
enterprise tactics.

Waking Up to Reality

Video is one the most ubiquitous and effective communication media
across broadcast, entertainment, enterprise, and consumer markets
today. Television and film production alone have generated millions
of hours of video content over the last 20 years. Furthermore, most
organizations produce significant amounts of video for a variety of
applications, such as sales and marketing, training, education, decision
support, and employee and customer communications.

As powerful as video is, however, it is not easy to manage, distribute,
and use. As a result, any enterprise that handles video content faces the
difficult and expensive proposition of finding, accessing, and deploying the right video segment. In most cases, the inability simply to locate
desired footage means wasted content, reacquisition costs, and lost
opportunities. In addition, as all content migrates to digital form, the
problem of managing these massive, opaque media assets actually gets

worse. Even a tape label conveys more information than a cryptic file name on a remote server.

Just as organizations are struggling to control their existing media assets, new channels for video creation, distribution, and use are emerging rapidly. High-speed Internet access, broadband distribution, and set-top boxes are just a few of the technologies presenting revolutionary new revenue opportunities that complement existing business models, such as broadcasting. Almost all these initiatives promise to provide much greater levels of interactivity with video.

Video in its native form, however, does not lend itself to user interaction, and video use is largely a one-way experience, where the viewer is relegated to a passive role. Traditional video does not take advantage of established Internet usage patterns characterized by short personalized exchanges of information and entertainment content.

From video archives on a corporate intranet to video-enhanced e-commerce sites on the Web, the common elements required to turn video into useful information are fine-grained access and control over the content. In short, video must have an accompanying index to be useful. While the extracted metadata and digital video have enormous value alone, it is the solution-oriented deployment of these data that makes video truly useful as an informational data type.

Taming a Wilderness of Data

"There is one unstructured data type, however—arguably, the most unstructured of data types—that has so far proved largely intractable to systematic management. Video data represents a rich, unexploited source of enterprise content and knowledge."

—Chuck Luce, senior analyst, Delphi Group

The next 10 years of digital media will have an impact comparable to that of the past 50 years of analog media. Figure 12.1 illustrates the evolution of digital video.

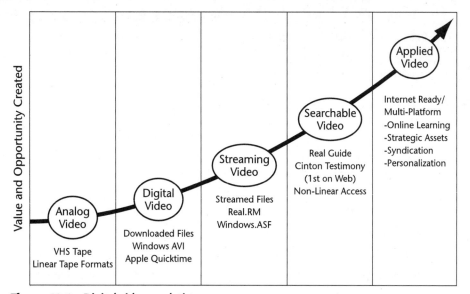

Figure 12.1 Digital video evolution.

Clearly, analog video, in the forms of broadcast, cable, and tape, has been with us for a long time. Digital video formats first appeared in the broadcast production environment and in the last decade have expanded to consumer formats and Web-based streaming formats. The recent migration to digital media assembly processes and digital TV (DTV) delivery has been a lengthy and painful process, one that is not yet complete.

Web-based video, on the other hand, has evolved much more rapidly. Beginning with QuickTime, Microsoft Video for Windows, and MPEG-1, digital video files became available for download in the early 1990s. The hypergrowth of the Internet brought forth new video standards based on streaming, such as RealVideo and Microsoft's WindowsMedia.

In November 1998, we saw the advent of searchable video, enabled by indexing and search technology from Virage, Inc. It debuted with the complete video of the Bill Clinton grand-jury testimony on the

AltaVista site available as a fine-grained, searchable, interactive, and streamable library of video clips. In the past year, more than 100 premium content owners have taken the steps to publish interactive video on their Web sites.

Digital Video Comes of Age

Recently, (refer to Figure 12.1), digital video has reached the next stage of maturity, where the video not only is searchable but also can be used for many advanced purposes, including targeted advertising, syndication, personalization, and multiplatform delivery. Further, video now can be synchronized easily with additional rich media data such as presentations, animations, transcripts, and related documents.

As a result, digital video now has become a first-class data type enabled for the emerging broadband infrastructure. It can be transformed into a body of information content that can be managed and exploited in the same manner that text and numbers have been in the past. Digital video now has reached a certain stage of maturity, by becoming *applied video.* Digital video is far more agile than film and tape because it can leverage metadata.

The Digital Video Value Chain

The driving force behind the recent evolution of digital video is the opportunity to monetize content in new ways that go beyond traditional delivery and commerce mechanisms. Applied video introduces new value opportunities that allow content owners to realize new revenue streams. Figure 12.2 illustrates the overall value chain for digital video and the discrete steps required to capitalize on the features and benefits of applied video.

Digital Video Value Chain

Acquisition	Production	Transformation	Publication	Distribution	Consumption
-Capture -Authoring -Smart Cameras	-Event Production -Post Production -Media Assembly -Stock Archives	-Video Captures -Video Indexing -Smart Encode -Editorial Metadata	-Multi-platform Delivery -Content Neetization -E-Commerce -Personalization/ Targeting	-Video Hosting -Backbone -Cache & Edge Services	-Web-Top Players -Set-Top Boxes -Wire Devices, PDA's, Phones

Figure 12.2   Digital video value chain.

Courtesy of Virage, Inc. © 1997-2001. All rights reserved. Used with permission.

Many of the steps in the value chain are shared with traditional video production and delivery processes. However, several new mechanisms are required to fully enable video for intelligent interactive delivery in the broadband paradigm of "What I want, when I want it, and where I want it." For example, something of interest is found using a wireless personal digital assistant (PDA) while commuting on the train and is then sent to the user's desktop at work for viewing when he or she arrives. If there is one central ingredient to the recipe, it is the capture and intelligent use of video *metadata*, index information about the contents of the video.

Transforming Video for Interactive Delivery

The preparation of video for film, broadcast, training, or strategic enterprise purposes follows essentially the same production and media assembly process that applied video does. The key departure from traditional preparation workflow occurs when the finished content is transformed into intelligent, indexed, and purposefully annotated content. The transformation process is accomplished by using a new breed of video.

Metadata, as shown in Figure 12.3, consist of time-stamped data elements such as keyframes, spoken text, speaker and face identification, on-screen text reading, logo detection, and so on. Each of these metadata elements acts as a reference back into the video content—in much the same way a card catalog unlocks the wealth of information in a library.

The video index enables searching, fine-grained navigation, previewing, and association with ancillary activities, such as personalization and content rights management. Metadata also enable video content to be managed effectively and delivered with targeted advertising and content relevant to e-commerce opportunities. For example, if a user is watching a skiing video:

- Show him or her an ad for snowboards
- Provide him or her with an option to enroll in a drawing for a ski-weekend getaway
- Allow him or her a one-click buy opportunity for lift tickets at a nearby resort

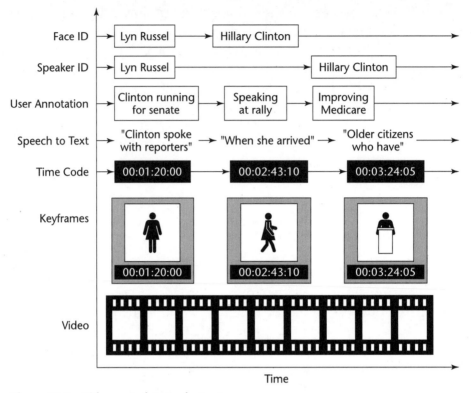

Figure 12.3 Video metadata track structure.

For premium content owners, indexed video is the basic starting point for broadband delivery mechanisms such as syndication, pay-per-view, and subscription business models. Consequently, metadata standard efforts are the most exciting evidence of the digital media evolution.

Meeting the Multiplatform Challenge

"To date, homegrown, piecemeal streaming solutions have frustrated content providers and held back broadband video both within the enterprise and on the Internet. But with the advent of integrated video application platforms, content providers can now stop experimenting and start efficiently exploiting their rich media assets, either as strategic information or monetized content."

—Jeremy Schwartz, senior analyst, Forrester Research

The video-logging tool is only part of the story. Metadata are managed and offered to users through an application-server mechanism, whereas the video content itself is distributed through content distribution networks (CDNs) and edge-caching infrastructure (see Chapter 13). The metadata must refer, in a time-accurate manner, back to the video content itself. In a multiplatform delivery model, this actually means referring back to many different physical renditions of a given piece of content. Modem users need 56-kbps streams, whereas broadband users need 300-kbps and above streams.

Video content for set-top box delivery must be of broadcast quality, whereas wireless devices currently are best served with text and thumbnail images rather than actual video, otherwise known as WAP (wireless application protocol). Therefore, the transformation process not only must produce a rich metadata index of the content but also must prepare a wide variety of renditions of the content, all of which are time-synchronized with the metadata.

NOTE One popular solution to this problem is the SmartEncode process from Virage, which orchestrates video indexing with any number of simultaneous encoding processes in various bit rates and formats. SmartEncode-processed video is the first step to searchability and interactivity, allowing users to pull snippets of video of interest to themselves from repositories of long-form video. For example, "I don't want to watch the entire debate. I just want to see what the candidate said about Social Security and education."

Evolving Formats and Standards

To address the new requirements of increased interactivity and multiplatform delivery, the popular digital video and streaming formats are evolving rapidly, and new standards are emerging to handle metadata. De facto standards such as RealVideo, QuickTime, MicrosoftMedia, and the Virage VDF metadata format have a solid foothold today, but new formats will become a factor in the future.

MPEG-7 is an emerging standard that provides a standardized description of various types of multimedia information. MPEG-7 is formally called the *Multimedia Content Description Interface.* The standard does not specify the (automatic) extraction of video metadata, nor does it specify the search mechanism that can make use of the description.

Several other metadata standards are also gaining acceptance, such as:

- The efforts of the SMPTE Metadata Working Group
- The Advanced Authoring Format
- The interesting things being accomplished with the highly flexible MPEG-4 format

Delivering Applied Video

"The advent of digital video data, however—and, in particular, of Web-friendly streaming standards—meant that video immediately became as easily browsed, searched, downloaded, and shared as any text document or Web page, right? Wrong. A major stumbling block to date has been the lack of an application framework robust enough to tackle the extraordinarily complex chore of video signal analysis."

—Chuck Luce, senior analyst, Delphi Group

An important sign that digital video has matured to the point where one can rightfully call it *applied video* is the emergence of complete-solution offerings. In other words: delivery of video that supports the intelligent applications previously discussed, in a platform-independent manner.

Today, frameworks such as the Virage video application platform (Figure 12.4) have matured to a level on par with traditional Web-authoring and content-management solutions for text and graphics media. Turnkey video-publishing platforms that support all the advanced capabilities and delivery platforms of interest can be licensed or outsourced as hosted applications. Virage has established relationships and tight integration with content distribution networks (CDNs). Therefore, it can provide not only basic video indexing and application hosting features but also value-added editorial assistance to fully exploit e-commerce and ad-targeting opportunities. Some vendors even provide layered application frameworks, allowing the addition of syndication engines, personalization support, and community-building features.

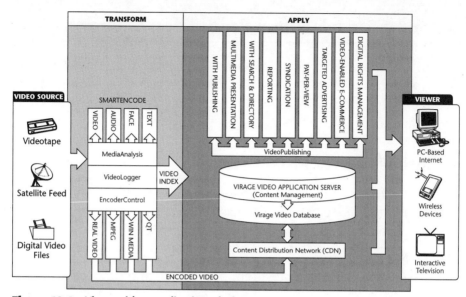

Figure 12.4 Virage video application platform.

Video metadata and streaming media, effectively managed by a video application server, are key ingredients to achieving device independence in the delivery chain. For example:

- Most wireless devices such as those from Palm cannot today receive and display streaming video at any bit rate. However, they can display thumbnail images and transcript text, and provide functions to redirect the applied video back to your desktop or to a friend.

- Alternately, at the broadcast-quality end of the spectrum, a set-top box can deliver high-quality video that is time-synchronized with auxiliary Web-based content.

Exploring Today's Video Production Environment

In today's marketplace, we are witnessing the convergence of traditional broadcasting with the digital revolution. Many changes and technological advances are taking place. The following sections offer a snapshot of what I mean.

The Current State of Broadcasting

"We were getting buried in video and realized that it was critical for CNN to invest in a more modern newsroom in order to manage content more efficiently. For us, that meant a transition from analog to digital and some type of asset management system."

—Kevin Ivey, vice president of research and development, CNN

Television broadcasters are actively seeking to improve the bottom line, while processing greater volumes of video. In today's tape-based environment, the management and distribution of video are inefficient and expensive. With the current economic conditions and the intense competition to improve content processing, quality, and delivery, broadcasters are seeking mature solutions to address these demanding requirements.

The transition to digital video is the key to improving productivity and creating operating efficiencies. A first step for many is updating and preparing current infrastructure to embrace the transition. Solutions must integrate into existing and planned workflows, promote open standards, have a proven track record, and provide performance and scalability to meet the rigorous demands of a broadcast environment.

Going Digital

Going digital improves productivity by allowing staff to view, review, and edit video on the corporate intranet. This eliminates or greatly reduces the need to find and handle videotapes. Digital video allows media companies to produce new content more quickly and to reuse existing content more effectively. Therefore, the most cost-effective and efficient solutions are able to process incoming content only once, and then apply it to multiple uses. For example, a digital environment allows broadcasters to extend their brands beyond traditional television to Internet Protocol (IP)-based delivery mechanisms, such as the World Wide Web or even wireless devices.

News Automation

Short time to air is essential, the costs are high, the process is slow, and the creative process is hampered by time spent searching for content. With increasing competition from 24-hour channels and the Internet, maintaining leadership in news broadcasting proves to be a difficult task. TV networks have to shorten time to air, handle more information, produce high-quality programming, and reduce production costs—all in an environment of significantly stiffer competition for viewers' attention.

The solution is to process video more efficiently, reduce production costs, and access high volumes of content with speed, accuracy, and reliability. Video indexing and metadata management enable broadcasters to:

- Centralize video and data acquisition and manage their content effectively.
- Save significantly on the costs associated with tape duplication and program creation.
- Access video from their desktops without having to shuttle through miles of tape, giving producers, journalists, and editors more control over the story content and presentation. This streamlined process saves expensive screening and editorial time and allows broadcasters to reallocate staff to more creative, productive assignments.

The Virage Broadcast Solution

In response to the needs of modern broadcasting, the Virage video application platform, with its open architecture, can integrate easily with existing systems—such as nonlinear editors, newsroom control systems, video encoders and servers, and asset-management systems. Virage also provides the foundation for broadcasters to build compelling digital video applications to help automate news production, manage video archives, publish video to Web sites, or securely syndicate video across the Internet.

Designed to scale to any broadcast facility, the Virage platform:

Transforms content. Virage SmartEncode is a simultaneous real-time process for optimizing and automating the video-transformation workflow that includes:

- The ability to control and monitor ingest processing and index content
- The ability to automate encoding of multiple formats and bit rates

Applies video. The Virage video application server provides the foundation for managing, publishing, distributing, and repurposing video across any IP network (Figure 12.5).

- Archive video can be managed intelligently for quick browse and retrieval of content.
- Clips can be published to your Web site automatically and integrated with other applications.
- Video can be distributed across the network at anytime or to any viewing device.
- A rough edit of new and old clips can be repurposed and assembled to quickly create new assets.

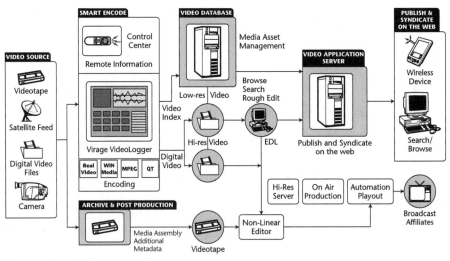

Figure 12.5 Video network.

Digital Video Archiving

The opportunity here lies in the ability to repurpose content effectively for new projects by managing an archive efficiently. Currently, broadcasters spend a significant amount of time and staff hours archiving content manually.

Often, these tapes get lost or are not cataloged properly. Even when companies have instituted a so-called card-catalog system, producers, production assistants, and editors still must shuttle through volumes of tape manually in hopes of locating the desired content. Thus, many talented and creative people spend most of their time locating, moving, and identifying the content rather than making important decisions, creating compelling programming, or preparing promotional material. The solution is to eliminate manual searching and cataloging, so information can be more efficiently accessed and shared throughout the organization.

A centrally indexed digital video archive allows for a much more streamlined communication process. It saves time in production, improves video services, and creates better-quality programming or promotional material. Material can be accessed on demand and reviewed at any time, right from the desktop. An efficient video indexing process eliminates much of the manual cataloging by automatically creating an accurate and reliable video database that maintains the integrity of the archive. By automating and controlling the encoding and indexing process, producers, promotional departments, and licensing departments experience greater productivity and control.

Web Publishing

By digitizing content efficiently and publishing instantly with effective distribution control, content can be monetized online. The Internet is fertile ground to repurpose broadcast content, create an on-demand experience, extend a brand or viewership, provide highlights, and promote television programming. Although broadcasters recognize the Internet's potential, many have found that repurposing video online in a compelling and user-friendly way can be a frustrating and labor-intensive process. Broadcasters need to find a cost-effective way to extend their programming online or even generate new revenue through advertising or archive environments.

Defining a Structured Web

All standard business school textbooks describe the evolution of an industry, which can be paraphrased as follows:

- An innovative phase engaging early adopters
- A growth phase characterized by rapid expansion and the emergence of industry leaders and standards
- A mature phase of optimal efficiencies and leads
- And a final phase of full maturity

This picture is classically known as the *adoption curve* or *S-curve* and has been extended to global economic cycles by Henry Dent. However, as Dent shows, large industries and economic trends do not simply emerge and follow a nice, smooth curve. They experience a period of *shakeout*, when many firms, attracted by the opportunity, join the fray and experience increased competition and market saturation.

Consider the advent of railroads, aviation, or the automobile. Typically, the shakeout is followed by a new growth period with more mature innovations and products, which is often called the *maturity boom*. Thus large industries experience oscillations in their growth owing to the extended geographic, economic, and social impact they bring about. Each oscillation has its own subphases of early adoption, rapid expansion, and so on.

The Web is the most significant industrial emergence of our times, with global economic and social impact. It is also oscillating. The first wave of the Web occupied the last half of the 1990s, and we are currently in a shakeout awaiting the arrival of the second wave. The key driver of the first wave was *infrastructure*. I assert that the second wave is about *superstructure*.

The survivors of the first wave are the companies that went beyond the plumbing and gee-whiz graphic user interfaces (GUIs) to deliver comprehensive, solutions-oriented products and services on top of the first-wave infrastructure. Just as you cannot build a building using only plumbing and a facade, you cannot deliver value on the Web with just fast pipes, hosting facilities, and GUI builders.

One of the clearest areas of Web superstructure consists of solutions built around rich media and video as first-class informational data types. The ability to manage, publish, syndicate, personalize, and synchronize video with presentations and other media effectively offers real value to content owners, corporations, and consumers.

Web Video Infrastructure

During the first wave, most of the necessary digital video infrastructure was put in place in terms of streaming technology: CDNs (both public iCDNs and private eCDNs), and video indexing tools. Streaming media also leveraged the early adoption of broadband access and improvements in Internet backbones.

However, the streaming industry as a whole has fallen as the early assumptions and business models of the first wave failed. The focus of streaming technology on the media and entertainment aspects of the Web proved faulty. Some examples:

- Content aggregation by third parties seems to be a flawed business proposition because many firms that attempted content aggregation are now out of business. Premium content owners (especially) want control over distribution and branding of their content.

- Efforts to create unique Web content also have failed (such as Pseudo, Atom Films, and so on).

- The end of the first wave was fraught with issues of digital rights management (DRM), secure transmission and encryption, watermarking, and the like. These are the last components of the needed infrastructure and are now largely resolved with DRM standards such as XMCL and improvements in the streaming platforms to handle secure delivery.

Web Video Superstructure

There are clear signs that at least a part of the larger digital video industry, specifically Web video publishing, is starting to catch the second wave. Part of the second wave is driven by the realization that applied video in the corporation offers tangible benefits and efficiency gains—for communication, distance learning, and exploitation of strategic information (such as best-practices and focus-group video). In the public Internet space, we see the emergence of business models and solution offerings to support syndication, pay-per-view, and subscriptions that work for content owners and allow them to monetize their content. Actual deployments of high-quality, indexed, and interactive video are reaching critical mass, both inside and outside the firewall.

The emergence of Web video publishing as the second-wave superstructure is a result of standards, technology maturation, partnerships, and workable business models, all of which are converging. Video-encoding formats and compression efficiencies have stabilized and are grounded in de facto standards (Real, Microsoft, and QuickTime) as well as industry-standard protocols such as SMIL, RTP and RTSP.

"On TV Previews" are published automatically, based on air date and time. Discovery also uses Virage to insert streaming ads before previews without having to encode the combined piece as a new asset.

Metadata Make the Difference

Metadata are the main driver that makes Web video a second-wave solution. Metadata unlock the latent value in video assets and expose a wide variety of opportunities for use and delivery. Nonlinear access, content-distribution management, and media synchronization are core features derived from metadata that bring video to center stage in Web environments. Video indexing and publishing platforms can now provide quantifiable value and targeted solutions for corporations and content owners. The coming wave of Web superstructure will be characterized by the successful vertical application of metadata.

Web Publishing Spotlight 1: The Discovery Channel

Discovery Networks uses audio and video indexing to publish on-demand previews of upcoming shows and for-sale videos on the Discovery Channel and its sibling channels, allowing the TV network side of the business to use the Web site as a promotional space for its cable programming.

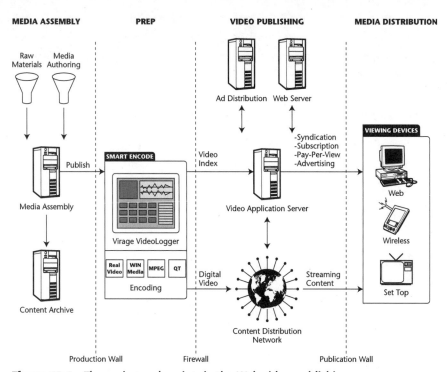

Figure 12.6 The main touch points in the Web video-publishing process.
Courtesy of Virage, Inc. © 1997-2001. All rights reserved. Used with permission.

The Emergence of Touch Points

In the past two years, the process of publishing rich media and video on the Web has matured significantly. Companies in adjacent categories such as video encoding, streaming, indexing, media management, and content delivery have worked together to solve the core problems, by which touch points have emerged. Web-time partnerships and Web-time technology have rapidly bridged connections between these touch points, and the technology and business-model boundaries have been drawn. Figure 12.6 presents a high-level view of the Web video publishing process in which you can see the main touch points.

A primary touch point is the integration of video-logging and metadata-analysis tools with asset-management systems and their data models. Synchronized video indexing and encoding (in multiple formats)—a process that Virage calls SmartEncode—is crucial not only to the media assembly process but also to publishing processes. Indexing and encoding processes occur more than once for good reason: Video formats and metadata structures are significantly different for different parts of the process. SmartEncode touches the archive, the publishing process, and specialized CDNs that cache the video at the edges of the network, close to consumers.

The Clear Distinction of Process Areas

The maturity of Web video publishing is revealed by the clear distinctions between the various processes that create the value chain:

- Media assembly
- Preparation
- Video publishing
- Distribution

Each process area is served by application and service vendors and is well understood by vendors and system integrators. The emergence of these specialized roles is analogous to the functions of printing, shipping, and retailing in the print publishing realm. Each of these processes plays a critical role in the value chain from content creator to consumer. Each area also exhibits workable business models with commercial offerings in each area.

Web Publishing Spotlight 2: Major League Baseball

Major League Baseball Advanced Media (MLBAM) uses audio and video indexing to develop and distribute video coverage of the entire Major League Baseball season on MLB.com. Virage provides MLBAM with the infrastructure services to create and publish a searchable video database of all games played, allowing every pitch of every game to be available on demand.

For example, the Virage-enabled "MLB.com Custom Cuts" feature transforms television coverage of baseball games into interactive, on-demand video programming that lets individuals choose the exact game highlights they want to watch. Users can search for and create customizable video highlights of daily game coverage and can easily compile and review footage of their favorite teams and players on a daily basis.

The Media Assembly Environment

Media asset management (MAM) systems debuted in the early 1990s, driven largely by the explosion in digital imaging. MAM system vendors struggled in a tight market that had long development and deployment cycles. Early-adopter projects helped the vendors to hone the feature sets of these systems, tackling mass storage interfaces, workflow management, schema design and evolution, rights management and tracking, and a tangle of representation issues stemming from too many formats and versions. What, after all, is the definition of a *digital media asset* when it may exist in many forms targeted at several types of delivery?

In recent years, MAM system vendors have evolved powerful data models and processes for keeping track of the virtual media asset and most recently have tackled video management. The MAM industry has spread into new vertical markets, and MAM system vendors have specialized their offerings for these markets. Broadcast production, digital libraries, corporate archives, Web production, and brand management appear to be gaining the most traction.

The term *media asset management* now refers to an overly broad set of applications and verges on being meaningless. In the present view, *media assembly* becomes the more accurate term to describe the function that the traditional asset-management systems play in the Web video-publishing process, where the video-publishing process becomes the recipient of assembled content.

The Critical Step-by-Step Flow of Metadata

Video metadata are the single most important ingredient of the Web video publication process. Here's why:

- Video logging and indexing applications extract information from the video that is used by management and publishing tools.
- Video indexing occurs at several points in the full process, where different forms of metadata are applied for different purposes.
- Likewise, video encoding usually occurs multiple times, with each encoding format having certain strengths.

- Video loggers ingest raw video content into the media assembly process and provide baseline metadata and encoded video suitable for searching and browsing (refer to Figure 12.6).

- Produced content is fed back into a media archive, where librarians apply a sophisticated vocabulary and quality assurance (QA) processes to index the video for posterity and reuse.

- The media assembly system ultimately pushes produced content across the production wall to a preparation stage, where video logging processes endow it with specialized metadata tags to enhance ad targeting, e-commerce, syndication, and personalization.

- At the same time, video-encoding processes generate an array of streaming formats and bit rates tuned for Web delivery.

- The video index and streaming content is then uploaded to production servers for publishing and delivery.

Streaming bumper ads are added flawlessly before and after the featured clip without the need for additional encoding. CNET is also able to syndicate content to multiple online affiliates, controlling content quality and distribution.

The Role of the Video-Publishing Platforms in the Value Chain

Video-publishing platforms are the most recent key technology to reach a mature stage and solve one of the last thorny problems in the value chain. Prior to the emergence of these platforms, individual content or Web site owners had to build their own Web-based solutions to the publishing problem. This barrier to entry has now been removed, and this is the main reason the industry has entered the rapid growth phase.

Web Publishing Spotlight 3: CNET

CNET has made video an integral part of the CNET Web site experience. Video- and text-based product and technology information is integrated seamlessly. Topical searches yield both text and video results.

Articles flow around corresponding clips. Hits are tracked to publish results automatically, such as "Most Popular Video." Ads are targeted to the selected video and are displayed in the player window.

Video-publishing platforms distinguish themselves from media assembly by providing Web-style consumer interactions with digital content. Interactive video begins with fine-grained access, search, and pull metaphors for consuming content on the consumer's terms. Exploitation of metadata is a critical requirement of such systems, enabling the baseline search but taking the next step—also enabling synchronized presentations of multimedia content, personalization, video-driven e-commerce, community building, and targeted advertising. Video-publishing platforms also exhibit strong remote administrative and reporting tools, allowing content owners to interact directly with and control the content they choose to publish. Content owners can manage syndicated content in packages for distribution to affiliates, where critical business syndication rules and usage-tracking tools help make the process efficient.

Video-publishing platforms also offer an ideal outsourcing opportunity for the main tasks of indexing, Web-format encoding, and publishing. Application service providers (ASPs) can speed the time to market for content owners, while preserving each owner's brand identity, by injecting indexed content right into their own Web site.

New Distribution Modalities

In the experimental phase of Web video, it became painfully obvious that bandwidth was a problem. The favored solution today employs local caches of thick content (images, graphics, video) at Internet service provider (ISP) points of presence (POPs) to alleviate congestion on Internet backbones. This *edge-caching* tactic is also combined with dedicated networks, including satellite links and advanced routing algorithms, to speed the movement of thick content. In the past 2 to 3 years, a large number of CDNs have built significant infrastructures that make Internet video a usable and consumable medium.

Distribution of fat video streams is only part of the story, however. The other part is distribution of the video index and the associated applications that constitute Web video publishing. The syndication engines of the video-publishing platform mediate between the content owner's central video index and the potentially large number of actual affiliate sites that manifest that content. This mediation occurs across the publication wall that controls and monitors access to the published content in a similar way that a firewall controls and monitors data access.

The CDN Alternative: Transcode on Demand

I've shared this new trend in content distribution with you in a previous chapter, but it bears repeating here. Basically, certain companies, such as Generic Media, Telestream, and Vingage, are convinced that encoding and maintaining multiple copies of video assets (in different formats and bit rates) and distributing those multiple copies to the network's edge is a thing of the past. They argue for the encoding of a single, high-quality master, which can then be transcoded on demand.

This translates into optimal access for each end user, in his or her preferred format and at the bit rate best for the connection speed of the moment, and, perhaps of equal importance, a substantial savings on storage and distribution fees. This advanced technology, may also render format obsolescence a concept for the history books.

Web Tactics for Content Owners

Creating streaming for the Web is just the start. Many companies must develop an objective in terms of why they want to stream and how they will obtain a return on their investment. I have created the following topics to give you something to think about.

From Information Wants to Be Free . . .

Free information has been a long-standing meme in our society, crystallized by John Perry Barlow when he said, "Information wants to be free." The idea that information wants to be free stems from the way people communicate and carry ideas around in their heads, in books, or on laptops. Humans are happier when their communication is unfettered. Information in this context is relatively raw and unprocessed; it is information such as facts, statistics, how-to information, and lightly interpreted data. This thought gains momentum in the communication explosion (that is, the Web or e-mail); it gains global awareness and creates phenomena such as the Freedom of Information Act, freeware, and open source.

Information in this view is part of a classic progression (Figure 12.7) adapted from spiritual and philosophical thinking. It begins with the void, progressing to noise, signal, and data, and builds to information. This is the domain of *acquisition*. Information, in turn, is the beginning of the domain of *interpretation* that progresses from information to knowledge, wisdom, and beyond into the spiritual views of enlightenment.

To the Evolution of Content . . .

Content, however, is not simply information or data, nor is it knowledge or wisdom. Content is a branch off the preceding progression that merges data, information, and knowledge into the *creative process*, the actual producer of content. The creative process primarily adds value by providing an interpretation and editorial perspective on the raw information. The added value of the creative process might serve commercial, aesthetic, or noble interests. Content then proceeds into the distribution chain, where publication and consumption take place.

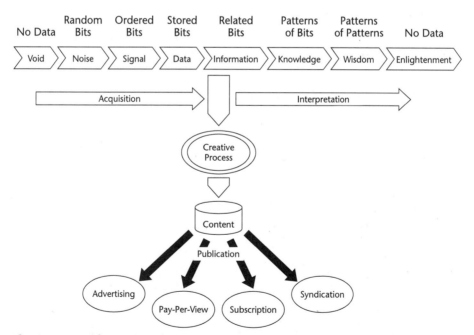

Figure 12.7 Video progression.

Content has the benefit of creative authorship and the art of storytelling (be it news, documentary, artistic entertainment, how-to information, or research reports) that add significant value. The content is packaged and has a brand identity, further contributing to its value. Premium content also exhibits scarcity in quantity and comes through restricted distribution channels that can elevate the perceived value to the consumer. Commodity content such as a news headline, which verges on raw information, can have elevated value if it is time- and location-sensitive and can be delivered quickly.

To Gaining a Return on Investment . . .

The majority of content authoring, packaging, and distribution occurs today fundamentally as a business proposition. Content, by its nature, wants to be monetized to support the delivery chain. Content always has faced the distribution hurdle, from ancient playwrights to early authors at the dawn of the printing press. Mass media such as radio and television altered the equation, and the methods available to monetize content, and now media such as the Internet and interactive television, have altered it further. Several prime mechanisms for content monetization evolved long ago, and these have remained fundamental in the face of massive technical change:

- Advertising-supported delivery
- Subscription services
- Pay-per-view
- Syndication

Today, the Internet is a new and exciting medium for content delivery and monetization. The available channels of delivery are broader and more complex than ever, and this has introduced new business model opportunities.

There is nothing really fundamentally new in the prime mechanisms available, but the tactics are changed significantly. We are in a realm of thousands to millions of Web sites with global audiences and pull access.

Content in digital form can carry rich metadata with it that allow the consumption process to be directed by the consumer instead of the producer. Techniques such as video search (nonlinear access) and personalization are the newest mechanisms that must be considered in any distribution strategy. The accelerated pace of the Internet offers new opportunities for time-sensitive content. Let's consider each of the prime distribution mechanisms in the context of the Web and metadata.

Advertising-Supported Delivery

Advertising was the first prime mechanism used on the Web, and it has met with partial success. It has fared better with portals and services than it has with premium content publication. Content metadata are now driving a revival in advertising models, using the content to help target the advertising—evolving from banners to video-based ads. As targeted advertising injection into video streams becomes common-place, look for advertising models to take an appropriate place in distribution strategies, although probably less prominently than in traditional broadcast media with captive audiences.

E-commerce is one aspect of Web advertising that changes the value equation as compared to traditional media. E-commerce is not a fundamentally new mechanism; rather, it is instant gratification in advertising. All advertising, directly or indirectly, strives to consummate a purchase. Web and e-commerce technology simply brings this transaction to the consumer's desktop.

Subscription Services

Subscription models also were attempted early in the Internet era and were met mostly with failure. However, digital music, finance, and sports are driving new subscription value propositions, and we can expect growth in this model, especially when premium video content is the driver.

As broadband adoption accelerates and time-sensitive content migrates to the Web in a vertical fashion (such as financial news and sports), we can anticipate new life for this tried-and-true distribution mechanism. Personalization further compounds the attractiveness of this model because the value delivered to subscribers increases dramatically. In a fast-paced world, where no one has time to sift through irrelevancies, the accurate targeting of content offers a way out, and consumers are willing to pay for it.

Pay-per-View

Traditional video-on-demand and pay-per-view services have proven to be a highly successful mechanism, especially in the cable industry, where it is a multi-billion-dollar business. The prospects also look attractive on the Web, although the model is still in the infant stage.

The combination of broadband, digitized long-form content and search capability allows consumers to find what they want when they want it and for how much they are willing to pay. Metadata enable search and pull from vast archives that dwarf what is available at your local video store. Ancillary tactics, such as recommendation systems, leverage personalization technology to further increase revenue generation and the attractiveness of this model to the consumer. The advent of interactive television systems drives a combination of delivery models and heightens the need for good video metadata.

Syndication

Strictly speaking, syndication is a metadistribution mechanism. When content is syndicated to other Web sites, it can be monetized locally by any or all of the preceding prime mechanisms. The new Web tactical viewpoint for content owners starts with recognition of the vast number of syndication sites available. With a potential global consumption base on the order of a large fraction of the population of the earth, the business economics of syndication must adjust.

Beyond price/volume concerns, multitier syndication must be considered. The nuts and bolts of syndication now revolve around usage management, delivery logging and tracking, and syndication rules engines that automate the transactions between a content owner and potentially thousands of syndication sites. Once again, metadata about the content drive the syndication engines, while simultaneously offering added value once the content eventually is consumed under one of the other prime distribution mechanisms.

To Tackling the Hurdles of a Web-Based Value Chain

Content owners face a significant hurdle to being successful in Web distribution but can capitalize on an equally significant opportunity on the other side of this hurdle.

- The good news is that the rules have not changed fundamentally.

- The bad news is that most of the tools and techniques have changed, and time cycles have accelerated. Merely publishing content on a Web site does not realize the vast potential of the Web or allow a distribution strategy to scale effectively.

Syndication emerges as the most effective prime distribution mechanism for Web content. As they have in the past with book and movie distributors, content owners now must embrace an emerging industry centered on Internet video publication platforms that provide video indexing, publishing and searching, personalization technologies, syndication engines, and collaboration with CDNs. These are the new distribution tools that tackle the new hurdles for the Web-based value chain from the creative process to consumption.

Looking at the Future of Video Metadata

In recent years, much progress has been made in the area of video indexing and metadata extraction. These efforts are aimed at transforming video into useful, searchable information. Examples of video indexing techniques include keyframing, closed-caption text extraction, speech-to-text processing, speaker identification, face identification, on-screen text recognition, dropout detection, object (or logo) detection, and so on. The Virage VideoLogger is the premier example of the commercial deployment of these technologies.

Each of these indexing approaches uses some form of algorithmic signal or text analysis to extract meaningful metadata, which are then time stamped to correlate the occurrence of the metadata item with the location within the video where that metadata occurred. These indexing approaches can be thought of as *observations* derived from some form of signal analysis within a signal modality (for example, video pixels, audio samples, and text). They have significant value in terms of forming the basis for a searchable index that can be exploited in a variety of application areas (for example, Web publishing, media asset management, and video archives) to make the video accessible and useful in a fine-grained, nonlinear way.

The Next Generation of Video Indexing

The next generation of video indexing technology will build on the observational modalities of present systems to provide higher-level semantic information and structure, resulting in a more useful and powerful video index. The primary goal of current research is to automatically determine meaningful boundaries within the video, wherein the subject matter of the video is coherent. This process is known as *video segmentation* and results in a higher-level structure of clips (defined by in- and out-points within a larger piece of video), thereby providing richer opportunities for search, retrieval, classification, and summarization of video content.

Currently, human beings mainly perform video segmentation in commercial applications by interacting with a video indexing system to mark the clip boundaries and assign categories and summaries in a manual process. The next generation will largely automate this process, as well as produce additional value, with such features as summarization, topic identification, and proper noun identification.

Virage long ago anticipated the emergence of second-order analysis techniques and pioneered a framework capable of supporting the multimodal fusion approach to analysis. Not only can media analysis plug-ins subscribe to raw signals (pixels, audio samples), but they also can access any metadata track generated by other plug-ins. Moreover, groups of plug-ins can cooperate and exchange information with human beings, providing the framework for the next generation of video indexing.

Virage Media Analysis Framework

Virage's VideoLogger has a rich, open, and extensible architecture supported by a robust software development kit (SDK). One of the central interfaces in this architecture is the media analysis framework.

Multimodal Fusion

In the past few years, a number of new technologies from leading-edge companies, academic research institutions, and government-sponsored research programs have reached a level of maturity that will allow them to become commercially viable in the near future. Examples include various forms of linguistic analysis (in English and other languages) that can identify and track topics, produce summaries of news stories, identify proper nouns and their type (person, place, organization), and place content segments into one or more categories for keyword retrieval. These types of analysis are second-order, in that they operate on metadata generated by the first-order observational and signal-analysis techniques.

By themselves, second-order technologies can offer real value by enriching the video index and producing results that formerly required human intervention. The real breakthrough for next-generation indexing, however, comes about through the coordinated and intelligent use of several first- and second-order technologies. This approach is known as *multimode fusion*. By using information from several observations simultaneously and taking hints from the second-order language-analysis techniques, we can achieve the goal of intelligent video segmentation.

The ability to automatically chop video content up into *semantically coherent segments* is of immense value in video production, monitoring, and archive environments. The meaning of semantically coherent segments for video varies greatly across domains. For example:

- For news, the goal is to segment a newscast into individual stories or sections such as weather, finance, sports, and so on.
- For entertainment content (such as a movie or a soap opera), the segmentation should map to the scene structure.

Another way of looking at this is to explore the traditional method broadcasters use to present their content. If you were to view a length of videotape representing just the content for a full-length news or entertainment segment, you would observe occasional black frames and an audio dropout, indicating the space needed for a commercial break.

> **Metadata Standards Synergy**
>
> Various metadata standards are gaining momentum concurrent with advances in indexing technology. MPEG-7, AAF, RDF, the Dublin Core, NewsML, and SMPTE standards all address various aspects of content description. Metadata authoring will rapidly become a core function in all media assembly and production processes.

Each domain of content, therefore, has its own unique structure and corresponding cues that indicate segment boundaries. As a result, there is no one single algorithm that can intelligently segment all video.

The key to effective use of the multimodal fusion approach is to:

1. Build probabilistic models for state transitions within the video that can be trained and tailored for the various content domains.

2. Serve each domain (for example, news or entertainment) by a specific set of observations mapped onto a specific state-transition model.

3. Then train the model against a known corpus of ground truth— evaluated, and tuned for optimal performance.

Much of these metadata will be derived from automatic indexing functions. As the standards find their niche in the content value chain, the need for more and better metadata, requiring little or no human intervention, becomes paramount. The timing is perfect for second-generation indexing to meld with metadata authoring in accordance with new standards.

Synthesizing E-Commerce and Streaming

How else do you intend to make money? At the time of this writing, e-commerce is a major source of income for most Internet companies. In the case of streaming, the basic business plan for most companies is to charge customers a fee in order to see or hear the stream. Audible.com and HelloWorld are good examples of this type of structure. A user pays to listen to a reading, a live Webcast, or some music.

One could make revenue from advertising. However, in the case of streaming, advertising has a tendency to draw visitors away from your site, thereby making it counterproductive to the whole point of the media you intend to stream.

Legal Ramifications and Opportunities

In the wake of the Napster lawsuits and court decisions, other proprietary and copyrighted media probably will end up becoming protected under future laws and acts. This will benefit streaming Web sites because it will allow them to charge a fee for media that is either proprietary, copyrighted, or exclusive.

Others who either distribute or facilitate the distribution of media for free (as Napster did) will face civil lawsuits, and may also face punishment under the law, in the form of charges, fines, or even imprisonment. Licensing content and digital rights management can be used to prevent unauthorized copying and distribution of streaming media.

The Considerations of E-Commerce Streaming

It's important to consider the following factors when setting up an e-commerce streaming media enterprise:

- There are numerous types of Internet-based e-commerce platforms, such as:
  - One-time credit card fees
  - E-cash services (including debit accounts)
  - Intermediate e-commerce firms
- Pricing structures are very important in considering an e-commerce platform.
  - The creation of a one-time setup fee capability is an easy task for any programmer familiar with e-commerce.
- A complicated multilayered system of various charges, items, account/customer information, discounts, and so on is something that requires a lot of planning and personnel. (Look at Amazon.com and you will see a complicated but very well run e-commerce system.)

Table 12.1 E-Commerce Resources

COMPANY	E-MAIL ADDRESS	PRODUCT(S)
Brainshark	www.brainshark.com/	Brainshark
Convera	www.convera.com/	Screening Room
gForce Systems	www.gforce.com/	gForce Central 2.5
InfoLibria, Inc.	www.infolibria.com/	MediaMall
Lariat Software, Inc.	www.lariat.com/	StationManager, MediaReports, MediaReportsOnline
Network Appliance	www.netapp.com/ products/netcache	NetCache
Pictron, Inc.	www.pictron.com/	Video Gateway, Audio Gateway, Image Gateway, Media Gateway Search Server
The Fantastic Corporation	www.fantastic.com/	Channel Editor Center (CEC), Channel Management Center (CMC), MediaSurfer
Viewtran	www.viewtran.com/ en/product/viewcast/ viewcast.htm	ViewCast

Streaming Media Resources

I encourage you to develop a plan of action, based on the information contained in this chapter, before you communicate with the products and services companies listed in Table 12.1.

Taking the Next Step

In the realm of streaming media, emerging strategies for the development of effective management techniques are of paramount importance. Solutions-oriented approaches to this vital need have been the focus of this chapter.

As the next logical step, Chapter 13 will introduce further enhancements to the integration of your streaming enterprise, such as asset watermarking, management, production requirements, and digital broadband distribution.

Enhancing the Streaming Enterprise

Streaming in itself is a complex process, but it can be made easy by using the correct components. The same applies when creating the streaming content on an enterprise scale. In this chapter, I will cover enhancements for your streaming enterprise. Concepts and technologies such as watermarking, media asset management (specifically related to IBM's Media Production Suite), the issues involved in leveraging rich-media content over the internet, and a case study pointing up the features of video collaboration systems are introduced and dealt with in appropriate detail.

Watermarking Your Video Assets

Watermarking is an excellent way to identify and protect the content of your video assets. In essence, the watermarking process embeds a unique symbol in each frame of video. Perhaps you've seen a station or network watermark symbol—often displayed in the lower-right corner of your TV monitor screen—while watching cable television. Most current encoding software, such as Real, Microsoft, and Apple QuickTime, allows for watermarking, as does most video-indexing software.

A unique watermarking process developed by IBM's Tokyo Research Laboratory is robust enough to survive multiple generations, compression, cropping, aspect ratio conversion, and downsampling. Different watermarks can be applied at different stages of the production process. The watermark currently is detectable within a period of 1 minute, depending on the compression ratio. It has passed the test of the golden eyes in Hollywood, and further detection tests can be conducted using picture-quality measurement devices.

In purely technical terms, the watermarking process:

- Functions as a separate real-time process that inputs a 601 serial digital video signal into a Netfinity computer, which embeds the watermarking information and then outputs the watermarked material for recording on a videotape recorder (VTR).

- Incorporates a detection process that uses a similar approach, and detection stations can be incorporated into separate workstation locations.

Moving into Media Asset Management

The video production business currently is undergoing a major transformation as a result of a number of converging factors. Some of these factors include:

- The advent of digital television broadcasting throughout the world
- The availability of low-cost digital storage on disk and tape
- The development of computer-based techniques for video composition and editing (including animation and special effects)
- The development of powerful digital video compression standards (in particular the MPEG standard)

This movement toward digital video standards has allowed the television industry to represent video programming as digital files, making the handling of video very similar to the handling of files in the data-processing industry. Video producers, therefore, can take advantage of the experience of the data-processing industry. They can leverage the deep expertise and technology of data processing, which is designed to manage data efficiently, and apply it to the management of video and other broadcasting assets.

IBM's Media Production Suite

In the past several years, IBM has made a fundamental commitment to the broadcasting industry, making substantial investments in the application of data-management technology to the area of broadcasting and video production. The IBM Media Production Suite (hereafter referred to as MPS) is based on these investments in technology. The IBM staff has brought all their expertise in managing data files and in providing task-oriented production systems in other industries to the implementation of MPS.

MPS provides the following significant benefits over tape-based manual production systems:

- Content retrieval time is reduced from hours to seconds.
- Years of assets are preserved and protected against media deterioration.
- The complete archive can be centralized and reached by all who need access.
- There is a significant reduction in expensive tape storage and space.

MPS has been designed specifically to provide overall management of video assets and to remove the mundane tasks that require creative people to manage production, allowing them instead to concentrate on the creation of superior content. MPS is built on open standards and is designed for the creation, management, and distribution of digital content of any media type. The result is a robust system that provides:

A content-management system based on IBM foundational database products. This results in a fully scaleable solution for handling the management of small television libraries to large enterprise-wide repositories. These repositories can be very large in size and in the number of clients that can have access to the content.

A fully networked environment with intranet connectivity. MPS is designed to be networked and can support an enterprise with multiple sites, all having access to content that resides throughout the enterprise intranet. MPS can search, find, and deliver that content as required to meet programming demands.

An industry-standard-compliant and open architecture. MPS is based on current international standards and will support future standards sponsored by such bodies as SMPTE and MPEG. (IBM has active membership in most international standards organizations.) In the future, MPS will support the MXF file format defined by the Pro-MPEG Forum and the MPEG-7 metadata standards as they evolve and are adopted more generally by the industry. IBM is also committed to supporting the AAF file formats, which will allow compatibility with future standards-based editing and server systems as they become available.

A flexible, adaptable, graphic user interface (GUI) environment with workflow. MPS is designed for easy customization in both GUI design and workflow functionality, allowing it to be adapted to an organization's specific requirements. A starter set of GUIs and workflows are provided with MPS.

A continually enhanced product. Additional features have been added to enhance the usability of the system for people with broadcasting skills. For example, the video viewer is designed to provide a complete visual scan capability, providing frame-by-frame viewing and thus simulating the hardware jog and shuttle controls of a VTR.

Frame-accurate MPEG-2 proxies. MPS also optionally can provide frame-accurate MPEG-2 proxies of broadcast-quality video. The IBM viewer can provide a rough-cut edit decision list (EDL) that can be passed to either a nonlinear editor for final editing or a rendering engine if speed to air is more important than tight editing.

The Design Features of MPS

The MPS product design was driven by the basic set of features, functions, and overall specifications required for a system designed for the storage and collection of media content. The key specifications and features of the MPS design are as follows:

Workflow management. Includes a workflow system to manage the requests and interactions between the processes of the production team, as well as the interface with the external processes and legacy systems.

Create/enhance/edit and register. Includes a function to capture and register new or modified media content in the system. This process can be fed by external sources or follow search/browse/retrieve activities.

Capture and register (ingest). Accepts media content supplied from outside the system. Examples include photos from the news wires, satellite feeds from remote studios/locations, and existing videotapes.

Catalog/index. Provides annotation beyond the basic registration of new or modified content in the system. While registration provides basic metadata about the entire media object, the catalog process typically provides annotation of the media object's elements and internal characteristics.

Search/browse/review/retrieve. Uses the power of either the registration metadata or the catalog metadata to identify relevant media content for retrieval and subsequent use.

Distribute/fulfill/playout. Delivers the media content and metadata, if required, in the right format, at the right time, and to the right (authorized) processes/systems/users/devices. Also delivers a collection of content assembled in a requested order.

Media management. Stores and manages the media content and the metadata in a secure, safe, and media-type-appropriate manner.

Scalability. Provides for departmental systems that can grow and communicate with other systems within the enterprise as the requirements of the organization grow.

Standards. Adopts industry-accepted standards for representing content and metadata as they are adopted to enable the seamless exchange of data between systems.

Openness. Maintains an open-system architecture to enable organizations to take advantage of new technologies as they are introduced.

Flexibility. Provides for the accommodation of changes in operation after the system is installed and organizations learn and adopt new processes.

Reliability. Provides reliable and high-availability implementations, where necessary, in mission-critical applications.

The MPS Asset Manager

The IBM MPS product is designed to fully support the broadcasting industry in managing and producing digital video assets. This section describes the current IBM MPS. However, IBM has reserved the right to alter the release plan, the schedule, and scope of these product plans.

The current MPS release includes the following functions:

- Capture of content from videotape
- Catalog

- Search
- Fulfillment to videotape
- Workflow management
- Media management

MPS is designed to provide sufficient functionality for customers to build and use a production repository. All video material and corresponding metadata that are ingested and archived with this release will be supported by subsequent releases. When a system is upgraded to a higher release level, it will not be necessary to ingest the content again. It may, however, be necessary to enhance the associated metadata.

Other features of MPS include the following:

- Scalability from relatively small systems with Gigabytes of assets to very large systems with petabytes of assets. (Three classes of systems have been predefined for small, medium, and large applications.)
- Ability to store production-quality video as well as browser-quality video in a variety of formats.
- Ability to configure user-interface screens, workflow processes, and metadata database to meet the requirements of the user organization's business.

Adherence to international multimedia standards includes the following:

- MPEG-1, MPEG-2, and MPEG-4. (Support of MPEG-4 is based on a future IBM product direction and will be available through the IBM DB2 Content Manager Video Charger product.)
- Pro-MPEG Forum MXF—material exchange format. (Support of MXF depends on the pending approval of the standard by SMPTE—Society of Motion Picture and Television Engineers—and on the consequent availability of the appropriate hardware from OEM vendors.)
- Ability to interface with IBM or other e-business products for electronic fulfillment.

Based on well-established IBM products, such as the DB2 Universal Database, IBM Content Manager, WebSphere Application Server, and MQSeries, MPS does not include integrated facilities to support the editing and production of media content but will provide mechanisms to easily transfer content to and from creative tools and production systems.

NOTE To find out more about IBM's Media Production Suite (MPS) and how you can incorporate it into your streaming media plans, contact www.ibm.com.

Leveraging Rich-Media Content over the Internet

The media industry tracks with great interest the continued rapid technical developments in compression, transport, digital rights management, media asset management, and other technologies surrounding the secure transport of digital media over the Internet. However, it is the vexing business problem of how to leverage rich-media content over the Internet, separate from the technologies that will enable it, that is the most critical issue facing media executives at the present time.

For technology, service, or consulting organizations wanting to facilitate the movement of content on the Internet, the questions not only surround technology and architecture but also involve the root business problems faced by both the media companies and the content creators.

- What is the ideal architecture that solves the fundamental business problem?
- How do present technologies apply?
- Which problems can be solved now and which ones later?
- What is the time horizon for the various plausible solutions, and how can they be applied across an industry that must act in a coordinated fashion and yet whose very nature is sharply competitive?

At this stage of the game (see the sidebar in this chapter for background on the pressures facing media executives), a framework for analysis will need to be constructed that examines the key domains involved in the process of broadband media distribution, pointing to a rounded and comprehensive solution set.

It is far too early to predict how the chips will fall for content providers and media companies in this new century of ubiquitous, plentiful bandwidth. However, since the issue of Internet-based digital media distribution is so scorchingly hot, posing both a tremendous threat and a tremendous opportunity to media companies, one thing is certain: Decisions regarding the direction of Internet-based distribution of rich-media content for media companies will be made at the highest levels.

Media Pressures Facing Media Executives

The pressure, fear, and uncertainty involving the leveraging of rich-media content over the Internet are best exemplified by the recent rise and fall of Napster in the music space. To the music industry, Napster was like a shark terrorizing the beach at a summer resort. It came, it ate, and it was killed (more or less), but the sense that sequels to this familiar story are not far away offers little consolation. (The dorsal fins of Audio Galaxy and Bearshare have been spotted in the distance, causing renewed consternation.)

The root concern is *disintermediation,* a term you can hopefully define for yourself as you read on. Media companies mediate; at present, they bridge the gap between the creative endeavor and the public. True, they make every effort to own their own content, and some succeed admirably. And also true, some content creators are able to go directly to the public. By virtue of owning airwaves (or pipe), cable plant, broadcast facilities, movie studios, movie theaters, printing presses, or so-called eyeballs, however, the media companies are the gatekeepers of the large majority of content for the public.

To be fair, the number of gatekeepers is expanding, with an increasing number of media outlets, including cable television, satellite distribution, and the Internet. And gatekeeping per se is not a bad thing because we rely on the editorial sense of the gatekeepers to separate the wheat from the chaff for our continued viewing pleasure (and for their continued profit).

What happens when the gatekeepers lose their gates, however? The peer-to-peer service of Napster began the process of disintermediation for the record companies. Napster pulled down the gate. Worse, the media companies themselves became unwitting accomplices in the process by spending millions to promote new acts, only to see profits eroded by the free exchange of content made desirable by virtue of the buzz they created. It was like a supermarket chain spending millions on advertising a free food giveaway. A nice promotion perhaps, but no way to run a business.

Having weathered the challenge from VTRs (analog at least), and now confronting personal digital recorders like TIVO, media companies with digital video (or digitizable video) now live in a schizophrenic world. They both fear some kind of video Napster and simultaneously hope that a secure and comprehensive system will evolve for them to capitalize on the Internet for the distribution of digital video.

They will tread with caution because they do not want unwittingly to aid and abet the enemy (mass pirating of content). Yet they must be ready to move, rapidly if necessary, because if it has done anything, Napster has proven that successful systems can explode on the scene and disintermediate the gatekeepers. When peer to peer suddenly can mean buyer to seller (a concept surely demonstrated by eBay), then new rules are written for the industry.

Case Study: Video Collaboration Systems

Developing streaming alliance customers or partners is very important. This case study is an example of what types of initiatives are taking place in today's marketplace.

Project Overview

Collaboration among video producers and programmers from separate production entities has long been a difficult and time-consuming process. To exchange full-motion video, physical dubs must be made and shipped to collaborating partners. The high-bandwidth nature of video has limited Internet collaboration efforts to exchanging scripts and stills or the trading of low-bandwidth proxies. In fact, with the limited amount of materials exchanged routinely, in any given collaboration project, between geographically dispersed entities, true collaboration in video production has been at worst nonexistent and at best extremely difficult and costly.

The emergence of Internet2 raises the possibility that new video collaborative environments and communities may now be possible and reasonably cost-effective. These environments require the following:

- Low-cost video encoding
- Flexible metadata standards
- Easy transport of video assets to a central storage repository
- Searching and viewing of shared video assets in a central storage repository
- A viable editor's workbench to prepare rough-cut sequences
- Ability to conform rough cuts to new video assets
- Retrieval and downloading of assets from the central repository

These and other features are needed for a true collaborative video production environment, and in this new collaborative paradigm, many critical questions emerge. Among them are:

- Can a viable and cost-effective system be created to allow real collaboration for disparate production groups?
- Once created, how will producers and programmers actually use the new environment, and will it contribute positively to the production and programming capabilities of participants?

- What is the impact on the changes to process flow within these new collaborative communities?
- How will collaborative communities work together?

IBM and a prominent university, referred to here as the *University of Extension/Public TV Video,* have teamed up to work together to define and architect a video collaboration system that takes advantage of the latest media asset-management software, as well as the high bandwidth enabled by Internet2. The mission of this project and the proposed utility-concept system is to demonstrate that an individual PTV (public television) station can maintain and enhance its local value by adopting collaborative technologies and processes for media asset creation, management, and digital distribution.

I believe that this mission is critical to the long-term survival and growth of individual public TV stations as they continue to seek creative and cost-effective ways to serve the underserved in their communities by extending the richness of their programming and the reach of their resources into global communities. This requires a thoughtfully crafted framework—one that will protect the autonomy of each station, while extending each station's resources and its ability to leverage the information and material available throughout the global communities of common purpose.

This proof-of-concept model will deliver a system with no custom development, using commercial off-the-shelf software and hardware and allowing multiple geographically dispersed programming entities to participate. It will be constructed both to support the participating programming and production entities in their immediate production goals and to assess the key questions raised by this new model of sharing and collaboration.

System Description

The video collaboration system (Figure 13.1) offers a straightforward hub-and-spoke design. The hub is a rich-media utility (RMU), hosted by IBM, that will run the main system applications, provide security and backups, and allow central storage of shared rich-media assets. The spokes represent contributing participants with low-cost encoding workstations and Internet2 connectivity.

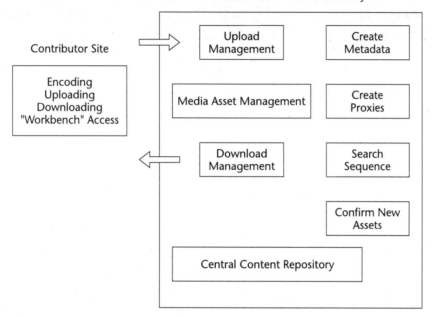

Figure 13.1 Video collaboration system.

At each end node or contributor site, a simple encoding station will allow participants to take either fully produced video or assembled segments and encode them in high-resolution, industry-standard MPEG-2 digital video of a quality suitable for editing and airing. Once the video is encoded, the system provides a flexible model for entering metadata about each encoded asset. The metadata application is part of a suite of software tools available over the Internet from the central RMU. Contributors then, quite literally, e-mail their video assets to the RMU, a hosted Web environment that provides a central storage facility to be shared by all participants. Additionally, any digital artifacts, such as scripts, stills, and so on, can be linked to the main video asset and uploaded along with it.

The RMU is a collection of applications, from media asset management to Web servers, that lives in a hosting facility that provides security, backups, and ongoing maintenance to the hardware and software that are at the core of the video collaboration system. By accessing the RMU through the Internet, participants can search and retrieve video in the system, view it in low-resolution streaming formats, and mark it for later use. The search mechanisms can evolve from the most straightforward parametric searches (matching fielded data) to advanced fuzzy-logic or controlled-vocabulary access.

The RMU toolbox will permit editors and producers to:

- Create rough cuts by finding and sequencing video clips
- Enter time-code in-points and out-points
- Create edit, save, and share decision lists (EDLs)
- Reconform rough cuts into new high-resolution video assets by assembling those assets based on the instructions in the EDLs
- Jointly view rough cuts

All these functions are performed over the Internet (Internet2) through a standard Web browser using streaming technologies. No special configuration at the workstation level is required—only browser plug-ins.

Finally, contributors can search and select any high-resolution asset (and its linked artifacts), either uploaded from a contributor or newly formed in the RMU, and download that asset back to their local workstation. Assets can be downloaded in either Avid format, standard MPEG-2, or both. From there, the video asset can be moved to an air server, moved to an edit bay, or spun off to tape.

The overall system supports the exchange of both ready-to-edit and ready-to-air video. In the case of ready-to-edit video, the intent of uploading media assets is to offer them into the collaborative environment. In the case of ready-to-air video, uploaded assets are meant to be shared in their entirety with other contributors.

The Benefits of Partnership

Beyond the stated mission of this project, there is no substitute as effective and compelling as a proof-of-concept and proof-of-value in-market experiment that defines and validates the value and advantage expected from this collaborative solution. The inherent design of the architecture, the explicit functional requirements, and the operational success of this project are based on the direct input of the public TV professionals who ultimately will subscribe to and use this utility service.

The basic determination of value—both quantitative, in terms of explicit time and cost savings, and qualitative, in terms of richness of programming and increased ability to serve individual markets—lies in the hands of the project participants. The participation of this broad base of educators, public TV professionals, and technology groups provides the opportunity to build a uniquely cost-effective model for growth and quality.

IBM's opportunity lies in the ability to develop and deliver a utility service that has broad appeal. By the end of the project, a proven value and business model should also emerge, one that enables not only educational organizations to leverage the public television network but also other industries who have the need to reach and educate specific communities—health care organizations; local, state, and federal governments; and financial institutions, to name just a few.

The university involved has an unparalleled reputation for providing both quality and service to local communities. Combined with its extensive network of subscriber stations, it has the ability to provide a well-founded service design with a proven business model. The goal is to offer trusted delivery of content to organizations with broad and diverse needs. The services provided should extend the reach of public TV stations and enable them to provide more meaningful public service, rather than simply push information into the daily lives of their subscribers.

NOTE

For more information on the status of this project, its details, the concept of RMUs (rich-media utilities), or how you can participate, contact www.ibm.com.

Taking the Next Step

This chapter has given you a clearer view of the types of media enhancements you can integrate into your streaming enterprise. It's also demonstrated the creative ways this technology can enable the construction of meaningful, dynamic, and cost-effective collaborative environments.

Chapter 14 will discuss network infrastructure software for global enterprises, another step toward developing your own successful streaming system.

Employing Network Infrastructure Software

B efore too long, moviegoers will no longer go to the theater but to their living rooms to watch a movie on their Web-enabled device, pushed (served) from a local server in their home "media closet" directly from the Internet. The files will be downloaded to their video server during the middle of the night. Applications like this one are the promise of new content-distribution systems coming online. Combining elements of caching, content selection, and application development, these systems will enable profound new network-aware applications to make intelligent use of caches installed in the network.

Meeting the Challenge of Managing and Distributing Content

The scenario I used to introduce this chapter, however, brings up a problem in search of a solution. The rapid growth of Internet traffic and the increasing complexity of internetwork communications create serious challenges for managing and distributing content. At the same time, networks struggle to manage newer forms of communication, such as streaming media, that have the power to overload the network if handled incorrectly.

Intelligent Edge-Network Devices

The development of intelligent edge-network devices (such as the server in the home "media closet" posited earlier) is enabling better performance by taking on a greater share of the processing burden, thereby relieving overworked traditional types of servers. The way networks used to be built, you would have a central office with racks and racks of very expensive, very complex equipment. From there would emanate a bunch of copper wires, and at the end, you would have a device with very few working parts, like a plain old telephone system (POTS) telephone.

However, there are companies, such as Inktomi, creating various network solutions to help overcome these challenges. By providing an intelligent end-to-end solution for the distribution, delivery, and management of all Internet Protocol (IP) content throughout your network, the Inktomi Content Networking Platform (CNP) enables your network to overcome these problems.

Effective Content Distribution

Many server networks do not address the real needs of content distribution over the Internet. Latencies, buffering, poor performance, and other frustrating experiences cause viewers to stay away from watching poor video streaming transmissions. After reviewing Inktomi's product line, I find that it has addressed many of the hurdles in this area, starting out with their product called Traffic Edge, which is a superintelligent content-aware edge server that caches and delivers all types of rich media and traditional media content—from PowerPoint presentations to live streaming audio and video. Traffic Edge servers and technology can:

- Simultaneously distribute Web content, streaming media, and applications to thousands of employees and customers around the world
- Improve performance and reduce upstream bandwidth usage by storing frequently requested content at the edge of the network, physically closer to end users on the Internet infrastructure
- Reduce hardware expenses by caching static and all major streaming formats in one integrated edge device

- Ensure availability and boost performance by accepting and serving preloaded, on-demand content at the edge of the network

- Offer easy integration of key features, such as filtering, user authentication—lightweight directory access protocol (LDAP)—pay-per-use, and more

- Capture real-time audience data on usage and preferences during streaming sessions

Efficient Bandwidth Utilization

Bandwidth utilization can be a problem for many companies that do not have a subscription-based or revenue model for streaming media. Inktomi enables bandwidth savings by transmitting only one copy of a stream or static content to multiple recipients and by prioritizing streaming content based on author, title, department, content category, and so on. In this way, your chief executive officer's Webcast is broadcast with higher quality than, for example, a business news report or sports wrap-up (Figure 14.1).

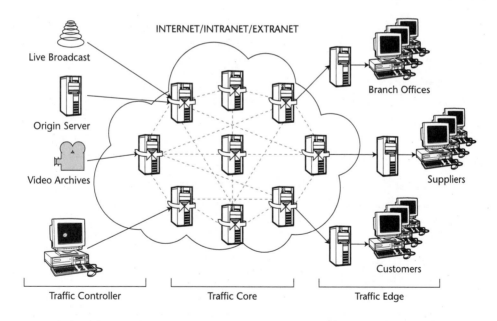

Figure 14.1 Internet traffic flow using the Traffic Edge solution.

NOTE

Inktomi Enterprise Search integrates with leading enterprise solutions by Broad-Vision, Epicentric, eRoom, IBM, Lotus, Netegrity, Oracle, Plumtree, Viador, Watchfire, Coporate, Yahoo!, and many others. As the market-leading OEM provider of Web search services, Inktomi provides search capabilities for many of the largest portals and destination sites on the Internet. Inktomi Web search provides a customizable private-label solution that offers the ability to serve differentiated, highly relevant search results as well as to monetize your site's traffic.

The concluding sections in this chapter begin with a case study completed by Inktomi that produced some very interesting results, followed by an overview of the challenges of streaming, storing, and maintaining rich media, as characterized by the solutions offered by the products of Akamai. These are success stories, which I feel it is important to share with you.

Delivering Effective Corporate Communications: The Inktomi Story

Inktomi, like most middle- to large-sized companies, communicates a tremendous amount of information to a number of different audiences as part of its daily business routine. Employees must have the latest technical specifications, marketing collateral, human resources information, and so on, and must be able to access training and support information as well as news on product updates. Partners must also be kept informed of all technical and marketing updates that have an impact on their businesses.

This information comes in a wide number of forms, including e-mail, conference calls, Web pages, CD-ROMs, videos, and so on, and it must be distributed to people all over the globe. In addition, the information must be communicated over a mix of heterogeneous networks, including virtual private networks (VPNs) and dialup home-office connections using different protocols and format standards. Distributing all this information through traditional methods can be expensive and time-consuming.

The Problem

After a thorough analysis of spending on internal communications to employees, Inktomi concluded that it invested over $1 million in just 1 year alone. These costs included:

- Travel expenses associated with flying employees to biannual sales conferences and quarterly regional training sessions
- Facility rental and maintenance fees
- Telecommunications charges for audio conference calls
- CD-ROM and video production and distribution expenses
- Outsourcing fees for company-wide Webcasts

There also were hidden costs associated with these communication efforts. These included the amount of time it took sales reps to absorb the information being presented to them in the predominantly text-based formats. Streaming media frequently was not deployed for fear of overwhelming the wide area network (WAN) with hundreds of employees accessing the same content simultaneously.

Most communications also were underutilized because so much of the information was distributed in a way that was not archived easily for future use. For example, on-site training sessions that were delivered by technical and marketing people flown in from headquarters were not easily available for use by employees who missed the sessions.

The Solution

Inktomi realized that to remain competitive, the company needed to optimize delivery of these communications in terms of both making them more cost-effective and increasing their impact. As a leader in scalable, reliable content networking and search technology, Inktomi knew that the way to do this was to move these communications online. As a result, they naturally turned to the new Inktomi Enterprise Communications Suite (ECS) to accomplish this.

Inktomi used ECS to create InkTV, a proprietary online training and information resource for Inktomi employees. Through InkTV, Inktomi now broadcasts CEO Webcasts, an annual sales conference, weekly brown bag training sessions, training courses, and marketing videos created by product managers over the corporate network.

Employees can view all these communications right at their desks, and all the material is archived, making it easy for employees to access it at their convenience.

How It Works

To create InkTV, Inktomi installed ECS in five locations, including Needham, Massachusetts; Herdon, Virginia; San Francisco, California; London, United Kingdom; and the Inktomi headquarters in Foster City, California. The network is configured in a traditional multilayer hub-and-spoke topology. Foster City is the main hub. Other cities, such as San Francisco and Needham, are the spokes. There is a dedicated network connection between San Francisco and Foster City. Other cities are connected via a VPN from a major interexchange carrier.

In terms of software, the Inktomi deployment includes the Inktomi Content Networking Platform (CNP), comprising Inktomi Traffic Edge, Traffic Core, and Traffic Controller, as well as Inktomi Media Publisher. In addition to facilitating scalable delivery of rich-media content, the software offers built-in redundancy so that if any location is ever compromised, content will be routed around that location, ensuring that communication will be maintained.

"The Inktomi ECS as deployed in InkTV is fundamentally changing the way we communicate with our salespeople," said Al Shipp, senior vice president of worldwide sales at Inktomi. "This is helping our salespeople become more knowledgeable about our products and is enabling our employees in regional offices to feel much more connected to the flow of information and the company's corporate culture."

Cameras, microphone kits, and encoders were deployed in three of the locations to automatically translate analog audio and video signals to Real or Windows digital media streams and enable content to be streamed into the IP-based network from any of these points. Traffic Edge servers, which cache content and speed content delivery to remote employees, also were deployed (Figure 14.2).

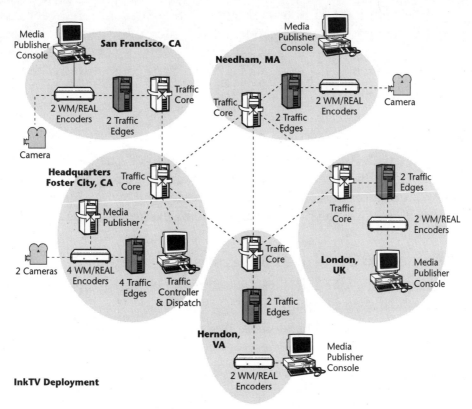

InkTV Deployment

Figure 14.2 InkTV deployment.

Once streamed into the network, prerecorded or on-demand content can be preloaded into the Traffic Edge caches to optimize performance. Live content is sent to the edge offices on user request.

The total cost of the deployment was approximately $550,000. This includes $325,000 for Inktomi software, which reflects the estimated cost of a comparable deployment. The estimate also includes $190,000 for hardware expenditures and another $30,000 for additional software—such as WindowsMedia and RealServer player software, and their encoding software.

It is important to note that since ECS creates an intelligent software layer above the existing router and switch infrastructure, Inktomi did not have to invest in costly upgrades of its IP network to achieve the maximum benefits from InkTV. Nor did the company have to purchase any additional bandwidth.

The Results

The impact of Inktomi's development of InkTV using the Inktomi ECS software has been dramatic. By moving a large portion of corporate communications online with InkTV, Inktomi will save more than $1 million in just the first year alone. Some examples of the annual savings include:

- $100,000 saved by reducing conference call fees
- $150,000 saved by eliminating the travel and facilities expenses for the quarterly product road shows
- $300,000 saved by eliminating outsourcing of weekly Webcasts and Talktomi CD production
- $285,000 saved by moving one of the two annual sales conferences online
- $240,000 saved by conducting technical training online

Assuming an initial outlay of $550,000, these savings translate into a payback period of just 6 months. In addition to providing considerable financial benefits, InkTV also delivers other significant benefits, including:

More effective employee training.   The ECS software makes it easier to publish and distribute streaming audio and video, enabling Inktomi marketing and technical managers to provide employees with more frequent and more timely training.

Enhanced network reliability.   ECS improved network reliability by enabling administrators to limit the amount of bandwidth allocated to streaming content without having a negative impact on the quality of a broadcast.

Increased productivity.   With InkTV, product managers, salespeople, and engineers are freed from traveling 3 to 4 days every quarter for training.

NOTE
■■■■■ You can access further information on Inktomi and their complete line of products at www.inktomi.com.

Streaming, Storing, and Maintaining Rich Media: The Akamai Story

Today's Internet users demand exciting, dynamic content with superior performance; and business-class Web sites require the liveliest, most compelling media possible.

The Problem

Streaming media can enhance a Web site experience, or it can slow it down. Webcasts often degrade as a result of Internet congestion, inconsistent servers, and interrupted streams. The challenge is to ensure consistency and reliability so that Web site visitors enjoy a compelling streaming experience. However, the expense and technical challenges inherent in storing and maintaining a large collection of media files— racks of redundant servers, constant upkeep, and endless administrative details—can prevent a Web site from looking its best.

The Solution

Akamai's line of world-class streaming media services enable Internet content providers and enterprises to succeed in today's Web-centric marketplace.

- Akamai's FreeFlow Streaming has been delivering streaming content to viewers worldwide with dramatic improvements in quality and reliability using the global Akamai platform.

- SteadyStream is Akamai's technology to ensure that only the highest-quality streams reach the audience.

- EdgeSuite content storage is Akamai's way of surmounting the obstacles associated with storing rich media. EdgeSuite customers get the most advanced, fault-tolerant storage solution for streaming media.

How It Works

With streaming servers located closer to the edges of the network and closer to end users, FreeFlow Streaming offers performance with unlimited scalability. It delivers live-event Webcasts (complete with video production, encoding, and signal-acquisition services), streaming media on demand, 24/7 Webcasts, and a variety of streaming application services based on the Akamai platform. All services include comprehensive usage reports so that customers can measure the effectiveness of their streaming content.

For live broadcasts, SteadyStream uses sophisticated error correcting to send multiple copies of streams to the edges of the network, where they are recombined into their original quality format (see Figure 14.3). For on-demand files, SteadyStream locates the original files at the edges of the Internet so that the last mile is all that limits the delivery of a perfect stream. SteadyStream also supports all leading formats.

SteadyStream: Live Streaming Media

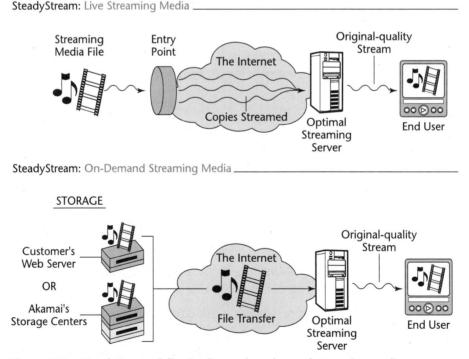

SteadyStream: On-Demand Streaming Media

Figure 14.3 SteadyStream delivering live and on-demand streaming media.

EdgeSuite content storage uses multiple Terabytes of storage capacity, geographical replication, a massively scalable architecture, and proprietary mapping and routing technology to ensure that rich-media content is available to users on demand. EdgeSuite customers simply upload their content to a designated FTP directory. As soon as the upload is complete, EdgeSuite content storage replicates the content, placing copies of the files on each of Akamai's multiple storage centers.

When an end user requests a streaming media file—one that is not already cached in the Akamai streaming server that was determined to be optimal for the end user—the server fetches a copy of the requested file from the optimal storage center. Then, EdgeSuite fulfills the user's request. It also keeps a copy of the file in its cache so that it can fulfill subsequent requests for that content.

The benefits of this approach are:

- Enhanced performance
- Enormous scalability
- Ease of use
- Comprehensive reporting
- A turnkey outsourced solution

NOTE To learn more about Akamai and the product solutions mentioned in this chapter, go to www.akamai.com.

Taking the Next Step

In this chapter, we covered the rapid growth of Internet traffic and the increasing complexity of internetwork communications that create serious challenges for managing and distributing content along with solutions. Chapter 15 will discuss in further detail the topics associated with managing your media assets, including content storage, virtual multicasting, and managing video-on-demand content.

Managing Media Assets

So far this book has covered many topics, including digital devices, editing, preprocessing, indexing, and network congestion, to name just a few. This chapter digs deeper into storing and managing your content, including video-on-demand issues.

Exploring New Media Asset Technologies

At the IBC 2000 Exhibition, Sagitta demonstrated a large-scale storage-area network (SAN) in operation over several halls. To implement this demonstration, Sagitta spent 5 to 6 weeks setting up both the IBM enterprise storage server (ESS) and the IBM fiber channel RAID storage server (FCRSS) in video production environments (see Figure 15.1).

The objective of the IBC demonstration was to show that large media companies such as broadcasters and postproduction companies can implement production-level SANs using storage that can be managed centrally. The demonstration used five partners, 5 TB (Terabytes) of storage, and 5 km of fiber-channel cable in a single SAN.

Sagitta has spent the last several years working in the video, postproduction, graphics, broadcast, and nonlinear editing markets. It has developed a wealth of understanding of what these markets are looking for and trying to achieve.

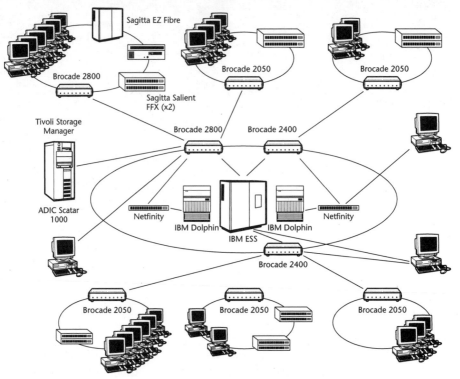

Figure 15.1 SAN demonstrated at IBC 2000 by Sagitta and IBM.

Essentially, the scope of new technologies in media asset management—such as SANs—can be broken down into four industry segments (briefly overviewed as follows, and dealt with in detail later in the chapter):

Nonlinear editing in postproduction. Both Sony and Lightworks use nonlinear editing applications that can benefit from storage area networks (SANs) incorporating centralized storage. The Sony system can run two nonlinear editing machines that require that dual-stream uncompressed video be sent to each machine. The two machines share and edit video clips and then allow three DVD authoring machines to pick up the video clips and create a DVD master.

NOTE

A significant number of opportunities are arising for these midrange systems. The IBC implementation at the IBC exhibition used the IBM FCRSS (Dolphin) connected to the Sony stand across 1 km of fiber-optic cable. This type of solution is being used in departments within broadcasting companies, postproduction houses, educational establishments, and corporate media departments. The main criteria for these systems are performance and a high level of availability.

Broadcast and playout.   Once content has been created and is ready for playout, customers are looking for highly available storage systems that can deliver streams of video reliably via satellite or terrestrial feeds. Both traditional broadcasters and outsourced playout centers have the same requirements. Playout centers are looking to manage playouts for multiple channels, storing vast quantities of video and program information. Typically, the vendors selected for these solutions are the ones that are able to supply highly available, enterprise-class products that can scale to Terabytes and remain manageable.

Content management and repurpose of assets.   A number of customers are looking to create new business models in which they can digitally store vast quantities of video and metadata that can then be repurposed and sold via a number of delivery systems. While the material may be played out or simply transferred in a number of different formats, the baseline requirement is to store the material in the highest-quality format possible. Since the business model is often an e-commerce environment, both high availability and performance are critical.

NOTE

Significant amounts of money are being invested in these new business models, and the competition for these solutions consists of vendors of enterprise-class systems that meet the video requirements. This is arguably the most demanding sector because systems must be highly available and highly scaleable, and support the highest quality of video streaming (dual-stream uncompressed per port).

Video on demand and e-commerce.   The requirements for video on demand (VOD) and e-commerce are often a combination of the ability to support playout centers and content management and the ability to repurpose assets. The use of storage is the same in these two applications. It is essential that the systems can scale to store massive amounts of content while at the same time being able to support as many multiple streams of video as possible. While the streams may be only MPEG-1 or MPEG-2, the cost per user is the ultimate measure in this business. The more streams that the VOD supplier can deliver from a given solution, the more competitive he or she will be.

NOTE ▬▬▬ **There is a drive toward interactive VOD, and this places more demands on the storage systems. (For more information on video indexing, please refer to Chapter 12.)**

Meeting the Technical Demands

The demands and workload profiles placed on the back-end storage systems in the broadcast and production industries vary quite widely, depending on the specific application and application area. Having said this, certain common factors can be identified, and critical requirements exist within each application area, some spanning the entire range of the industry space.

The following sections examine the critical factors for success in each of the four industry segments already identified (that is, postproduction, broadcast playout, content management, and VOD). The key requirements will be examined in terms of the vectors of performance, resilience, availability, and quality of service (QOS), focusing on the business objectives of the customers and how the storage system and SAN must be designed and configured to support those requirements.

NOTE ▬▬▬ **This information is derived from experience in implementing SANs in these industry segments over the last 4 years and from the common requirements highlighted by customers. Where appropriate, the requirements are expressed in terms understood within the broadcast and production industry, and then translated into terms meaningful within the computer and, specifically, the storage industry. No attempt has been made here to fully expand or explain the broadcast-specific terminology or concepts because that is beyond the scope of this chapter.**

Nonlinear Editing

Nonlinear editing (NLE) is the process of bringing captured material from whatever format—film, analog tape, digital tape, news feeds, and so on—into the digital domain within a workstation or edit station, transforming it in some way (that is, editing, effects, compositing, and compliance), and producing a final version for the processes that follow it. *Nonlinear* simply means that the process is random access within the digital domain, which is a significant advance on the linear-editing, tape-based processes that were used in the past (and still are used).

Performance

Except for very specialized applications (for example, film effects editing), NLE until recently has been performed mostly on compressed material. The new generation of editors, such as Sony's ES-3, is now capable of real-time editing of uncompressed material up to International Telecommunications Union (ITU) 601 standards. Future edit stations will be capable of editing material at high-definition TV (HDTV) standards in real time.

Resilience

Resilience tends not to be a major issue in NLE because most assets exist in the video domain and can be recaptured or redigitized if they are lost. There are, however, certain critical exceptions:

- In ENPS (entertainment, news, production, sports) environments, news feeds are brought directly into the editing environment to be edited ready for air. Time to air is a critical competitive issue in this environment, and the material typically is not reproducible.

- The output of some rendering, effects, and compositing operations can represent many hours of creative and computer time and can be expensive to re-create, while not impossible. It is in this environment that facilities such as AVID Unity's Clip Mirror score highly.

- In film capture to video for digital effects, the cost of the telecine and of the skilled operator are enormous, and the grading of the material at capture is a creative input that is difficult to reproduce accurately. The captured material therefore represents, effectively, a unique asset that must be stored in a resilient way.

NLE Technical Factors

Given that an editing process normally consists of the merging in some way of two streams of material to provide a single output, with transitions and effects being incorporated, and that there is an output stream to be returned to the storage medium, a fairly simple calculation can be performed. Assuming the data rate needed is equivalent to serial digital interface (SDI)—270 Mbps to 34 MBps—then the three streams (two input and one output) for each uncompressed edit take up slightly more than 100 MBps of bandwidth. Thus the storage system and the SAN must be designed to provide at least this bandwidth capability *per edit station* in a reliable fashion.

The preceding represents the streaming rate of material transfers between the storage system and the edit station. Internally, there are additional performance factors to consider:

- In the simplest case, two input streams will be taken from separate storage pools, combined, and written back to a third storage pool. This represents a very cache-friendly workload for each of the storage pools because there are only single large sequential transactions (reads or writes) at each pool.

- At the next level, and more likely in reality, given the way storage pools are assigned to edit stations, all three streams may be to one storage pool. In this case, the cache-management algorithm must be capable of sustaining two read and one write streams as isochronous transfers, compensating for the latency caused by the mechanical movement of the disk heads and arms. This is less cache friendly than the first case but still within the capabilities of modern cache algorithms.

- In a studio or facility environment that uses a SAN infrastructure for asset sharing and cooperative workflow, the situation is worse yet. In this case, there may be several edit stations accessing different material from the same storage pool at the same time. Here, the cache algorithm may need to deal with more than three streams of real-time data and still maintain isochronous streaming. This is where the systems design of the SAN and the overall solution become critical, and where a proper understanding of both the technologies employed and the workflow and needs of the clients is essential.

- Finally, in the worst case, an edit stream may consist not of a sequential stream of a single asset or media item but rather of a collection of short clips that are dispersed randomly around one or more storage pools. This is common in the production of music videos and advertising material, where rapid cuts between streams are used to give the feeling of action and pace. In the extreme case, an asset may be played backwards, where each frame is followed not by the next frame but by the frame that precedes it in the stored format. In this case, each frame within the asset must be read forward, and then the storage system must seek backwards to the start of the preceding frame and play it forward. This is extremely difficult for many cache algorithms as well as for traditional linear editing.

Availability

Availability is generally not a major issue in NLE, except that the facilities houses charge by the hour for the use of their edit suites, and thus downtime is an operating cost. One increasingly common and crucial example of where NLE availability is critical is in operations such as ENPS, where editing is done very quickly in order to make material available to air quickly and where time to air is a competitive factor.

Service

Quality of delivered service is crucial in NLE environments. Digitization or ingesting of assets absolutely requires isochronous capture facility. The editing, rendering, and final cutting of material will fail if the streaming transfer is interrupted.

The storage system and SAN architecture must be designed and implemented to take this into account and must allow for tolerance in the event of parts failure or infrastructural interruptions. This is why FC-al (fiber channel arbitrated loop) is not recommended in NLE.

Broadcast Playout

The broadcast playout operation is a unique environment in its own right. It is absolutely crucial that this operation continue uninterrupted because the client's entire revenue stream, customer satisfaction, and potential operational survival are based on it.

Performance

Performance in playout is highly deterministic. Each playout channel consists of a single stream of totally sequential data sent to the playout server. Bandwidth requirements per channel usually are relatively low due to the nature of the delivery mechanism, which requires compromises. The important performance aspect is to maintain the streaming transfer of data to the playout server under all conditions. Because of this, it is normal to do a FRT (fractional fourier transform) transfer of the asset to the server in a cache-ahead mode and ring-fence the delivery stream to the actual broadcast server or head end.

Resilience, Availability, and Service

Resilience is an absolute requirement for playout. The playout stream must continue to be delivered to the server at the right speed and on time under all circumstances. Highly resilient and fault-tolerant architectures are employed in the servers and in the back-end storage supporting them.

Availability and service must be 24/7 × 365 guaranteed, with no compromises—ever. Ring-fenced, replicated architectures are the norm.

Content Management and Asset Repurposing

Content management represents a very large opportunity and is one of the most rapidly growing, dynamic industry segments at the moment, and will be for the foreseeable future. Fundamentally, the concept is that broadcasters have a huge back catalogue of already produced and used material in the form of programs to which they own the rights. Once this material is stored in the digital domain, along with relevant metadata to describe it, the assets can be searched for and retrieved easily. Therefore, they can be repurposed to provide saleable new programs for the burgeoning group of broadcasters in the cable, digital, and satellite fields. This is broadly what the computer industry would recognize as data warehousing or data mining, but with program assets as the data objects.

Performance

Performance in this environment places several different and conflicting demands on the storage system:

- First, there is the metadata database that contains the asset descriptions. This must be able to handle large numbers of unstructured, random queries from a very large population of distributed users. This is a fairly typical, large database application with a performance focus on transaction and IO delivery.

- Second, there is the need to support a large number of relatively low-resolution (typically MPEG at 1.5 Mbps) browse streams to allow users to review, approve, or select the clips that are suggested by the preceding queries. These represent many short, sequential transfers that are distributed randomly throughout the object storage space.

- Once clips are selected, the system must support either the real-time streaming of the actual clip to edit stations, as is done for NLE, or transfer the clips to local storage or SAN islands, potentially across distributed networks at rates up to fractional T1. Obviously, streaming must be isochronous, whereas transfers can be synchronous or asynchronous.

- In addition, the system must support one or several ingest streams at the highest retained quality (potentially uncompressed). These streams must remain isochronous during the ingesting because this is likely to be done from sequential linear material.

Resilience

Resilience is very important in this field because large amounts of material become associated with the system, and the workflow within the organization becomes dependent on it. Thus, the system rapidly becomes critical to the business, and the stored material cannot be lost. The assets stored within the system also may represent a significant business opportunity in terms of repurposing and sale of the asset rights, so their retention and availability may represent an important revenue generator.

Availability

As with the resilience of the system, availability tends not to be a prime consideration at the outset of this type of project, but it can become so very rapidly. The workflow of the user organization tends to become dependent on the centralized asset store, and production and retrieval operations also become focused on it. It is also common for repurposed asset delivery to become a revenue earner, and thus availability of the system becomes critical.

When developing and deploying this type of project, it is critical that the architect does nothing in the early or pilot phases that precludes the deployment of enterprise-class storage solutions and infrastructures. This becomes especially critical as the importance of the new system within the general business grows.

Service

Service delivery is an extremely complex issue in this type of project. Thousands of users may be connected to the system and doing database queries and browsing at one time, with simultaneous streaming and/or transfer of selected assets occurring at the same time. Obviously, the system must be capable of sustaining these streams under all conditions, whereas the browsing and query activities, and indeed the transfers, are less critical. However, if browsing or transferring is too slow or unreliable, the system may be seen as user-unfriendly and may not be adopted within the business. Thus, proper solutions design to provide the necessary QOS for all available services is critical. This design must take into account scalability from early pilots to, potentially, very large and business-critical implementations.

Video on Demand

VOD has been a growth area for some time, although much of the actual work has been experimental or has focused on localized pilots. As the public infrastructure to support VOD has started to become more widely available through digital delivery and asymmetric technologies such as ADSL (asymmetric digital subscriber line) so has the potential market grown and is beginning to mushroom.

Performance

The root of VOD is to provide movies or other material to a subscriber base on demand. The actual quality of delivery tends not to be very great, using quite highly compressed MPEG streams. The performance demands of VOD stem more from the need to address the variability and scalability needs related to the demand for stream provision.

VOD Technical Factors

In true VOD, many thousands of users can be viewing the same piece of material, at different points in the material, at the same time. This obviously presents a significant challenge for storage if the material is to be delivered directly and dealt with at such a high level. Either large cache pools can be used at the servers to smooth the access profile and make the workload more cache-friendly, or the VOD may be limited to allow viewers to access the material in discrete time increments (for example, movies starting every 15 minutes). As the user base becomes more sophisticated, the latter technique will become unacceptable, so the root issue must be addressed by the systems.

In order to support demand when large numbers of users are calling for the same material, techniques such as load-balancing servers are used. This allows for an extra playout server to take on part of the load as demand grows, and then move to another use (that is, supplying different material) when demand falls. To accomplish this, it is necessary to be able to connect new servers to a stored copy of material as required or to spawn a new copy very quickly, without having an impact on the existing streams.

Key performance factors, along with the ability to maintain streaming as demand grows, are the ability to access material very rapidly when demanded, either from online or near-line storage, and the ability to respond promptly to user requests and instructions.

Resilience

Resilience is quite important in VOD applications but not so critical as availability. Material once ingested into the system must be protected, but this can be done in the form of near-line or offline archiving. The ability to retain the appropriate number of copies of heavily used material and to manage the material effectively, as data in an HSM (hierarchical storage management) environment, is more important.

Availability

Availability is critical in VOD applications because the streamed video material represents the primary source of revenue, and customer satisfaction with the service is highly important. Video streams must maintain isochronous transfers under normal operation, and background housekeeping tasks—such as spawning copies, transferring material to and from archive, or searching and starting new streams—must not interfere with the foreground streaming.

In the event of a failure of a component or storage server, the system must be designed so as to fail the active stream over to an alternate unit without pausing the transfer. While it may be acceptable to interrupt the isochronous stream (that is, drop frames) during the failover, the transfer must resume and continue within a very short period.

Service

Service levels with VOD tend to be very clearly defined because of the nature of the material involved. Once a stream is initiated to a client, it must be maintained within the performance criteria defined or required for the type of video material being employed. Service levels must focus on being able to provide clusters of sufficient load-balancing servers to satisfy peak demands, and systems architectures must incorporate features to support this, as well as to deny service gracefully if the operating parameters for the system are becoming exceeded (for example, by excessive demand).

Discovering Some Common Threads

The descriptions in this chapter provide an introduction to the key features required of storage solutions and SANs within the broadcast and production industries. While the individual requirements vary and their prioritization may differ between particular industry segments or applications, the following common threads can be seen:

♦ Basically, all broadcast and production systems need to be able to sustain a defined number of streams of a known performance reliably and without interruption.

♦ The actual performance levels required vary from application to application but always can be defined clearly.

♦ It is critical that the components and solutions offered have the determinism of performance and behavior, the flexibility of configuration, and the scalability of both performance and capacity to support the target industries.

♦ The systems also must allow sufficient management and control to support the architecting of the resilience and availability required into the total solution, not just at the individual-component level.

Reviewing Some Key Storage Products

This section will look briefly at some of the key storage products and how they fit the demands and requirements outlined earlier for the broadcast and production industries. Much of the ability to meet the requirements of individual organizations depends on the proper design of the overall system, rather than on the individual components chosen. It is critical, however, to have the right components available when designing a solutions architecture and to understand which components provide which key features in the overall design.

ESS

The ESS (enterprise storage server) is the flagship of the storage server range. It provides massive resilience and availability through a fully fault-tolerant internal architecture. It uses SSA (serial storage architecture) as the back-end disk system, which is arguably the fastest and most resilient disk subsystem available today.

Performance. The performance of the ESS, from the broadcast and production perspective, quite frankly is disappointing. Given the very high performance of the back-end SSA disk subsystems, the number of SSA loops employed, and the amount of processor power available for RAID and cache management in the two clusters, it is very difficult to justify why any of the fiber channel (FC) connections to the ESS can provide only about half the delivered performance of which FC is capable.

NOTE

━━━━━ Worse than the poor absolute performance for streaming is the lack of determinism of that performance. When any streaming operation is in progress, operations such as configuring new disk groups anywhere else in the machine can cause performance to plunge to the point where the stream cannot be maintained. The inability to assign particular groups of disks or external hosts to specific ports on the ESS makes system planning and design for performance almost impossible.

Resilience. The ESS intrinsically provides very high levels of resilience, and material stored within it is almost perfectly protected. PPRC (peer-to-peer remote copy) potentially provides a good measure of resilience beyond the individual unit, although there is some concern that PPRC performance may be too poor for video applications.

Availability. Availability is also intrinsically good with the ESS. The lack of port-to-LUN configurability limits the systems-level design for availability, and the multiaccess LUN (logical unit number) feature is likely to be a significant detractor because of this. SDD (subsystem device driver) is most unlikely to gain wide acceptance within the broadcast and production industries.

Service. There are no service-management features within the ESS as such, and the severe configuration limitations already highlighted make most of the common extensions and design philosophies used to overcome this invalid.

Scalability. The ESS can grow to very large capacity internally (~22 TB). However, the poor performance of the interconnects and the inability to partition the SAN, as discussed earlier, mean that it is unlikely for there to be very much use in retaining this capacity in a single machine. Scalability by adding machines is also compromised by the lack of configuration features and is unlikely to prove cost-effective for most applications.

Fiber Channel RAID Storage Server

The fiber channel RAID storage server (FCRSS) is a dual RAID controller system that provides FC (fiber channel) access to LVD (low voltage differential) Small Computer Systems Interface (SCSI) disks. There are two FC ports, one to each RAID controller, and six LVD disk busses. It is alleged that the FCRSS is about to be withdrawn, and it is unclear what will replace it.

Performance. The performance of the FCRSS in streaming applications is excellent. The FCRSS probably was the first product that was capable of equaling or excelling the Ciprico RAID arrays, which had become ubiquitous in this industry. Streaming performance from each of the ports could be made to approach the FC limits, although lack of sufficient cache compromised performance when delivering multiple streams per port. Very high levels of configurability make the performance of the FCRSS both tunable and highly deterministic.

Resilience. The FCRSS is reasonable in terms of resilience, although the bus-based nature of the SCSI disk subsystem compromises this. It is generally on a par with competing products in this area. There are no interunit data replication facilities, but internal battery backup and cache mirroring enhance unit resilience.

Availability. Availability on the FCRSS is equivalent to that of other products of this generation. Again, the highest risk is the SCSI busses, which may compromise the whole unit.

Service. The FCRSS is a straightforward RAID subsystem with no QOS-specific configuration or features. Limitations of ports and busses restrict solution design.

Scalability. This factor is poor due to the paucity of ports both upstream and downstream. Scaling of the solution is limited to adding discrete and independent FCRSS systems.

There are products in the IBM PSG range that show potential, such as the FAST 500 (FCRSS replacement) and its smaller siblings. These appear to have demonstrable advantages for the video-based industries, and would provide a more well-rounded and comprehensive product arsenal for solutions design.

Future IBM Products

At the current time, it is unclear what IBM products will be available to support the specific needs of the broadcast and production industries. The ESS is a very high-end solution in this arena and has some problems, as identified earlier.

With the withdrawal (potentially) of the FCRSS, it is unknown what products will replace it in the SSD portfolio. The Hewlett Packard storage products are an unknown in this area, and judgment must be reserved until they can be analyzed properly and proven from a video requirements perspective.

Virtual Multicasting Technology from CacheStream

CacheStream's Virtual Multicasting technology allows broadband network providers to benefit from scalable one-to-many distribution of rich media (TV-quality video and CD-quality audio) *without the need to enable Internet Protocol (IP) multicasting in the network*. CacheStream accomplishes this within its StreamControl point-of-presence (POP) server, as follows:

- This special POP server, collocated with an associated DSLAM (digital subscriber line access multiplexer), provides SoftRouter functionality that manages communications with its client base: personal computers (PCs), set-top boxes, and other StreamControl servers provisioned within the network.

- The StreamControl POP server looks for the Internet standard IP multicasting protocol (IPMP), and if it is not available at time of communication with a client, StreamControl maintains a dynamic table of the clients and the associated IP channels they wish to listen to. It then replicates packets that need to be sent to multiple addresses from the dynamic tables it maintains and translates the outbound packets into a standard UDP (Universal Data Protocol) unicast format, thus eliminating the need to turn on multicasting on the network.

The benefits are as follows:

- Scalable rich-media streaming applications *will not* require the incremental investment of implementing IP multicasting by the network provider.

- Rich-media broadband applications can be provisioned and scaled economically throughout the entire network; for example, with StreamControl servers provisioned within partner regional data centers, single output streams of content can be virtually multicast to multiple consumers, thereby simultaneously saving bandwidth costs.

- This approach retains the simplicity and security of the unicast network while adding the bandwidth efficiency of the multicast network.

The requirements are as follows:

- CacheStream StreamControl POP servers will need to be collocated with DSLAMS and in partner regional and edge data centers.

- CacheStream client software will need to be resident on all client devices (for example, PCs, set-top boxes, and so on) that will access the broadband streaming applications.

Currently, execution of the product deliverables in a video-friendly offering and coherence of the overall message, especially in terms the industry understands, would appear to be restricting progress.

Measuring the Competition

Broadcast and production represent a very competitive and discrete marketplace when deploying storage solutions. Several companies are building on footholds in the arena and are producing products that have appeal to broadcasters and the larger production companies. Notably:

- ◆ EMC is producing scalable solutions with integrated management, and its Celera media server provides a very attractive proposition with its direct video and audio feeds.

- ◆ Discrete Logic is a traditional player in this marketplace and is again bidding for recognition and market share under its new management.

The market is enormous and is expanding more rapidly than at any previous time. IBM appears to have a potentially extremely attractive product and technology set, especially given its span of control and knowledge.

Taking the Next Step

Having completed the first four parts (Chapters 1 through 15) of this book, you have covered the basic aspects of how to enrich your streaming enterprise system. Part Five, "Working with Advanced Technologies," will wrap things up with a look at more intricate applications, as well as a vision for the future of streaming media. Chapter 16 starts off with an exploration of wireless devices, specifically, the wireless application protocol (WAP).

Working with Advanced Technologies

Implementing Wireless Technology

M obility is one of the key factors shaping how companies and end users conduct daily affairs. Constant availability is fast becoming an essential part of future competitiveness. Businesses embracing the idea of the mobile information society can reinvent themselves as real-time organizations, in which access and interaction are instant.

Now, with the masses having portable devices, more and more wireless streaming applications are becoming prevalent. Wireless application protocol (WAP) technology is one of the leading ways to communicate with a portable device. I have included this chapter for readers with a more technical bent who are up for challenges. Therefore, this chapter is for those who have a programming background and a fair working knowledge of Hypertext Markup Language (HTML).

Discovering WAP and the Wireless Markup Language

WAP stands for *wireless application protocol*. The idea comes from the wireless industry, which includes companies such as Openwave.com, Nokia, and Ericsson. The point of the WAP concept is to stream Internet contents and Internet services to wireless clients and WAP devices, such as mobile phones and terminals. WAP is not a single entity but a list of protocols and specifications. It is limited in its streaming resources and currently can support the streaming of text and graphics. Other more fully functioned devices supported by HTML—as opposed to *Wireless Markup Language* (WML), the language of WAP—can use more power resources and support full multimedia streaming, such as audio and video. WML, therefore, is what HTML is to a Web browser.

WAP is an Extensible Markup Language (XML) application. If you are going from HTML to WML, with no prior knowledge of XML, chances are that WML may appear to be very strict. Just like HTML and XML, WML is read and interpreted by a browser built into the WAP device. For WAP devices, the browser is commonly called a *microbrowser*, an indication that its capabilities are somewhat limited. These capabilities, of course, are also limited by the capabilities of the WAP device in which it lives.

NOTE
The authoritative source for information on the Wireless Application Protocol (WAP) is www.wapforum.org. For further details on XML, contact: http://www.w3.org/TR/REC-xml.

WML Instead of HTML

WAP specifications require the use of WML. Although you may have heard of WAP devices that support HTML, this really is not the case. There are several other wireless devices similar to WAP devices, but these use straight HTML—such as devices with the Microsoft Mobile Explorer (www.allnetdevices.com/faq/?pair=06.21), which supports both HTML and WML. The MME devices are really two completely separate devices in one.

Then there are the variants on HTML, such as the iMode (www.allnetdevices.com/faq/?pair=12.002) browsers, which use Compact HTML. In short, if you are talking about WAP devices, the markup language *is* WML.

WAP's Bandwidth Resources

There are many reasons why WML is used in the WAP environment instead of HTML. Currently, the most important reason is that WML requires very little bandwidth resources compared with HTML. The technology supports streaming of text and graphics, and in most cases WAP devices can be very effective in getting the message distributed.

A Brief Glossary of Wireless Terminology

WMLScript is a client-side script language based on ECMAScript. It might seem a lot like JavaScript, and in a very general way, it is meant for the same type of application, which is to actually run simple code on the client side rather than just render a display—the job of the markup language. WMLScript obviously has been modified to fit the limitations of the WAP environment.

WAP server. A frequently misused term, a WAP server by itself is really nothing more than a Hypertext Transfer Protocol (HTTP) server—that is, a Web server. In order to confuse everyone, Nokia has a product it calls a WAP server, which is a WAP gateway and an HTTP server all in one—actually a content-providing server and a gateway. The gateway takes care of the gateway stuff, and the Web server provides the contents.

WAP gateway. A WAP gateway is a two-way device (as is any gateway). Looking at it from the WAP device's side, since a WAP device can only understand WML in its tokenized/compiled/binary format, the function of the WAP gateway is to convert content into this format. Looking at it from the HTTP server's side, the WAP gateway can provide additional information about the WAP device through the HTTP headers—for example, the subscriber number of a WAP-capable cellular phone, its cell ID, and even such things as location information (whenever that becomes available).

WML Script. This is a scripting language for WAP devices, based on JavaScript but less powerful.

XML (Extensible Markup Language). The World Wide Web Consortium's (W3C's) standard for Internet markup languages. WML is one of these languages. XML is a subset of SGML (standard generalized markup language).

PDA (personal digital assistant). Usually a handheld device, such as the Palm Pilot. WAP at http://www.palmpilot.com/ is not just for cellular phones.

This is proven by the millions of messages being streamed daily by people around the globe from business associates, family members, teenagers, and even grade-schoolers. With the introduction of technologies that provide higher bandwidth for WAP devices, the low-bandwidth rationale becomes less important. However, it will take many years before these higher-bandwidth technologies are available globally.

NOTE HTML also requires relatively great processing strength to render, and processing strength means power. This requires more energy from batteries. Less processing power means longer-lasting batteries, which are ideal for thin clients.

WAP Devices and Graphics

WAP specifications allow for the use of a graphics format called *WAP Bit Map Protocol* (WBMP), which is a 1-bit (either black or white) version of the Bit Map Protocol (BMP) format. Therefore, to be compliant with the specifications, all graphics must be converted into WBMP.

NOTE HTML really requires larger displays than the displays on such devices as mobile phones. Although the display can be larger on a mobile phone, the trend is to make the phone smaller and more portable. Even with iMode, which supports colors and a page layout similar to simple HTML, the displays are already at the maximum size you would want to carry every day.

Because WAP screen devices are very limited, when using WBMP, an image should not be larger than 150×150 pixels. For instance, the Nokia 7110 (www.nokia.com/phones/7110/index.html) screen is 96 pixels wide by 65 pixels high, so 150×150 pixels would look very large and take up more than the entire screen. Additionally, the size of the graphics cannot exceed 1461 bytes because of WAP phone memory limitations.

Not all WAP devices can display graphics. Consequently, the Alt option in the `<img>` tag must be used so that users of nongraphics WAP devices will be able to see an alternate textual representation instead of the graphics.

Image Preloading

There is no such thing as preloading any images using WML or WMLScript, whereas in HTML, images can be preloaded using simple JavaScript commands. The images, if small enough, can then be read from the WAP device's cache quickly. It is then also possible to animate images, and if all the images are able to fit into the WAP device's memory, you may not get a "Connecting to service . . ." message between each image.

Color Images

As of this writing, there is only one browser that accepts color images—Openwave.com's (www.Openwave.com/) UP.Browser version 3.2. Currently, this browser is only in one cellular phone, the Hitachi C309H, and has not yet been released to the market.

Since WBMP images are monochrome, Openwave.com wisely has chosen the very popular Portable Network Graphics (PNG) format for color images. The format of PNG images is described in RFC-2083 (ftp.isi.edu/in-notes/rfc2083.txt). If you are thinking about generating dynamic images, most good graphics packages fully support the format.

Openwave.com has released an SDK (version 3.3) to emulate this browser, and this is available at http://www.openwave.com/products/developer_products/sdk/index.html after registering. Note that there are a few limitations to this SDK. It is more of an HDML browser with WML and PNG capabilities. Unfortunately, all Openwave.com's Web documentation on the SDK version 3.3 is in Japanese.

The WAPCAM, available for WML browsers at www.allnetdevices .com/faq/wapcam.php3, supports the new color image format. After downloading and installing the SDK, simply paste the preceding Uniform Resource Locator (URL) into the emulator and have a look. To use PNG images in your code, simply point to the image file the same way you point to a WBMP image.

Standard Domain Names

As you already know, when a domain is registered either via your Internet service provider or directly through one of the domain registration companies, such as Network Solutions or Register.com, you register the domain part, that is, mydomain.com. A domain name server (DNS) is then assigned to hold a list of names and addresses for the hosts that live in this domain.

The DNS simply translates textual human-readable host names into Internet Protocol (IP) addresses and IP addresses into human-readable host names. Your Web site will have at least one host in this list called *www* that points to an IP address. When someone attempts to access your site, the DNS for the domain is asked, "What is the IP address of the host called www.mydomain.com?" and the DNS replies with the IP address, for instance, "193.143.2.90," which the requester then uses to access the site.

To add a WAP host to your domain, you basically just need to add a host in the DNS for the domain, and you can call this host *wap*. Any user requesting the IP address of wap.mydomain.com now receives the IP address of this WAP host.

The WAP host and the Web host can have the same IP address, which, in effect, means you serve both Web and WAP content from the same Web server. Since Web browsers read HTML and WAP browsers read WML, your Web server needs to be able to tell which type of browser it is talking to, and this can be done with a simple script on the server. This is explained at www.allnetdevices.com/faq/?pair=04.006. Since the host names www.mydomain.com and wap.mydomain.com both point to the same IP address, WAP users can access www.mydomain .com, and Web users can access wap.mydomain.com. After all, the textual host name is just a human-readable representation of the IP address of the host.

If you have one server for Web content and another for WAP content, you obviously need to point the Web host name (www.mydomain.com) to the IP address of the Web server hosting the Web contents and the WAP host name (wap.mydomain.com) to the Web server hosting the WAP contents.

WAP Device Registration

As I mentioned already, there is no difference between a Web domain and a WAP domain. If you already have a Web site, then you also have an Internet service provider who has hooked your site to the Internet. The common host name for a Web site is www or www.mydomain .com, and the typical host name for a WAP site is wap.mydomain.com.

WML in Europe and Other GSM Areas

The short answer to how to communicate via WML in Europe and other GSM areas is that Openwave.com's WML Extensions can be used if you target your code for the UP.Browser version 4 or higher. The slightly longer answer is that according to the WAP specifications, every gateway should pass unrecognized markup along to the browser unencoded. This has been seen to work on common gateways used by network operators in GSM (global system for mobile) communication areas—for example, UP.Link, Ericsson, and Nokia. If you target your application for the UP.Browser (that is, if you use multiple versions of your application), you will be able to exploit the possibilities offered by the extensions.

Size Limits of WML Decks

On the Web, a Web page is a file (document) stored on a Web server. In WAP, the documents are called *decks,* and each deck contains one or more cards. The content of each card is what is displayed in the WAP browser window. Given that WAP devices have very little memory, there is a limit to how big each WML deck can be. There is also no standardized limit, so it varies from browser to browser. Table 16.1 shows the limits on some browsers.

NOTE The limits shown in Table 16.1 state the size of the WML deck in its plaintext XML code (compiled/binary form)—the one you most likely send out from your server—not the compiled form the gateway passes along to the WAP device. An uncompiled WML deck can be quite large, and then end up as a fairly small compiled deck once it passes through the gateway.

Table 16.1   WML Deck Byte Size Limits

WML BROWSER	COMPILED WML DECK LIMIT
UP.Browser, version 3.2	1492 bytes
UP.Browser, version 4.x	2048 bytes
Ericsson R320	Approximately 3000 bytes
Ericsson R380	Approximately 3500 bytes
Ericsson MC218	More than 8000 bytes
Nokia 7110	1397 bytes

Metatags in WML

By default, metatags such as `<meta http-equiv="refresh" content="1;http://somewhere.com/">` are not supported by WML browsers. A few gateways, however, do support a very limited subset of metatags, but tests show that if you need to use them, there is something wrong with the gateway. For instance, one gateway does not support normal bog standard HTTP cache control, and the only way to control its cache is to use special metatags. Obviously, a user coming in from another gateway would not be able to use the same code. The bottom line is: Do not use metatags. There is bound to be a proper way to do what you want.

NOTE
The most commonly attempted metatag is:

```
<meta http-equiv="refresh" content=";http://somewhere.com/">
```

This tells the browser to load the specified URL after a certain amount of time has passed. WML already contains a tag for this called:

```
<ontimer>
```

Cookie Support

Normal HTTP cookies are to some extent supported in the WAP environment and are getting better. Openwave.com's UP.Link gateway has had support for this for some time.

NOTE
To test cookie support, you can use the script located at www.allnetdevices.com/faq/apps/cookietest.php3. The script is also available in the demos section at www.allnetdevices.com/faq/demos.php3.

All the major WAP players are developing solutions to this problem, but for now, these solutions create other problems. Developers of so-called WAP servers or Web servers with WAP gateway capabilities provide end-to-end security in a way because the data stream leaves the content server (the WAP server) already encrypted with WTLS.

A Question of Security

Secure Sockets Layer (SSL), which is used widely in the Web world to encrypt the data stream between a browser and a Web server, is actually also used in the WAP environment. However, SSL is used only between a Web server and the WAP gateway. Between the WAP gateway and the WAP device, a similar system called *Wireless Transport Layer Security* (WTLS) is used. WTLS is specialized for the wireless environment.

Security is a touchy subject. Although no systems are totally secure, SSL and WTLS on their own, in my opinion, provide adequate security for most applications. However, there is a potential security problem where the two protocols meet, and this is inside the WAP gateway.

SSL is not directly compatible with WTLS, so the WAP gateway must decrypt the SSL-protected data stream coming from the Web server, and then reencrypt it using WTLS before passing the data on to the WAP device. Inside the memory of the WAP gateway, the data are unprotected.

Let's assume, for example, that you are working with an online trading company that has made WAP service available to you. When the data leave the security of your system and your network, they are reasonably well protected. Then, when they enter the WAP gateway, which is commonly owned and operated by a third party, such as a mobile operator, the data are decrypted. All mobile operators are potential security risks. Trusting sensitive data to an unknown third party is hardly a good idea. The mobile operator in question could be any mobile operator in the world. Your customer might be on vacation in some country where security is considered a trivial matter. If the mobile operator's networks are vulnerable to attack, so are your data.

Exploring WAP Devices

The list is in no particular order. Phones are, as far as I know, GSM unless otherwise stated. Most of the information in Table 16.2 comes directly from manufacturers. Manufacturers not listed most likely cannot be bothered to tell developers that they have released a new device.

NOTE

Openwave.com also has an excellent list of released (and unreleased) devices with its browsers. To see Openwave.com's list, you must register at http://www .openwave.com/alliances/developer/membership.html (which you should do anyway if you are a developer).

AnyWhereYouGo (www.anywhereyougo.com) also has excellent tables of most WAP-enabled phones and PDA's located at http://www.anywhereyougo.com/. These tables even show technical information about each device, such as browser type, markup languages supported, screen size, and network bearer type.

There is also a list of released devices at WAPWala.net, located at http://wapwala .net/devices/.

Table 16.2   A Listing of WAP Devices

MANUFACTURERS	DEVICES	
Alcatel	One Touch 302 One Touch 303	One Touch 700/701 One Touch View db @
Audiovox	CDM4500	CDM9000
Benefon	Q	
Denso	1200 2100	2200
Ericsson	A2618s R320s	R380s
Mitsubishi	T250	T255
Motorola	i500plus (iDEN) i550plus (iDEN) i700plus (iDEN) i1000plus (iDEN) StarTAC ST7860W StarTAC ST7867W StarTAC ST7868W	Talkabout T2260 Talkabout T2267 Talkabout T2282 Talkabout T2288 Talkabout T8160 Talkabout T8167 Timeport 250

Table 16.2 *(Continued)*

MANUFACTURERS	DEVICES	
Motorola	Timeport 260	V series V2282
	Timeport P7382	V series V3682
	Timeport P7389	V series V8160
	Timeport P7389e	V series V8162
	Timeport P8167	V series V100
	Timeport P8767	V series V2288
	V series V2260	V series V50
	V series V2267	
Neopoint	1000	1600
Nokia	6210	9110i Communicator
	6250	9210 Communicator
	7110	
Panasonic	GD93	
Philips	Az@lis 238	Xenium 9@9
	Ozeo 8@8	
Qualcomm-Kyocera	QCP2000 Series	Thinphone QCP1960
	Smartphone PDQ1900	Thinphone QCP2760
	Smartphone PDQ800	Thinphone QCP860
Sagem	Sagem MW939	
Samsung	SCH3500	SCHi201
	SCH6000	SCH-N105
	SCH6100	SGH-A110
	SCH850	SPH-N105
	SCH8500	SPH-T100
	SCH-A105	Uproar SPH-M100
Siemens	C35i	S40
	M35i	S42
	S35i	SL45
Sony	CMDJ5	CMDZ5
Trium-Mitsubishi	Aria-@	Mars
	Cosmo-@	Mondo
	Geo-@	Neptune
	Geo-GPRS	

WAP is not the Web on your mobile phone, and WAP should have all the prospects of a long life, as long as developers understand: It is what's inside the application that matters, not necessarily how it's packaged.

Working with WML and WAP

The following sections address the day-to-day issues of actually working with WML and WAP—topics such as: WML page access, direct Internet connections (bypassing your operator), surfing sites with WAP device emulators, and the basics of WML programming.

WML Page Access

The easiest way to access WML pages, or cards, is to go through an existing gateway. Most cellular providers will have this functionality on their WAP home pages, which you access through your WAP device. The gateway link is commonly called *Go to URL*. When selected, the WAP device will access the URL you specify through the normal IP via the gateway. In this case, it is the gateway that reads the WML contents for you and passes them on to your WAP device. The contents are read the same way a PC-based browser reads them.

Some operators have chosen not to allow their users access to sites other than their own. This could be compared with an Internet service provider (ISP) only allowing its users access to the ISP's own sites. Such a policy shows a clear lack of brains, and any such operators may find their customers going elsewhere.

If you are stuck with such an operator, it is possible to get around this by connecting to the Internet via a local ISP's dialup service and using a public gateway to access WAP resources. An e-mail explaining the error to the operator in question probably also would help.

WAP Devices defined

WAP devices are used in mobile phones, but WAP is not in any way limited to phones. A WAP device should also not be considered a Web browser. WAP can be used to offer services and applications, similar to the ones you find on the Internet, in a very thin client environment. *Thin* here means virtually no processor power, very limited display-rendering capabilities, and so on. How well these applications work are up to the developers. Although WAP deployment currently is limited, the technology is new, and there are ways around almost every obstacle.

Because WAP devices are limited in terms of display size and by the lack of a keyboard, many people see the death of WAP when they are shown handheld micro-personal computers (micro-PCs) and personal digital assistants (PDAs). Although carrying only one device is more convenient, many people need to carry both their mobile phone and their micro-PC/PDA. Manufacturers have tried and continue to try to solve these problems by combining the PC and the mobile phone. The problem then becomes size. For a device such as this to be usable by a human being, there are certain size restrictions.

The typical combination PDA and mobile phone today is something like the Nokia Communicator. The drawback with this is that you cannot use the device comfortably unless you have one hand free to hold the device or the device is firmly seated somewhere. A normal mobile phone can be operated with just one hand, both holding and typing. Some people argue that it is impossible to type using the numeric keypads of a mobile phone. It is true that this is more complicated than using a normal keyboard, but then again, you are not meant to be writing an essay on a WAP device. The billions of SMS (Short Messaging Service) messages sent from mobile phones every day prove that this is not impossible.

Direct Internet Connections

If you are stuck with an operator unwilling to allow access to other WAP resources, or if you simply want to bypass your operator for development purposes, most WAP devices will let you do this. Even though different WAP devices work in different ways, you should be able to figure it out.

First of all, you need the telephone number of a local ISP with which you have a normal dialup account (the same type of account you would use for your home computer, for instance), either one you pay for or something you get for free. Many ISPs actually offer dialup access to the Internet for free. The ISP does not have to be local, but remember that you are going to pay mobile call prices for this. The ISP needs to support the PPP protocol. Obviously, you need a user ID and a password with this ISP, and you also need the IP address of a public gateway.

Configure your WAP device with the telephone number, user ID, password, and IP address for the gateway. On the Nokia 7110 at www .nokia.com/main.html, this is done under "Services, Settings, Connection." Some public gateways include:

Ericsson: 195.58.110.201

wapHQ: 212.1.130.132

Other gateways are listed at www.allnetdevices.com/faq/?pair=03.006.

WAP Device Emulation

Any microbrowser or user agent can read WML content. The best way to read WML content probably would be to use one of the many WAP device emulators because the contents are written for real WAP devices. These are heavy applications, however, and some of them require installation of additional components such as Java Runtime (Table 16.3).

Table 16.3 A List of Browsers, Emulators, and Related Items

BROWSER NAME	ENVIRONMENT	DESCRIPTION
WAPJAG.DE	Internet Explorer	Web-based browser; good for surfing
AU Systems WAP Browser	Palm OS 3.3	An alternative to a WAP phone, for instance

Table 16.3 *(Continued)*

BROWSER NAME	ENVIRONMENT	DESCRIPTION
WinWAP	Windows 9x/NT	A simple browser; good for application testing during development
Wapalizer	Internet Explorer/ Netscape	A simple browser; good for application testing during development
Fetchpage	Any HTML browser	Not really a browser, but useful for developers; displays HTTP header info
WAPman	Windows 9x/NT	Pretty looking browser; even has skins
WAPman	Palm OS 3.1	Pretty looking browser; same as above, but it is only for the Palm OS 3.1 operating system
Nokia WAP Toolkit 1.3 Beta	Windows 9x/NT+Java	Preferred developers' kit of many developers; *must* register first
Nokia WAP Toolkit 1.2	Windows 9x/NT+Java	Preferred developers' kit of many developers; *must* register first
Openwave.com UP.SDK	Windows 9x/NT	UP.Browser SDK (4.0 and 3.2)
Ericsson R380 Emulator	Windows NT 4.0	Ericsson's R380 emulator
Nokia SDK 2.18	Windows 9x/NT	Good development kit and a good 7110 emulator; again, the preferred choice of many developers
Wappy's Wapview	Internet Explorer/ Netscape	A simple browser-based WML viewer
Opera 4.0	Standalone browser	The Norwegians do it again; a great HTML browser, now with WML support
EzWAP CE, and Pocket PC	Windows NT, 2000,	Nice looking multiplatform browser; only $25; demo available

WML Programming

Most of you probably find it easier to learn by doing rather than by reading lots of documentation first and then trying. I recommend, however, that you at least take a quick look at the following overview of WML programming before starting. This section will be short and to the point.

Before you start, however, it is important to note that it's virtually impossible to get a grasp on WAP without some prior knowledge of HTML and Web servers. Such a basic grasp is required for this introduction. If you do not know any HTML, stop now and learn some before returning. Those of you who already have prior knowledge of WAP may notice some white lies and shortcuts. Ignore them please. This section is for newbies.

NOTE

For more information on WML programming, you might want to check out the *Beginner's Guide to WAP/WML* at www.wap.com.

You can also search for other articles on this topic at Wap.com (www.wap.com/). Eventually, you may find the article that was the basis for this chapter at www .asptoday.com/articles/20000717.htm.

Further searches can be made on the ASP Today site (www.asptoday.com/), and another source that takes you through the first steps of writing WMLScript can be found at www.allnetdevices.com/faq/?pair=11.001applications.

As you already know, a Web page is a file (document) stored on a Web server. In WAP, the documents are called *decks*, and each deck contains one or more cards. The content of each card is what is displayed in the WAP browser window.

On the Web, the common language for documents is HTML. In WAP, the language is WML. The two look very similar, and for this demonstration, I will pretend they are very similar (but, in fact, they are not).

To better understand what is involved with WML, here are some sample code comparisons. A very simple HTML page may look like this:

```
<H1>Have a great day!
```

This HTML code may not be formatted correctly. First of all, the end tag </H1> is missing, and there really should be a <HEAD> and <BODY>

section, and so on. However, all normal Web browsers will be able to display the preceding page correctly.

In WML, it is a different story. The WML code is much more strict. For example, all tags must be closed. In other words, the code must be formatted correctly, and there is no room for error. The reason for this is that a so-called WAP gateway with very little intelligence may convert the WML code to a compressed format before it is sent to the WAP browser. The same previously described code in WML would be something like this:

```
<?xml version="1.0"?>
<!DOCTYPE wml PUBLIC "-//WAPFORUM//DTD WML 1.1//EN" "http://www.wapfo-
rum.org/DTD/wml_1.1.xml">
<wml>
<card id="mycard" title="My first card">
<p> Have a great day!</p>
</card>
</wml>
```

Most important is the header. The absolutely first character received by the browser must be the < character that starts the line <?xml version="1.0">. Any other character (even a space, a carriage return, or something else) will break the card.

If you want, you can now take the preceding code and put it into a file called greatday.wml. Notice the .wml file extension.

NOTE All you need to know is provided by an excellent document from Openwave.com: available at www.openwave.com/products/developer_products/index.html.

Streaming Wireless Cellular Video

The video streaming industry is becoming very exciting, and along with WAP technologies, we now have video streaming communications. Video streaming enterprises may now be able to send video media to cellular phones, now considered full-featured communication devices. One of the companies leading this initiative is Nokia.

Accessing Additional Resources

Some good information on securing WAP is available at the following locations:

◆ Wapforum's WTLS specs (high caffeine factor): SPEC-WTLS-19991105 (www.openwave.com/)

◆ Baltimore Telepathy's secure demonstration: www.baltimore.com/telepathy/index.html

◆ Tantau's excellent article covering, among other things, WAP structures (Register first!): "An Introduction to WML Programming and Third-Party WAP Toolkits" (www.tantau.com/literature/WML+WAP.pdf)

◆ Openwave.com's excellent article on wireless security (Register first at http://www.openwave.com/alliances/developer/membership.html): "Understanding Security on the Wireless Internet" (www.Openwave.com/pub/Security_WP.pdf)

You can learn more about WMLScript at the following sites:

◆ For a beginner's guide to WMLScript, see this article from *ASP Today* at www.asptoday.com/articles/20000717.htm.

◆ WMLScript.com's site at www.wmlscript.com/ contains lots of WMLScript information and even an WMLScript library at www.wmlscript.com/script_library.asp.

◆ After registering with Openwave.com's Developer site (www.Openwave .com/), you may access its excellent reference to WMLScript.

◆ Doc JavaScript (and do not let this fool you) has a couple of articles at www.webreference.com/js/.

DEVELOPER SITES

◆ WapForum (www.wapforum.org): The authoritative source on WAP environment specifications.

◆ WMLScript.com (www.wmlscript.com/): Very promising site for WML and WML developers.

◆ Wireless Developer Network (www.wirelessdevnet.com/): Very good collection of resources and information

◆ Also check manufacturers' sites.

ARTICLES

◆ Luca Passani's WAP and ASP articles

◆ Luca Passani's WML/XML/ASP articles

◆ Wei Meng Lee's article on ASP-based WAP shopping carts

BOOKS

◆ The current WAP bible: *Professional WAP* (from Wrox) by Charles Arehart (Editor), Nirmal Chidambaram, Shashikiran Guruprasad, Alex Homer, Ric Howell, Stephan Kasippillai, Rob Machin, Tom Myers, Alexander Nakhimovsky, Luca Passani, Chris Pedley, Richard Taylor, Marco Toschi

MAILING LISTS

◆ The Yahoo (prev eGroups.com) WML and WMLScript Programmers List

◆ The WMLScript Discussion Forum

◆ WAPWarp's WAP-Dev mailing list at yoyo.org

MANUFACTURER SITES

◆ Nokia's WAP Developer Forum (http://www.forum.nokia.com//)

◆ Ericsson's WAP Developer's Zone

◆ Openwave.com Developer's Program

MISCELLANEOUS SITES

◆ WapRing (excellent catalogue of WAP services for both users and developers) http://flashcommerce.com/articles/00/04/10/161203340.html

◆ PPT WAP Resource Center (lots of information and links) http://www.palowireless.com/wap/

THE WML AND WML SCRIPT PROGRAMMERS LIST LINKS VAULT

Here are some excellent open-source sites that in some way relate to WAP and the wireless environment:

◆ OpenWAP.org, promoting open-source WAP development and informing the WAP community of news http://www.openwap.org/

◆ Kannel.org, an open-source WAP gateway project (previously wapgateway.org)

◆ WMLbrowser.org, an open-source project maintained by 5NINE to create a WML browser that runs in all Linux environments

◆ LEAP (Lightweight and Efficient Application Protocols), an open wireless protocol suite specification http://www.freeprotocols.org/LEAP/Manifesto/roadMap/

◆ Silocon Penguin Embedded Linux Authority (at present, there is only one that I know of, and it contains the Nokia 7110) http://www.siliconpenguin.com/

VISIO STENSILS

◆ Nokia 7110 Stensil http://www.nokia.com/

NOTE

▬▬▬▬ **Nokia is one of the world's leaders in mobile communications. The company has become the foremost supplier of mobile phones and a force in mobile, fixed, and IP networks.**

By the time you read this, the Nokia 9290 Communicator should have made its debut in the United States. Combining a vivid, active-matrix color screen with the Symbian operating system (Symbian OS, crystal category), this product features a full-color display, PersonalJava (which allows for any number of third-party software solutions), and offers a glimpse into the future of multimedia messaging.

Following introduction of the Nokia 9210 Communicator for European and Asian markets, Nokia also announced Java platforms for developers worldwide, which are to be available through numerous distribution channels.

"The Nokia 9290 Communicator demonstrates Nokia's commitment not only to provide unique, innovative products for its customers but also to do it using open standards, such as the Symbian OS, Java, and SyncML," said Paul Chellgren, vice president of business development for Nokia. I have found that by "Using the platform that the Nokia 9290 Communicator provides, numerous applications, ranging from business to entertainment, can be implemented, allowing the user to customize their Nokia Communicator to their individual needs."

Incorporating the ability to send and receive images, sound, and video clips, the Nokia 9290 Communicator is the first product announced in the United States to reveal the next steps toward multimedia messaging. With over 200 billion SMS messages sent during 2001, multimedia messaging builds on this success by adding rich content to messages— making this form of communication more unique and personal.

The Nokia 9290 Communicator is a fully integrated mobile terminal combining phone, fax, e-mail, calendar, and imaging functionality. Internet access is possible via both a WAP- and HTML-based WWW browser, which also supports frames. Along with proprietary word-processing and spreadsheet applications, support for many of the most used PC applications (including viewing and editing of Microsoft Word and Excel documents, and a PowerPoint viewer), is built into the Nokia 9290 Communicator. SyncML support allows for seamless synchronization of contact, calendar, and to-do information across SyncML-enabled PCs, PDAs, mobile phones, and other devices.

NOTE

━━━━ Additional product features and technical specifications can be found at www.nokia.com, and information for the developer community is located at www.forum.nokia.com or www.americas.forum.nokia.com. (Some features depend on network capabilities.)

Taking the Next Step

Text streaming on handheld devices is becoming more mainstream. On many phone systems, you see this when people exchange encrypted messages using their own shortened glossary. Audio and video streaming devices are now following this trend. Gear your streaming enterprise to target these markets.

Chapter 17 will cover another unique topic—security and surveillance using your streaming enterprise system.

Streaming for Security and Surveillance

This chapter brings together many of the enabling and emerging technologies discussed in this book to form a basis for using streaming media in the realm of security and surveillance—a particularly important topic in our present age. As digital video technology advances and is integrated with the Internet, the paradigm for CCTV (closed caption television) applications is moving from dedicated cabling toward fully digital solutions. In making the transition, much is to be learned from the evolution we have seen in computing: from the dominating mainframes to the ubiquitous networked personal computers (PCs) of today. The same transition can be expected in the CCTV area, where available computer network resources are used increasingly for the transmission of CCTV signals, thereby eliminating the need for dedicated video cables.

Other advantages are scalability, flexibility, fault tolerance, and ultimately, no more multiplexers. What's more, the networks of today, combined with state-of-the-art compression technology, provide many parallel and full-frame-rate streams of video, whereas multiplexers have so far provided few frames per second.

Reviewing the Technological Landscape

The video camera, a commodity item by today's standards, will regain its reputation by integrating into itself more and more functions, intelligence, and digital network interfaces. Once it is in the digital domain, other advantages really come for free. The following are just three of the many advantages that can be tapped in the digital domain:

- Global access to remote video at a mouse click
- Video recording without wear and tear
- Seamless integration with databases and other media

Networked video also opens up the door to a whole new class of tapeless (that is, hard disk) video recording systems, namely, networked video recording. Based on standard PC server technology, cost-efficient mass storage is here. A scheduling agent will access video streams over the network and record in the background so that if something happens, you are covered.

Networked Video: Advantages and Requirements

From the elements briefly reviewed so far, it is easy to recognize the parallels between today's CCTV and yesterday's computer technology, and to see the limitations of CCTV technology. By adopting computer network technology, whereby all cameras are linked to a network system in the same way as PCs, the digital alternative avoids any disadvantages while presenting the following advantages:

- Camera signals can be stored anywhere on the network and can be accessed from anywhere within the network.
- They can be displayed, recorded, and transferred into other media.
- The network may be limited to a single room, or it may extend around the globe.
- Thanks to its structure, the overall system is inherently fault tolerant.
- Digital video technology brings higher-quality video; faster, more efficient access to stored data; higher reliability; and distributed, even global, monitoring over networks.

The following list details some of the even more striking advantages of networked video:

Installation and maintenance.   Having a single unified network— for example, one based on CAT5 Ethernet, for information technology, video monitoring, access control, telephony, and other applications—yields significant advantages in terms of installation and maintenance.

No dedicated video cabling.   Especially for large projects, a huge portion of the installed value is in cabling and associated workmanship. The additional cost for digital equipment is more than compensated for by the greatly reduced cost for wiring and workmanship.

True parallel video streams.   Digital networks are inherently parallel. Thus the usual trade-off between the number of cameras and fields per second is no longer valid. All packetized digital video streams travel the network in parallel—so the network really can be viewed as a large-capacity multiplexer.

Scalability, flexibility, and fault tolerance.   Standard CCTV equipment has a fixed number of inputs. For networked video, cameras may be added as they are needed, just as you would add a PC to your network. In the case of networked video, when cameras or viewing and recording equipment need to be rearranged, this is no problem. Contrast this with using dedicated coaxial cabling, whereby the whole installation has to be redone.

No wear and tear.   Unlike analog tape, the quality of digital recordings does not degrade with use. In addition, digital, wide-area transmission systems do not need equalizers and/or amplifiers, as is the case with analog transmission.

Wide-area connectivity.   Once in the digital domain, global access to video actually comes for free, as demonstrated by the success of the Internet.

Cost-effectiveness.   In addition to the savings already realized from the lack of coaxial cabling, networking equipment and PCs are really commodity items with rock-bottom pricing. By going digital, the large volume of networking gear and its associated pricing may be leveraged.

Seamless integration with standard databases. Digital networked video is no different from all the other data that travel your network. Digital video may be stored using the same kinds of servers that are already in use for other corporate data (for example, CAD files).

Standard printing, reporting, and archiving tools. Last but not least, all the tools available in the information technology (IT) world may be put to work for CCTV applications as well.

In order to tap into all the advantages offered by digital video technology, four main building blocks—compression, transmission, recording, and analysis—are required (Figure 17.1). It all starts with a standard camera, for example, based on a charge-coupled device (CCD) or the latest CMOS technology.

Compression

The purpose of compression is to reduce the data rate of the digital video signal down to a value that is compatible with the transmission capabilities of the considered network. A good compression scheme retains as much of the original information as possible. By filtering static information and filtering information that a human observer cannot perceive, and by producing the most efficient representation of the digital data, significant savings are obtainable. Typical compression ratios range from 10 to several 100, depending on algorithms and requirements.

Transmission

The compressed data signal needs to be adapted to the environment of the considered network. Compressed data are surrounded by the appropriate network headers and embedded into the respective protocols. For Ethernet networks, a packetization of the data is required. With knowledge of the underlying meaning of the payload data, packetization can be performed in a clever manner so that lost packets do not cause catastrophic failures but rather small artifacts, sometimes too small to notice.

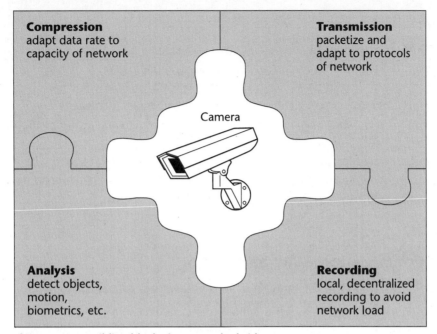

Compression
adapt data rate to
capacity of network

Transmission
packetize and
adapt to protocols
of network

Camera

Analysis
detect objects,
motion,
biometrics, etc.

Recording
local, decentralized
recording to avoid
network load

Figure 17.1   Building blocks for networked video.

Recording

About 90 percent of all recorded video is never viewed again but rather is overwritten or deleted. In order to avoid network utilization or loading, recording may take place at the camera site or even within the camera. Digital video is recorded in a decentralized fashion, allowing it to be used in a manner similar to the way data is used by today's computer users, who do not know, or even care to know, where a wanted file is located physically. For backup purposes and/or to increase the capacity of local recording, the network can periodically flush or copy the content of the local recording to another archiving medium. Local recording is also very powerful for assessing the prealarm history: Comprehensive coverage of the time before an alarm occurred aids in determining postalarm action plans ranging from alarm classification to prosecution.

Analysis

One of the most powerful advantages of digital video is signal processing. To name but a few of the endless possibilities, digital signal processing makes it possible to analyze the video scene for moving objects, particular motion patterns, license plates, even human faces. Especially with chips and algorithms becoming ever more powerful, formerly dumb CCTV components will turn into intelligent units. These intelligent cameras can effectively assist human observers without showing fatigue or distraction. They can even carry out automated recording tasks or other functions on an autonomous regime.

Video Compression: Why and Which

It was mentioned earlier that compression is one of the building blocks of a video network. This section will provide some insights into why compression of video data is required in the first place and which compression algorithm is best suited for a particular application.

Why It's Needed

When an analog video signal such as a National Television Standards Committee (NTSC) or Phase Alternate Line (PAL) signal is digitized, this is usually done in accordance to the CCIR 601 standard. This standard accounts for a true and high-quality representation of the video signal at the cost of high data rate requirements. Figure 17.2 depicts the data rates of two digital video representations and contrasts them with the bandwidth available over some popular networks.

As can be seen in the upper row, the digital format CCIR 601 requires a bandwidth of approximately 140 Mbps. Even if the video is subsampled to a lower resolution—for example, the Common Intermediate Format (CIF) with 352 pixels and 288 lines—and only every other field is transmitted, the resulting data rate is no lower than about 35 Mbps.

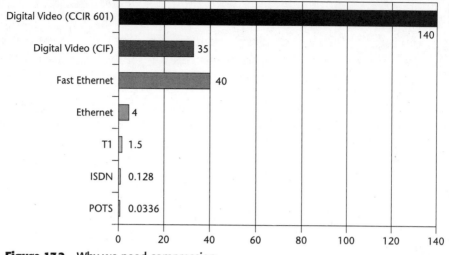

Figure 17.2 Why we need compression.

Even modern networks such as Fast Ethernet, for example, have a net capacity of approximately 40 Mbps. Thus, theoretically, a single low-resolution video stream already would completely exhaust the capacity of a modern high-speed network link. For standard Ethernet or even wide-area connections, the gap widens considerably. Compare the rate of a modem (POTS) at 33.6 kbps with the requirements of video, and it becomes clear why compression is needed and what compression can do.

Modern video compression standards such as H.263 yield about VHS-type quality at data rates as low as 500 kbps. Even over telephone lines, live video transmission with about 15 fps does not constitute a problem. All this shows that today's networks are indeed suitable to support many parallel video streams.

Which Method to Use

Now that you understand the need for video compression, the next question arises: Which is the best method or algorithm to be used? While it certainly would go beyond the scope of this chapter to explain all schemes in detail, along with their associated pros and cons, some general guidelines will be provided. Figure 17.3 shows the applicable operating ranges of different compression schemes, and it can be seen that the answer to the preceding question really depends on the application and the requirements.

A video camera can deliver up to 60 fps (frames, or fields, per second). If the application calls for very smooth motion rendition and best video quality (30 fps and above), the algorithm to look at is MPEG-2. Incidentally, MPEG-2 is also used on DVDs and for digital video broadcast, for which it was developed in the first place. Thus, quality is hardly an issue. On the other hand, MPEG-2 really makes sense only above data rates of 2 Mbps (DVDs run at about 6 Mbps), so a spacious local area network (LAN) and recording to hard disk are the typical environments for MPEG-2.

If data rate is at a premium, for example in WAN applications over ISDN or even analog telephone lines (POTS), it is better to limit the field rate to a maximum of 30 fps and use H.323, which is the standard for videoconferencing over the Internet (as used by Microsoft NetMeeting, for example). H.323 and its underlying H.263 video coding scheme are very efficient and introduce minimal delay. The lowest delay possible is important for live monitoring as well as for remote control of cameras, such as domes or pan/tilt/zoom drives.

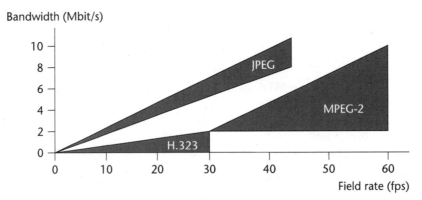

Figure 17.3   Which compression method to choose.

How does this relate to the ever-so-popular JPEG scheme? In general, JPEG is a still-picture coding scheme. The term *M-JPEG*, with *M* for motion, relates to a successive application of the JPEG method to each of the fields of the video source. Because static areas are not filtered, however, motion is not taken into consideration, and temporal redundancies are not accounted for. JPEG, therefore, is always less efficient than the aforementioned standards.

NOTE
As a rule of thumb, for any given frame rate and quality, JPEG or M-JPEG typically requires 10 times the data rate. Or, to look at this the other way around, at a fixed and given data rate, M-JPEG will yield a tenth of the frame rate.

The wavelet method is slightly more efficient than JPEG, but the same principal behavior still holds. Both JPEG and wavelet are well suited for local storage applications, where ease of handling, such as arbitrary extraction of images and backward single stepping during playback, are more important than raw efficiency.

Networking Basics II: Multicasting

In the analog world, a video signal may be connected to more than one receiver: Typically, a camera is connected to a monitor for viewing and, in parallel, to a VCR for recording. Additionally, the signal eventually is fed into a matrix or connected to a transmission unit. To this end, loop-through interfaces are used, or the termination of the video signal is switched off in all but the last unit of the chain. For an even larger distribution of the signal, special distribution amplifiers are capable of feeding eight or more inputs.

In the digital networking world, the simultaneous viewing or recording of a networked video source is called *multicasting*. In contrast to a point-to-point connection, also called *unicast*, multicasting offers the simultaneous reception of the same digital video stream at several receivers (Figure 17.4).

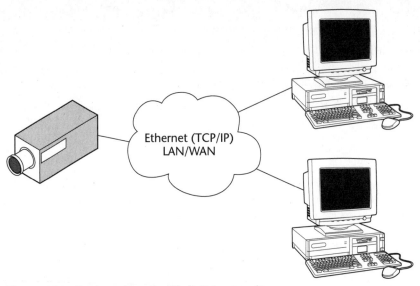

Figure 17.4 Basic multicasting in digital networking.

The most important aspect of multicasting is efficiency: The data stream is not duplicated by the transmitter but rather replicated inside the network on an as-needed basis. Therefore, the transmitter and the network link to the transmitter cannot be overloaded. Regardless of the number of simultaneous viewers, the same data rate is sent at the camera end.

Broadcasting is another well-known mechanism in networking. During network broadcasts, the information (that is, the data packets) is transmitted unsolicited to all devices on the network. Broadcast modes potentially impose a heavy load on a network. Therefore, broadcasting of digital video should be avoided, and the highly efficient multicast mode should be used even for large audiences.

Video over the Internet: System Architecture

Now that the main building blocks for networked video, namely, compression and networking, have been examined, a complete video over Internet Protocol (IP) system is the next step. Figure 17.5 shows a complete system built around a networking cloud. The networking cloud encompasses all networking gear required for local- or even wide-area connectivity, or any mix thereof. In order for a data packet to travel from a sender to a receiver, it might be necessary to pass multiple network segments, all with different characteristics. Explaining the specific properties and limitations of such complex networks is beyond the scope of this chapter.

NOTE
IP is synonymous with networking in general, due to the popularity of the Internet Protocol (IP). Of course, the basic aspects put forward here also apply to other underlying network types, such as Asynchronous Transfer Mode (ATM), for example.

Video Servers

When a standard analog video camera is to be connected to a digital network, a so-called video server is required. The video server digitizes and compresses the video signal and performs some or all of the functions mentioned earlier in this chapter. Most importantly, the video server provides an IP address that uniquely identifies the camera from anywhere in the network. The concept of IP addresses is the same for computers on a LAN or on the Internet in general.

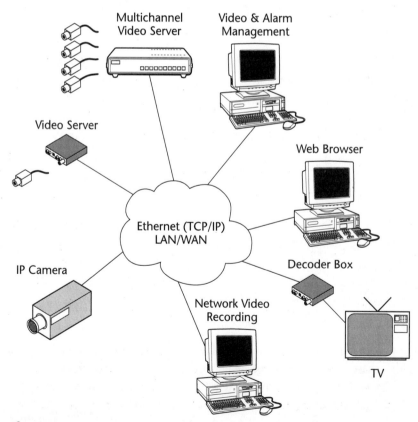

Figure 17.5 Systems overview: video over IP.

All functions and parameters of the video server are remotely controlled from the viewing side or any other controlling entity on the network. In addition to a video input, the video server may feature additional interfaces in order to accommodate bidirectional audio transmission—for remote listening or announcements, for example.

Full-duplex data interfaces allow for remote control of connected peripherals, such as pan/tilt/zoom drives or dome cameras. Other popular interfaces featured on most video servers are trigger inputs and relay outputs. While trigger inputs enable the connection of standard alarming devices, such as infrared (IR) motion detectors or simple doorknobs, relay outputs facilitate remote switching.

NOTE

The video server may be integrated into the camera housing, yielding a so-called IP camera. IP cameras are the easiest and most compact way to realize networked video. IP cameras are to be distinguished from so-called WebCams, which do require connection to a PC to operate.

Mutichannel Servers

For installations where several cameras are grouped together in close proximity, rather than using a separate video server for each camera, it might be more economical to use a multichannel video server. Such a system, for example, may combine a quad splitter and a multiplexer with a video server. Alternately, a video server also may be combined with legacy equipment—standard matrices or splitters for example.

Decoders

On the viewing end, a decoder is required to convert the digital video stream back to an analog composite NTSC or PAL video signal. Applications using this so-called box-to-box approach are fully compatible with existing analog CCTV installations. The computer network is used mainly as a replacement or extension of coaxial cable.

NOTE

Although the computer network is used for the transport of video, no computer is required. Arguments against the employment of a PC include: added security (no crashes), ease of use (no booting or fiddling with a mouse), compactness (servers that fit inside cabling ducts), and enhanced robustness (no ScanDisk after a power failure).

PC-Based Applications

On the other hand, software-only PC-based applications are available. They provide a wide range of functions and are economical. Often a PC is already available, and the software comes with the video server box. From the pricing and ease-of-use points of view, a standard Web browser offers the best solution. Specific software applications can provide a number of exclusive functions—multichannel viewing, over-archiving, alarm management, map-based operation—suitable even for alarm center use.

A special class of these applications is targeted toward recording and alarm logging. This type of recording is termed *network video recording* (NVR) because the cameras are not attached locally but logically over the network. Any standard PC on the network equipped with this recording software can act as a network video recorder. The examples explored in the following section provide more detail regarding network video recording.

Exploring Two of the Endless Possibilities

The system overview just given mentions only the most basic operations and possibilities. In practice, the possibilities and applications for network video are virtually endless. The following subsections give two examples that go beyond the common replacement of classic CCTV applications with digital technology.

Access Control

Most corporations today employ a LAN to connect all the company's PCs to a file server, printers, and other shared resources. Figure 17.6 shows a company with a head office and a branch office in different cities. Both LANs are connected by means of a leased line or a public network, thereby forming a corporate intranet.

Access control at the branch office is often a problem:

- On the one hand, employees want to work flexible hours and should not be prevented from coming to work at any time.
- On the other hand, it might not be economical to have a guard on duty 24 hour per day, 7 days per week.

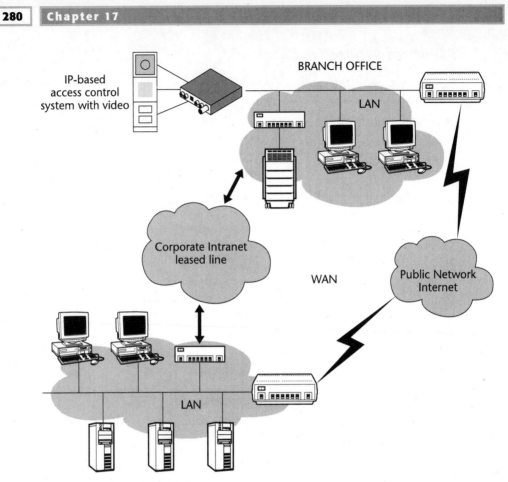

IP-based access control system with video

BRANCH OFFICE

LAN

Corporate Intranet leased line

WAN

Public Network Internet

LAN

HEAD OFFICE

Figure 17.6 Application I: IP-based access control.

An IP-based access control station can provide for an attractive solution, as follows:

1. The camera, the intercom, the card reader, the doorknob, and gate control are all connected to the video server.

2. As soon as an employee swipes his or her corporate ID card through the card reader, an IP connection is established to the central guard station at the head office.

3. Depending on the sophistication of the management software and the level of security required, the ID data may trigger a database lookup for the employee's data together with a picture taken at the time the employee was hired.

4. The guard on duty will then compare the picture with the live video feed from the entrance.

5. He or she can talk over the network to the access control station.

6. For visitors or people without ID cards—parcel services, for example—ringing the doorbell will trigger the connection setup to the central monitoring station.

7. With a mouse click, the gate may be opened remotely.

8. The complete transaction, together with associated video and audio, may be recorded in a corporate database, effectively providing a log of all (off-hour) company accesses.

Network Video Recording

As already mentioned, digital technology offers the possibility of network-based video recording (NVR). Any standard PC may be transformed into a hard-disk recording system by software only. Video streams delivered from video servers all over the network are recorded on a predefined regime and controlled by a scheduling agent. The PCs may be located anywhere inside the network, for example, in a server room. Unlike specially designed hard-disk recorders, network video recording is based on standard PC platforms, without the need for any add-in boards, such as frame grabbers, for example.

NOTE Standard equipment always represents the most economical and most widely available solution. For large storage requirements, RAID arrays are available ranging up to several Terabytes of storage capacity.

NVR will not replace local recording. Figure 17.7 shows a potential setup: a sample network video device without recording capability and a video server equipped with a hard disk for local recording. It has been observed that more than 99 percent of all recorded footage is never accessed and viewed but plainly overwritten. Local recording avoids network utilization. At the same time, the network may be used for archiving purposes or to increase the capacity of the local hard disk (virtual drive).

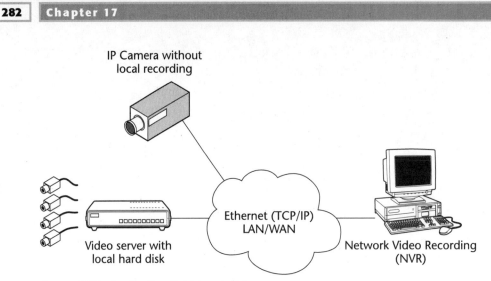

IP Camera without
local recording

Ethernet (TCP/IP)
LAN/WAN

Video server with
local hard disk

Network Video Recording
(NVR)

Figure 17.7 Application II: Network video recording.

The hard disk of the video server may also be mounted over the net-work for remote access. Searching and playback of archived video may take place from anywhere in the network, effectively blurring the line between local and remote recording. Just like the Internet, where the user mostly does not know or care where the information is stored, as long as access to the information is readily available, network video is becoming the universal and cost-effective paradigm for the CCTV industry and beyond.

Taking the Next Step

This chapter has given you a very good idea of how to integrate security and surveillance into your streaming enterprise system. Chapter 18, the final chapter in this book, presents a vision for the future, including a spe-cial interview with Roderick Snell at Snell & Wilcox about his lifetime work on breaking down the barriers of standards for television and help-ing the world's broadcasting community to communicate with itself.

Envisioning the Future

The concluding chapter of this book presents a special and insightful interview with Roderick Snell of Snell & Wilcox about his lifetime of work breaking down the barriers of standards for television and helping the world's broadcasting community to communicate with itself. I also offer you my vision of the future of the video streaming ecosystem.

An Interview with Roderick Snell

Roderick Snell is a winner of the John Tucker Award, which honors those who have made special contributions to the development of electronic media technology. His achievements, which are too numerous to list here, range from the creation of the YC and S-Video standards right up to creating technology for managing digital cinema displays in the home as well as in the theater. As he himself says, "The evolution of moving images can go a long way forward in the next decade or so." Expect Roderick Snell to be closely involved in that evolution.

Revolutionary Technology

Like many of his generation who have gone on to lead major companies, Roderick Snell was trained in broadcast engineering by the British Broadcasting Company (BBC), but he did not stay there long. "I was interested in television as a cultural and an educational tool more than as an entertainment system," Snell admits. This idealism led him not just to work for universities in the United Kingdom but also into a number of consultancies with international bodies such as UNESCO.

"One of the things I wanted to do within the university sector was to develop an open-access video library," he recalls. "This was at the beginning of the seventies, when playing a videotape required a technician to set it up and operate it. I felt that if the university had a library of tapes, then it should be used just like a library of books—people should be able to walk in and watch a program."

"That was primarily an engineering challenge," he continues. "There had to be good-quality copies of the material, and there had to be a replay system that was simple enough for academics to operate." The solution was to import Japanese VCRs and modify them for European standards. To maintain acceptable quality in tape copies, though, Snell had to import an American time-base corrector, which was, of course, a turning point.

Roderick Snell's enthusiasm for lightweight production and his inventive mind started to come together in the unlikely surroundings of a conference on television in the developing world held at Sussex University in the United Kingdom. "During the course of the conference, most of the big players at the time had been talking about their approaches to the status quo. My paper was the last session on the last day, and I introduced them [the audience] to the possibilities of lightweight equipment," he remembers. "Some delegates were certainly frightened for their jobs, but the light was seen by at least one or two."

"I was a great follower of Joe Flaherty," he adds. "He pioneered the idea of lightweight video cameras to bring immediacy into news reporting, what of course we now accept as ENG. This seemed to me to be such an obvious step. I was into lightweight kit when you needed 17 people to do a simple OB!"

"As a consultant for UNESCO, I was putting systems together. At this time I could source a lot of equipment from British manufacturers," explains Snell. "In order to make this lightweight kit work, I had to bring equipment, like the American TBCs, from abroad. That was how I got interested in building things."

By this time Roderick had gotten together with Joe Wilcox. He had been working for a major electronics company on a huge radio project for the British army, which had gone about as well as most large defense procurements tend to go. Wilcox, therefore, was desperate to get as far away as possible from large companies and unwieldy projects.

"Joe was a chartered engineer with useful things like an account at Radiospares, and I wanted to make things." This is how Snell describes the foundation of one of the industry's major partnerships, which in 30 years has gone from designing and building hardware on a kitchen table to being one of the leading suppliers of moving-image equipment, employing more than 500 people.

Standards Conversion

"We looked at the industry, being strangled then, as now, by a proliferation of standards and saw the need for a standards converter," Snell recalls. " To be precise, we looked at the needs of broadcasters in places like the Caribbean and identified the need for a noise-reducing, standards-converting time-base corrector at an affordable price."

"At a conference in 1979 I started talking about this idea, and the engineers in the audience fell off their chairs laughing," he adds. "At the time, standards conversion meant either hand-crafted systems such as the one the BBC bought for maybe a quarter of a million pounds—20 years ago—or the revolutionary new product from Quantel at maybe half the price. The idea that a box with any standard in and any out should be an affordable product was regarded as impossible."

"UNESCO gave us a small grant to continue study on our proposal. The project still nearly bankrupted us, but somehow we got through," Snell explains. "Our aim was to sell it for £12,000. One day I was talking to industry guru Jim Gambling, and he said, in no uncertain terms, that we were off our heads. If we sold it for three times that price, it would still be one-third the price of the competition for a higher specification."

"So that was how we pitched the price," he continues, "but we needed the money!" We had debts to pay and research to fund. Still, it was affordable. Our original idea was that it would be popular with universities, but broadcasters rushed to buy it."

There were two significant and long-lasting results of this project. First, it took Snell & Wilcox into the science of signal processing and standards conversion, which now, of course, is at the heart of everything the company does. Second, as Snell explains, "We had to learn to make complex digital electronics consistently."

"When I was working in the university, I had a very bright chap working for me who was headhunted by Sony. Four years later, the standards converter project gave me the opportunity to headhunt him back. During his time with Sony, David Lyon had learned a huge amount about production engineering. He came to us with the determination to make Snell & Wilcox at least as good as the Japanese in manufacturing. I am pleased to say that he is still our technical director, still achieving that goal."

And the success story has continued. The first high-definition (HD) systems came along, and the industry around the world turned to Snell & Wilcox for test systems, not to mention up- and downconversion. Then came digital television; the company developed test streams not only for DVB but also for ATSC.

Just as early video recorders suffered terribly from generation loss, so MPEG is fine as a transport stream but difficult to manipulate. Snell & Wilcox therefore developed the Mole, which preserves the original digitization information along with the stream, maintaining quality across multiple generations.

Digital Cinema

Now Snell's gaze is on digital cinema. "I cannot see why it will not be the next big thing," he says. "Look at what has happened to still photography. The technology is so obviously right for digital cinema. And technically it is fun—television is finally breaking free of the small screen."

Enough about the company, however; what about the man? In talking about this year's award that bears his name, John Tucker said, "Roderick is part of a breed of men we feared might have disappeared. He is a gentleman and a scholar. Apart from his considerable technical achievements, he has many human ones. In particular, he personally created the kind of environment at his company where excellence can flourish."

Tucker's analysis is an accurate one. Snell & Wilcox has become a very successful business. Earning over 100 awards in the last 10 years alone—including eight Queen's Awards for technology, four technical Emmys, and two IABM Peter Wayne Awards (the only company to do so twice)—much of this recognition comes from a dedication to innovation. Each year, at least 20 percent of the company's turnover of revenue is put back into research.

That research continues to be guided personally by Roderick Snell, too. His job title is president and research director, and his inquiring mind continues to drive the development program forward. His aim, now very much as it was in the beginning, is to make things that people need.

"Akio Morito used to talk about 'sand to silicon,' meaning that you have to make things," explains Snell. "Wealth creation involves coming up with a good idea and turning it into a product. When a business becomes successful, the temptation is to move from wealth creation to wealth manipulation—sell the company, go public, take the money, dabble in the stock market, whatever."

"I am not interested in that. I am interested in making things. Maybe I have not grown up," he jokes. "But it does mean that we can take the long-term view without being swayed by the short-term needs of the money men." Mole, for instance, was a 7-year project. "We have been working in high definition for more than 13 years, so now we are well poised to supply our skills into the new world of film-resolution electronic signals."

"The convergence of IT [information technology] and broadcasting is another thing that gets my juices going," he continues. "We in the broadcast world have a very great deal to teach IT people about moving images. This is another David and Goliath affair, where the skills of all of us in electronic media will be vital."

Breaking Down Barriers

The citation on Roderick Snell's IBC John Tucker Award, the international honor for excellence, reads: "Presented to Roderick Snell for his lifetime's work in breaking down the barriers due to different standards for television and helping the world's broadcasting community to communicate with itself."

How does this make him feel? Typically combative, he starts by looking to expand the definition. "It is not just about broadcasting. It is about taking our craft skills and experience beyond broadcasting, to IT and the cinema, to bigger areas just as IBC itself is doing."

"I [felt] particularly honored to receive the award the year after Ray Dolby," he adds. "Ray is a great hero of mine. He is a small guy who created world standards—and created wealth—without any of the trappings of big industry."

My Vision of the Future

Broadband continues to play an ever-increasing role in our society, and I operate my current company under the assumption that broadband technologies are our future, as evidenced by current and emerging businesses and technologies. My vision is to enable as much bandwidth and computer processing power as possible—to energize virtual offices, smart homes, wireless devices, biometrics, and any newly discovered applications—so we can grow and thrive in the video streaming ecosystem.

The following summarizes my snapshot of the near future:

- Parents have the ability to monitor their babysitters, gardeners, and children through security and surveillance systems using wireless devices remotely.

- Teleconferencing eliminates trips to the office and remote locations.

- Smart appliances notify homeowners and grocers of essential needs and the time for replenishment.

- When entering homes, flat-screen communication systems activate current video mail messages and prompt video mail callback through a voice-activated address book.

- The entertainment guide uses push technology to provide selections, while one accesses and engages in an eight-way conference call.

- Downloading movies in extended formats and special-edition releases and rereleases becomes a normal way to enhance home entertainment options.

- Recipes for special occasions are accessed through dedicated screens in the kitchen, as well as tutorials on how to prepare gourmet dishes and desserts like a world-class chef.

- Children push the limits using gaming entertainment systems with international teammates.

- Gated communities notify residents that specific people are about to visit their home, via license plate capture readers at the entrance.

- Security systems have monitored face- and fingerprint-recognition devices, which, when necessary, can record and automatically (wirelessly) alert police officers in their digital cruisers.

- Sophisticated keyless entry is enabled by simultaneous face- or fingerprint-recognition units.

The Internet has raised the bar significantly on what people expect from all types of digital content. Our society expects to easily browse, search, download, and share information anytime, anywhere. Until recently, these types of interactions applied primarily to text-based information because traditional video, even in digital form, did not lend itself to these levels of interactivity. Today, digital video has evolved into a new stage of maturity. Comprehensive solutions—for video capture, pre-processing, cleaning, editing, transcoding, indexing, management, and distribution—currently make video streaming as easy to work with as text.

Taking the Next Step

The next generation of video streaming will increase the quality of communications significantly and, more importantly, will enable us to develop and maintain a successful streaming media enterprise. This will be an extraordinary era for all of us.

Glossary

A/B roll   Technique of placing one scene on one videotape (and videotape player, or VTP) and another scene on another and then rolling (playing) both VTPs together, along with the editing videotape recorder (VTR), in order to fade, dissolve, or do a special effect using both scenes at once.

active matrix   A type of liquid crystal that changes quickly, appropriate for liquid-crystal display (LCD) panels that also display video.

analog   A signal that varies continuously, as opposed to a digital signal, which is made up of discrete levels. Also, a device that works with analog signals. Analog circuits suffer noise and distortion.

analog-to-digital (A/D) converter   A circuit that samples an analog signal and expresses the information as digital data.

analog VTR   A videotape recorder that records a continuously varying video signal onto the tape (as opposed to a digital signal).

ANSI   American National Standards Institute, an organization that, among other things, sets the standards for measuring projector brightness.

artifacts   Undesirable elements or defects in a video picture, such as dots crawling along the edge of colored graphics or color rainbows around shirts with stripes or herringbones.

ASCAP   American Society of Composers and Performers; an agency that licenses the use of copyrighted music.

aspect ratio   The shape of a TV screen expressed as height compared to width. Common TV screens have a 4:3 aspect ratio.

asynchronous   Not synchronized. Running independently without external sync circuits holding the device to the same rhythm as the rest of the studio equipment (usually used to describe communications in which data can be transmitted intermittently rather than in a steady stream).

ATM   Asynchronous Transfer Mode; a method of grouping data into packets and switching them along a route to their destination quickly.

ATR Audiotape recorder.

ATSC   Advanced Television Systems Committee; a group formed to study DTV and make recommendations to the Federal Communications Commission.

attenuator   Small electronic device that reduces the strength of an audio signal.

ATV   Advanced Television; a name that replaced high-definition TV (HDTV) as the specifications evolved, eventually being replaced by Digital TV (DTV).

audio   The sound part of a TV broadcast. Sound turned into an electric signal.

audio distribution amplifier or ADA   Electronic device that takes in one audio signal and makes several, each as strong as the original.

audio dub   Feature on video recorders that allows you to record new sound (erasing the old sound) on a tape while leaving the picture untouched.

authoring   Process of organizing the materials for an interactive disk and putting them into computer language.

automatic gain control or AGC   Electronic circuit that automatically adjusts the loudness of a recording.

autoscan or multiscan   A process whereby a multisync monitor or projector can be switched to a selected sweep frequency to match a computer or TV's scan rate; an autoscan or multiscan monitor or projector will sense the frequency and automatically lock onto it.

AV monitor or multimedia monitor   TV monitor with audio and video inputs to display picture and sound.

band   A range of radio frequencies used for a certain types of communications. Also a set of related frequencies. UHF (ultrahigh frequency) is one band at 470 to 890 MHz.

bandwidth   Electromagnetic room for TV channels or computer data on a wire, cable, fiber, or airwave. Also the range of frequencies over which a circuit or electronic device can function properly. National Television Standards Committee (NTSC) bandwidth is 4.2 MHz, meaning that the signals can have frequencies ranging between 0 and 4.2 million vibrations per second.

baud   Bits per second transmitted or received by a modem.

Betacam   Aging popular professional camcorder format using Betamax-like cassettes, recording separate colors at high tape speeds for high quality. Expensive.

Betamax   Introduced by Sony, a nearly extinct, ½-inch consumer videocassette format.

bit   A binary digit, a 0 or 1, representing a no or a yes answer to a question. A bit is the smallest piece of information a computer understands. A byte is composed of 8 consecutive bits.

bitmap   An image stored as pixels mapped across a screen.

BMI   Broadcast Music, Inc.; an agency that licenses the use of copyrighted music.

BMP   A bitmap format for an image file, capable of handling 16 colors, 256 colors, or True Color. BMPs are a subset of the Windows DIB format but do not support image compression.

bps   Bits per second; the speed that data travel through a wire or device.

byte   Eight bits; usually the number of bits necessary to represent an alphanumeric character such as the letter A (which happens to be 01000001).

C   The chrominance or color part of a video signal.

cable modem   A computer modem connected to cable TV coaxial cable, able to transport data at very high speeds (up to 30 Mbps). Also a device that connects between your computer and your cable TV source, able to transmit data quickly to an Internet service provider that is also on the system.

camcorder   A VCR and camera consisting of one unit or two devices joined together.

captioning encoder   Device that changes text data into the codes that go on line 21 of the video signal passing through it, essentially making closed (or open) captioned video.

capture   To digitize a stretch of videotape on a nonlinear editor or to digitize the first and last images of a scene and store the time codes on an analog nonlinear editor.

CAV   Constant angular velocity; the half-hour mode of an analog videodisk and player. Special effects are available.

CCD   Charge-coupled device; a popular type of image-sensing pickup chip in TV cameras; a transistorized light sensor on TV cameras.

CCITT   Comité Consultatif International Téléphonique et Télégraphique; an organization that sets international communications standards. CCITT, now known as the International Telecommunications Union (ITU) has defined many important standards for data communications.

CCU or camera control unit   A box of electronic circuits that can remotely adjust the operation of a camera as well as provide power and send signals to it.

CD-I   Compact disk interactive; a disk (or player) able to play, interactively, up to 74 minutes of limited-motion MPEG-1 compressed audio and video.

CD-R   Recordable CD.

CD-ROM XA   CD-ROM extended architecture; plays music CDs and CD-ROM data on one multisession disk. Disks can be recordable.

CGMS or copy generation management system   Method of making DVDs uncopyable.

chapter   One section of a level 2 videodisk program, similar to a chapter of a book.

character generator   An electronic device with a typewriter keyboard that electronically displays letters, numbers, and symbols on a TV screen.

chroma key   A key effect triggered by the color blue (or some other selected color other than black). Also a video effect where blue (or other selected color) parts of a TV picture are replaced with another picture.

chrominance or chroma   The color part of a video signal.

clip   A digitized audio sample. It could be a sound effect or a whole song or speech. Also a video and/or audio scene or shot, usually of raw footage. Nonlinear editors will digitize the clip so that it may be trimmed and added to the timeline.

ClipLink   Sony DVCAM mechanism for marking in/out-points of raw footage while it is in the camera. Thumbnail images and time-code numbers may then be downloaded quickly to the nonlinear editor, possibly guiding the editor in digitizing only the good shots.

clipping   Phenomenon where a signal is stronger than the circuits can handle, and, thus, they clip off the excess. In audio, this causes distorted sound; in video, it results in a chalky appearance.

closed captions   Signals invisibly encoded in the picture of some TV shows that can be deciphered by a caption decoder and turned into text appearing over the TV image, mostly for the benefit of the hearing impaired.

CLV   Constant linear velocity; the 1-hour mode of an analog videodisk and player. Special effects are not available.

coax or coaxial cable   Stiff, round wire used to carry video, sync, or RF (antenna) signals.

codec   Coder/decoder; a device used to convert video and audio into digits transportable via phone lines and then convert the digits back to audio/video for the recipient. Codecs also may employ digital compression.

color bars   Vertical bars of color used to test cameras and other video equipment.

color corrector   An electronic device that dissects the colors of a video signal and allows them to be individually adjusted (that is, the blues could be changed to aquas without changing anything else).

color difference signals   Component video signals that represent color parts of the picture. R-Y and B-Y are color difference signals.

colorize   Adding color to something electronically.

compact disk (CD)   Small, shiny disk embedded with microscopic pits representing digital data that can be read by a laser and converted into sound.

compand   Compress/expand; the technique of squeezing the dynamic range of a wireless microphone and then expanding that range at the receiver end to restore normal sound.

component video   Color video transmitted with the luminance (Y) on one wire and the color signals on other wires, or each color on its own wire. Examples: R,G,B; Y(R-Y)/(B-Y); Y/I/Q; Y/U/V; and 4:2:2.

composite video   The combination of three color video signals traveling on one wire. NTSC video is composite video. Also a video (picture) signal with the sync (timing) signal combined.

compression   A process for storing digital data in a smaller space than it would normally take. A 2:1 compression would squeeze the data into half its original size.

computer-assisted instruction (CAI)   Lessons presented interactively via computer.

convergence   On a three-tube video projector, focusing and aiming the three colored pictures so that they overlap, producing all colors accurately, without ridges along edges of objects. Also the precise overlapping of a color TV's three primary colored pictures to make one multicolored picture.

corner insert   A special wipe pattern that stops partway across the screen so that a corner of the TV picture is taken up by part of another camera's image.

CPU or computer chip   The heart of a computer; a single-circuit chip with millions of transistors programmed to interpret and carry out commands.

CRT or cathode-ray tube   A vacuum tube with an electron gun at one end and a phosphor screen at the other that glows when struck by electrons from the gun. Some computer screens and most TV picture tubes are CRTs.

cut   To Switch from one picture to another directly, in the blink of an eye.

DAT   Digital audio tape; a cassette with binary data representing stereo audio sound. Also, the machine that converts analog audio to digital and records it, as well as plays it back, converting the digital data to analog audio.

data compression   Storing data in a format that requires less space than usual.

data transfer rates The speed with which data can be transmitted from one device to another. Data rates often are measured in Megabits (millions of bits) or Megabytes (millions of bytes) per second, abbreviated as Mbps and MBps, respectively. Also known as throughput.

dB or decibel A measure of the strength of one electronic signal as compared with another. The higher the decibel number, the greater is the signal strength.

DBX A scheme for reducing audio noise in recordings by encoding and decoding a signal. The effect is more pronounced than with Dolby.

DDR Digital disk recorder; a device that records digital video (or other data) on a disk and plays it back.

deck A short name for a recorder; sometimes the VCR portion of a dockable camcorder; sometimes a standalone VCR.

decode The reprocessing of a signal to extract the desired part. In audio, a signal is encoded on recording; on playback, it is decoded so that it sounds normal, but noise is reduced.

depth of field The span of distance from a lens that appears in focus at one time. A wide depth of field means that far and near objects in the picture both appear sharp.

descrambler An electronic device (usually rented from a pay-TV company) used to convert scrambled TV signals to viewable ones.

desktop video The integration of several video disciplines (that is, titles, graphics, switcher, video editing) into one or several computers. Except for the cameras and microphones that gather the original footage, most of the production process can take place on a desktop computer.

DIB Microsoft Window's Device Independent Bitmap image file format, which is able to handle true color independently of the computer's graphics card. When used in 16 or 256 colors, the images can be compressed, but in true color, they cannot be.

digital   A signal consisting of a series of two discrete levels, on (or 1) and off (or 0), as opposed to signals that vary continuously between high, medium, and low levels. The opposite of digital is analog.

Digital-S   JVC's digital video compression and recording system that uses SVHS tape. It can also play analog SVHS tapes.

digital VTR   A videotape recorder that converts the video signal to 1s and 0s (digits) and records the numbers. On playback, the numbers are converted back to video.

digital zoom   An electronic way of blowing up a picture to make it look zoomed in. Used to any degree, it shows blockiness; that is, parts of the image turn into little squares.

direct broadcast satellite or DBS   A high-powered orbiting satellite that receives signals from earth and beams them back down, blanketing a part of the country so that they are easily tuned in to with a 3-foot dish antenna and a special (usually rented) receiver that feeds up to four channels to your TV set.

display monitor   TV monitor designed to make big, bright, pretty pictures for audience consumption.

dissolve (or lap dissolve)   TV effect in which one picture slowly melts into another. One picture fades to black, while another simultaneously fades up from black.

distortion   Poor-quality sound, usually raspy and loud, often caused by too strong an audio signal.

downlink   A receiver of signals from an orbiting satellite.

dropout   A speck or streak of snow on a TV screen seen when a videotape player hits a fleck of dirt or a bare spot when the tape is playing. Dust or scratches also can cause a dropout to be recorded on a tape.

DSL   Digital Subscriber Line; a digitized telephone line.

DSP or digital signal processing   A TV camera design that employs digital controls (menus and numbers) rather than manually turned knobs in order to set up and store the camera's adjustments.

DSS   Digital satellite system; a satellite that uses digital rather than analog signals.

DTH   Direct to home; another name for DBS.

DTV   Digital television; TV that is broadcast, recorded, and processed digitally, possibly with extended definition such as HDTV.

dub   In audio, to replace an old sound track with a new one, leaving the video unchanged. In video, it sometimes means to duplicate a tape.

duplication house   A company that duplicates videocassettes, usually hundreds at a time.

DV   Digital video format in which images and sound are recorded as digital data onto ¼-inch cassettes with very high quality.

DVD or digital video disk or digital versatile disk   Disk that can hold the data of seven CD-ROMs and play full-motion video and audio with good quality.

DVR   Digital video recorder; a VCR or computer disk recorder that records/plays digits representing audio and video.

dynamic range   A ratio comparing the lowest level of sound audible (above the noise of the machine) with the highest level; the range of loudness a device can handle without distorting.

dynamic tracking   Professional VTR feature that allows a tape to be played at various speeds, including still frame while making a clear picture.

ED Beta   Extended-Definition Betamax. A much-improved version of Betamax, downwardly compatible with it.

edit decision list (EDL)   A refined editing sheet listing each shot to be recorded; the exact time code of edit-in and -out prints for each shot, any effects to be included, their duration, and other details. Often the EDL resides on a computer disk and is the script to drive the editing VCRs during the final edit.

edited master   Same as a master tape but created by the editing process.

editing sheet   A plan showing which shots will be used to create the edited master. Usually time-code numbers and edit-in and edit-out points are included.

edit-in point   The first frame of raw footage video you wish to copy onto the master tape. Also, the point on the master tape where you wish to start copying the footage. Both can be described by time-code numbers.

edit-out point   The last frame of raw footage video you wish to copy onto the master tape. Also, the point on the master tape where you will stop copying the footage.

EFP   Electronic field production; producing TV shows outside the studio. This usually involves studio-quality equipment, techniques, and editing.

electrical-to-optical (E/O) converter   Device that changes electrical signals to light to go over fiber-optic cable.

electronic autofocus   Circuit that looks at a camera's picture to determine if it is sharp and focuses the lens appropriately.

electronic image stabilization (EIS)   Electronic mechanism used in cameras to reduce shakiness in the picture.

electronic viewfinder   A tiny TV monitor mounted on a camera showing the image the way the camera sees it. It also can be used to view tapes played back in the field.

encode   Modification or processing of a signal while it is being recorded, usually to make it less noisy during playback when the signal is decoded. Also to combine component video signals into a composite video signal.

encoder   A device used to compress picture data. You would send video through an encoder to make MPEG-compressed data. Also an electronic device to combine M-S audio signals in such a way as to create stereo.

ENG   Electronic news-gathering; portable video production for the news. Often quick-and-dirty techniques are used with minimal equipment and crew.

equalization   A tone adjustment for audio frequencies, often needed to boost high or low tones coming from a phonograph cartridge, microphone, or audiotape head.

external bus   A bus that connects a computer to peripheral devices. Two examples are the Universal Serial Bus (USB) and IEEE-1394.

fade out   Make a TV picture smoothly grow black.

fader   A slider or handle on a switcher that allows you to fade in or fade out a picture or dissolve from one picture to another.

fade up   Make a TV picture smoothly grow from black to normal.

feedback   A loud screech coming from a loudspeaker when sound enters a microphone, gets amplified, and then comes out the speaker only to be picked up again by the microphone and amplified more.

fiber optics   Glass fibers that are able to transmit light waves long distances and enable signals, coded into the light beam, to carry computer data or TV channels. Also the technique of converting a signal (such as audio or video) to a light beam, which is later converted back to an electric signal.

field   The TV picture created in one-sixtieth of a second by scanning an electron gun over every other line in the picture. In the United States there are 262 odd-numbered lines in a field, followed by 262 more even-numbered lines, making the next field one-sixtieth of a second later. The two fields together make a frame, a complete TV picture.

film chain or telecine   A device to project film into a TV camera.

filter   A small electrical device that can remove a certain frequency (that is, a certain channel) from a signal. Some filters can remove many frequencies, leaving just the desired ones. Audio filters remove certain tones from a sound signal.

fine cut   A final edited master prepared with painstaking care using the best editing equipment available. A fine cut is generally produced in an online editing session.

FireWire or IEEE-P1394   A standard for transmitting compressed video data used by DV format digital videocassette recorders.

FLIC   A large .fli or .flc file holding many image files for sequential playback to create an animation.

FMV or full-motion video   Video that proceeds at 60 fields per second, filling the whole TV screen (as opposed to a reduced size and frame rate).

focal length   The distance between the optical center of a lens and the surface where the image is focused when the lens is focused on infinity. The apparent magnification or angle of view of a lens.

footcandle   A measure of illumination; the level of brightness found 1 foot from a candle; about 10 lux.

format   The way that tapes, cassettes, and video recorders and players are designed so that one machine can play another machine's tapes. Machines of the same format should be able to play each other's tapes.

frame   A complete TV picture lasting one-thirtieth of a second, composed of two fields or 525 scanning lines (in the United States).

frequency   The number of times a signal or sound vibrates each second, usually expressed as cycles per second or hertz (Hz).

FTTC   Fiber to the curb; a cable TV or phone connection that brings wide-bandwidth fiber optics to your home or business.

fuzzy logic   An autofocus technology that increases focusing accuracy by rotating a camera lens by tiny amounts; not noticeable to the eye.

FX   Effects; a special effect such as text keyed over a picture.

gain　A projection screen's reflectivity. The higher the gain number, the brighter is the picture because more light is reflected back toward the projector (but less light is reflected to the sides). Also amplification of a circuit or camera adjustment that controls the strength of the camera's video signal, altering the contrast and brightness of the picture.

genlock　The ability of a camera or other TV device to receive an external video signal and synchronize its own video signal with it so that the two videos can be neatly switched or mixed.

geosynchronous or geostationary satellite　A satellite (usually for domestic communications or TV) whose position is constant relative to a point on the earth. An orbit 22,300 miles above the equator causes the satellite to circle the earth at the same speed at which the earth rotates.

gigahertz (GHz)　One billion hertz (Hz) or one billion cycles per second. Domestic satellites transmit at frequencies above 3.7 GHz.

graphic equalizer　Electronic audio device that cuts or boosts particular sound frequencies passing through it.

graphics accelerator card　Graphics card that performs high-speed rendering and video manipulations, relieving your slower standard graphics card of these duties.

grayscale　A standard of 10 steps from black to white used to measure contrast ratios. To be visible on TV, objects must be at least 1 grayscale step different in brightness from their backgrounds.

HDSL　High-Speed Digital Subscriber Line; a DSL with 750-kbps two-way service over two twisted pair wires.

HDTV (high-definition television)　A proposed method of displaying sharper, wider TV pictures than the present NTSC system. Pictures would be shaped into a 16:9 aspect ratio composed of 1125 scanning lines, each line having 1920 pixels.

heterodyne　Method of time-base correction used with common and color-under VCRs, yielding medium-resolution pictures. Also, the type of VCR that uses the color-under recording method.

high-band VTR   A video recorder capable of recording full-fidelity color signals (as opposed to color-under signals).

IEEE-1394   A new, very fast external bus standard that supports data transfer rates of up to 400 Mbps (400 million bits per second). Products supporting the 1394 standard go under different names, depending on the company. Apple, which originally developed the technology, uses the trademarked name FireWire. Other companies use other names, such as i.link and Lynx, to describe their 1394 products.

I encoder   An electronic circuit in a camera that mixes colors into a single color video signal. Responsible for certain colors.

image enhancer   An electronic device that makes a TV picture crisper (making it look sharper, although it really is not) by exaggerating the boundaries of parts of the image.

image intensifier   An electronic device that brightens the image fed to a TV camera—used in military and surveillance applications.

in-camera editing   Recording scenes chronologically, one after another, in the camcorder with the intention that all the shots will be used; a final tape emerges from the camcorder.

in-line amplifier   An amplifier inserted between two wires to boost the signal through them, getting its operating power through the same wires from a distant power supply.

input selector   A switch that determines which input (which source) a VCR will listen to.

insert edit   A feature that allows a VTR to record a new segment in the middle of a program, erasing what it is replacing. Also the recording of a new video segment amid old, prerecorded video; unlike an assemble edit, which places each new segment at the tail of the last segment.

instant video confidence   A feature on some VTRs that allows them to play back the picture hundredths of a second after it is recorded, while the VTR is still recording it. Handy for ensuring that the video heads are not clogged.

intelsat   An international satellite; one serving several countries.

interactive cable   Cable TV that not only sends shows and/or computer data to your home but also receives signals from you, such as fire/burglar alarm signals, orders to purchase goods, and computer signals (that is, to the Internet).

intercutting   Editing together several separate events or interviews to tell one story, make one statement, or answer one question using pieces from each.

interference   Unwanted signals that leak into your wires or devices and compete with your desired picture and sound, often causing grain, snow, or diagonal or wavy lines on a TV picture.

interframe compression   Digital reduction process that compresses data within a series of frames as well as within each frame. MPEG is an example.

interlace scan   A method of making a TV picture by drawing the odd numbered lines on the screen with one sweep and then filling in between them with the next sweep of even-numbered lines. The process is repeated approximately every $\frac{1}{30}$ second.

interpolator or universal format converter   A device to change one kind of DTV format into another.

intraframe compression   Using data-reducing compression within a single picture or within each picture individually in a series. JPEG and MJPEG are examples.

IRE   Institute of Radio Engineers; a measure of video level or whiteness that is marked off in units of 10 on waveform monitors. A 20 IRE level represents a dark part of a TV picture, and 80 IRE represents a light part.

ISDN   Integrated Services Digital Network; a souped-up telephone line that handles digital signals.

isochronous   Refers to processes in which data must be delivered within certain time constraints. Can be contrasted with asynchronous, which refers to processes in which data streams can be broken at random intervals, and synchronous processes, in which data streams can be delivered only at specific intervals. Isochronous service is not as rigid as synchronous service but not as lenient as asynchronous service.

ITFS   Instructional Television Fixed Service; a method of broadcasting TV programs throughout school systems via low-power, high-frequency transmitters.

ITU   International Telecommunications Union; a body that sets standards for videoconferencing.

jog   To move a videotape forward or back a very short distance (one or two frames) in search of the perfect place to edit.

jump cut   An edit from one scene to a very similar scene, causing the picture to jump from one position to another. Such edits should be hidden by video inserts of related scenes (cutaways).

juxtaposition   Editing together opposites, such as opposing views or conflicting responses to a question.

key (or luminance key)   Special effect in which the dark parts of one camera's picture are replaced with parts from another camera's picture.

kilohertz   One thousand cycles (vibrations) per second, represented by 1 kHz, which is near the sound frequency of speech.

LANC   Local Application Network Control; a Sony-developed system for controlling VCRs (mostly 8 mm, Hi8 camcorders) over a two-way communications link.

LCD   Liquid-crystal display.

leader   Unrecorded space (from 10 seconds to 3 minutes) at the beginning of a tape, often used to protect the actual program from threading damage. Also, unrecordable plastic tape attached to the beginnings of cassette rolls.

LED   Light-emitting diode; a tiny lamp that can blink very quickly, uses little power, and lasts a long time. Often used as an indicator on equipment.

lighting ratio   A comparison between the brightest part of a subject and the darkest. If the brightest white in a performer's shirt measured 60 fc (footcandles) and his or her black hair measured 2 fc, then the lighting ratio would be 60/2 = 30.

light valve projector or liquid-crystal light valve (LCLV) projector   Expensive, professional projector that creates bright images by bouncing light off a reflective surface inside. The reflective surface changes its reflectivity based on the video or computer images presented to it.

limiter   Electronic audio device that automatically reduces the volume of loud audio signals but does not change the normal or weak signals.

line   An external auxiliary input often used for a video signal. Can also be the final video or audio output signal from a device.

line or program monitor   TV monitor that shows the final signal being broadcast or sent to the VTRs.

LNA   A Low-noise amplifier used to boost a dish antenna's signal. Satellite signals are so weak that they have to be amplified (multiplied) 100,000 times. Special circuits with premium-grade transistors are needed to allow the signal to be amplified so much without adding appreciable visual noise to the signal.

lossy   A compression method that discards data and degrades the image quality. High degrees of compression are possible.

low-light-level camera   TV camera designed to see with very little light—used in military and surveillance applications.

LPTV   Low-power television; the technique of broadcasting local programming through a very low-power, inexpensive VHF TV transmitter. A limited signal range keeps LPTV stations from interfering with distant TV stations using the same channel frequency.

LTC or linear time code   Time code recorded in a linear stripe along a tape, perhaps on a longitudinal audio track.

lumen   A measurement of a source's light brightness. Lumens per square foot equals footcandles.

luminance   The black-and-white (brightness only) part of a video signal.

lux   A measure of illumination; the amount of light needed to make a 1-V video signal. Also a measure of the brightness of an object in a scene. Cameras need a certain degree of scene brightness to register a picture. Ten lux equals about 1 footcandle, another measure of brightness.

LV   Laservision; a videodisk read by a laser, the light of which reflects off microscopic pits in the disk. Not the same as CED videodisks, which use a groove.

Macrovision   A popular anticopy signal recorded on a videotape to make it playable but not copyable.

marker   A pointer on a timeline to show what part of it is playing. As the show plays, the marker moves. It can be positioned quickly to play a short segment of a show, perhaps to preview a simple transition.

master disk   A specially made original videodisk from which distribution copies are reproduced.

master tape   The original copy of the finished version of a tape. This could be original footage of a live show or a program edited together from other tapes. The master is the best-quality copy of this program in existence.

match frame edit   An edit in which a scene is edited onto itself so exactly that there is no apparent interruption in the scene.

megahertz   One million cycles (vibrations) per second, represented by 1 MHz, which is near the frequency of video signals.

microwave   An extremely high band of radio/TV frequencies used with satellites to relay TV signals.

MIDI or .mdi   Musical Instrument Digital Interface; a standardized way of sending digital instructions between audio devices and musical instruments, telling them, for instance, what notes to play.

modem   Modulator-demodulator; a device that turns digital data into tones that can travel over phone wires, as well as convert tones back to digits to be used by a computer.

modulator   An RF generator; combines audio and video into a channel number.

moire   A video artifact seen in NTSC pictures along the edges of brightly colored objects, text, and graphics. Moire looks like crawling dots or sawteeth.

monitor   A TV set that has no tuner and usually has no speaker (as opposed to a TV receiver, which has both). Such a TV displays video signals but not RF signals. Also, any device used to observe or hear the quality of a signal (that is, an audio monitor).

monochrome   Black and white (as opposed to color).

morph   2-D or 3-D graphic effect that gradually stretches one image into another, while simultaneously dissolving from one image to the other. Thus, the object changes shape while also changing color and surface character.

mosaic   A digital effect in which an image (or part of it) is broken into tiny tiles or colored squares.

motherboard   The main circuitry of the computer holding the CPU; the main brain of the computer, plus slots for memory and additional boards, such as a graphics board.

motion JPEG or MJPEG   JPEG compression performed on each video frame in real time (30 frames per second). Motion JPEG is used in nonlinear editors.

movieola   Device for viewing and comparing several reels of film at a time, while selecting segments to splice into an edited master film.

MPEG   Motion Picture Experts Group.

MTF or modulation transfer function   The ability of a lens to reproduce contrast, especially at high focal lengths.

MTS Multichannel television sound; a technique of broadcasting stereo audio on TV.

multimedia Audio, video, text, graphics, and other information delivered by computer.

multiplexer Mirror device that selects one (of several) projector's image and shines it at the TV camera. Also a mirrored device that selects one of several projectors and shines its image into a TV camera for transferring film to video.

multipoint videoconference A videoconference between three or more locations or individuals.

multiscan (or multisync) monitor A computer monitor capable of working with different horizontal and vertical scan rates to create the image.

network A group of computers communicating together via wire or optical fiber, sharing data, perhaps collectively rendering an image. Also a group of TV broadcasters or cable TV companies wired together to share signals with each other.

NLE Nonlinear editor or editing; assembling video sequences that are randomly accessible, typically digitized onto a hard drive. The process is much like word processing in that items can be moved, deleted, copied, or changed electronically before being printed or copied to videotape. Also a computerized video editor that permits scenes to be selected and rearranged on the computer's screen before being assembled (by the NLE) on the master tape.

noise Unwanted interference that creeps into a signal. Audio noise could be a hum or hiss. Video noise could be snow, graininess, or streaks in the picture.

noise bars Bands of snowy hash across a TV screen usually evident in still and scan modes and when mistracking occurs.

noise-reduction system Electronic device that attempts to reduce electronic noise when something gets recorded and/or played back.

noise temperature   Rating in degrees Kelvin for how quiet (does not make spurious signals) a satellite signal amplifier is; the lower the temperature, the better.

noncomposite video   A video (picture) signal without sync combined in it.

nonlossy   A compression scheme that reduces redundant data that will never be missed, thus retaining full picture quality while reducing the file size by a moderate amount.

NTSC   National Television Standards Committee; a U.S. organization that developed the NTSC video standards, which ensure that all TV signals in the United States are compatible.

NTSC video   A National Television Standards Committee method used in the United States for electronically creating a color TV signal. The color and brightness aspects of the image travel together on the same wire.

offline editing   Making a practice edit using inexpensive video equipment. The result is a lower-quality draft copy used for decision making and to create a list of edits to be performed later online.

online editing   Editing a videotape with the highest-quality VTRs and editor controllers. This process results in a final edited master but costs more than offline editing.

optical disk recorder   A device that records analog video onto a plastic disk, such as a laser videodisk.

optical-to-electrical (O/E) converter   A device that changes light from a fiber to electrical signals.

outtake   A shot that for some reason (for example, a flubbed line) you do not plan to use in the final production.

overdub   Recording sound on one audio track and then recording a related sound on another track.

overmodulating   Using too much video signal when making an RF signal, which results in buzzing from the TV speaker when white lettering appears on the screen.

overscanned   A TV picture blown up too big on the screen, causing the edges of the picture to be cut off and hidden from view.

PAL   Phase Alternate Line; a European video standard incompatible with the U.S. NTSC system.

palmcorder   A tiny camcorder that fits in the palm of your hand.

passive matrix   An inexpensive liquid crystal used in LCD panels that show static pictures and data.

patch bay   Several rows of sockets connected to the inputs and outputs of various devices. Plugging a patch cable into a pair of sockets connects them so that the signal can travel from one device to the other.

pay-per-view   Cable or broadcast television for which you pay to see each show, usually by activating a descrambler that makes the programs visible on your TV. Pay-per-view usually consists of movies and sports without commercials.

PCI bus   Peripheral Component Interchange bus that can pipe data between computer components at 132 MBps.

peak-level indicator   A tiny light often built into mixers and audio recorders that blinks when the sound volume is too loud.

pedestal   An electronic control on a camera that adjusts the brightness of the picture. Proper adjustment yields blacks that are the right darkness.

pixels   Picture elements; tiny dots that make up the picture. In a camera, pixels represent the tiny light-sensitive transistors that store the image.

playlist   The list of clips to be played in order on a timeline.

posterization   A visual effect in which a picture's varied brightness levels are reduced down to just one or two, giving it a flat poster-like or cartoon-like look.

postproduction house   A video service company that edits tapes, perhaps adding video and audio effects.

potentiometer   Also called a pot, it is a volume control on a mixer or other audio device.

POTS   Plain old telephone service; the analog telephone line that goes to most homes.

premaster   The videotape sent to the mastering facility and transformed into videodisks. Also, the act of making such a tape.

preread or read-before-write   A DVR's ability to play what is on a tape at the same time that it is recording new material on the tape a moment later.

preroll   Begin playing a tape so that it is up to speed and its signals are stable before the VCR switches to record.

primary colors   Three colors that can be combined together to create all the other colors. TVs in the United States use red, green, and blue as primary colors.

private network   A connection between sites that allows a group of subscribers to videoconference with each other but no one else. The system is leased from the phone or cable TV company on a monthly basis.

progressive scan   A method of making a computer picture by drawing all the scan lines sequentially from top to bottom.

protocol   A standard method of communication that allows one machine to send/receive data or commands to/from another.

quantization   The process of measuring an analog signal and assigning numerical levels to it.

QuickTime movie   A file format that takes a series of individual files (pictures), combines them into one file, and can play them in sequence, creating animation or motion.

RAID   Redundant array of inexpensive drives; a method of providing nonlinear editors with many Gigabytes of instantly accessible data storage by teaming together a group of slower, smaller, cheaper hard drives.

raw footage   Recordings made directly from the camera, intended to be edited into a final program later.

repeater   A receiver/transmitter that picks up a radio signal (or TV or microwave signal) and retransmits it. Repeaters usually are placed up high where their signals can reach farther than portable transmitters.

replicate   To duplicate a videodisk, CD, or CD-ROM.

resolution   Picture sharpness, measured in lines. The greater the number of lines, the sharper is the picture.

retroloop   A digital disk recorder's ability to continuously record audio and video on a disk and make room for the data by simultaneously erasing what was recorded some time earlier.

RF or radiofrequency   The kind of signal that is broadcast through the air and comes from a TV antenna. RF is a combination of audio and video signals coded as a channel number.

RGB   Red, green, blue; an RGB monitor displays a picture from three video signals, one for the red parts of the picture, one for green, and one for blue. Also, the name given to the kind of video signals that represent component colors rather than the combined colors.

RGB-to-video encoder   A device that changes RGB video signals to composite video signals. This is a part of the scan converter, and the term is sometimes used interchangeably with scan converter.

rippling edit   A nonlinear edit that pushes the following scenes later on the timeline, leaving them intact and lengthening the show. If a scene is removed, the following scenes move forward on the timeline, closing the hole.

rolling edit   An edit that adds or subtracts material to/from the timeline but does not push ahead the following scenes or close them up. Such an edit replaces other material or leaves a blank spot where material used to be.

rotoscope   A technique of carefully positioning a graphic object into a real picture so that an actor may appear to hold or interact with it.

rough cut   An approximation of what the edited master will took like. A rough cut is generally performed on offline editing equipment.

rule of thirds   A rule stating that the center of attention should not be dead center on the screen but one-third of the way down from the top, up from the bottom, or in from the edge of the screen.

sampling frequency   The number of measurements made per period of time (that is, per second). For digital video, 13.5 million samples per second is common (also expressed as 13.5 MHz).

SAP or supplementary audio program   A technique for broadcasting a third, additional sound track along with stereo TV signals.

satellite receiver   The tuner part of a satellite downlink; the part that resides in your house and takes commands from your remote control.

saturation   The purity and vividness of a color.

scan converter   An electronic device that changes the signals that a computer sends to its monitor into video signals that can be displayed on a TV monitor or recorded on a VCR.

scramble   To code the picture and sound signals so that they cannot be viewed without a descrambler (decoder) box.

SCSI   Small Computer Systems Interface; a hard disk drive controller. Various flavors include SCSI-2, SCSI-wide, and SCSI-Ultrawide for faster speeds.

SDTV   Standard definition television; digitally broadcast TV signals with about the same sharpness and screen shape as today's NTSC television.

SECAM   Sequential Color And Memory; a video standard used in much of Asia, incompatible with the U.S. NTSC system.

segue   Pronounced "SEG-way"; a smooth change from one sound, place, or subject to another.

serial   A way of sending computer data over a single wire, one command after another. Modems and mice are serial devices, as are RS-422 and RS 232 ports on a computer.

session   An event on a CD. A single session might be a series of songs on a CD or a file on a CD-ROM. CD players are capable of playing single sessions only, and CDs have a single session on them.

shot sheet   An index of all shots recorded on a tape (including time-code numbers for each shot plus a commentary on the quality of each take) or a brief list of the kinds of shots a camera operator will need to take during a show.

shutter bar   Occurs when a TV camera records a movie from a projector. A soft dark band runs through the TV picture when the projector does not synchronize its shutter with the TV camera's picture-making frequency.

signal-to-noise ratio (S/N ratio)   A number describing how much desired signal there is compared with undesirable background noise. The higher the S/N ratio, the cleaner is the signal.

slate   A visible and/or audible cue recorded at the beginning (or end) of a take, identifying the take number for later reference.

slave   In the tape-copying process, the videocassette recorder that actually does the recording.

slide chain   A slide projector connected to a TV camera for converting slides to video.

SMPTE time code   A time code used to address every frame on a tape with a unique number to aid in logging and editing. The time-code format is standardized in the United States by the Society of Motion Picture and Television Engineers.

soft wipe   A split-screen or wipe effect with a soft border where the two pictures join.

sound card   A circuit installed in a computer to change audio signals into data the computer can handle, and vice versa.

special effects generator (SEG)   An electronic video device that creates effects such as wipes, fades, keys, and so on.

speed   A measure of how much light a lens can transmit. A faster lens has a lower *f*-stop number.

split screen   A wipe that stops partway across the picture, revealing a section of the original picture and a section of the new picture.

standards converter   A device that changes one standard of video signal (say, NTSC) into another (say, PAL), or vice versa, bridging the gap of incompatibility between standards.

steadicam   An elaborate framework of levers and springs used to hold a camera steady while the camera operator walks or climbs. A harness straps to the camera operator, while the camera attaches to the other end of a movable arm.

storyboard   A script done in pictures showing the sequence of shots that will make a show.

streams   A technique for transferring data so that they can be processed as a steady and continuous stream.

stripe   To record time code on a tape.

studio production switcher   A large active switcher/SEG that receives all the video sources (inputs from cameras and so on) and is used to select the pictures or effects to be shown.

super VHS (S-VHS)   An improved VHS format that uses special tape and yields 400 lines of resolution picture sharpness (also Hi8, ED Beta 3/4U-SP, or any improvement to a VCR format—sometimes called high band).

SuperBeta   A slightly improved, totally compatible version of Betamax.

superimposer   A circuit that lays computer text over videodisk scenes so that both can be viewed together on the same TV monitor.

sweetening   The manipulation of recorded sound to give it echo, filter out a noise, boost a particular frequency, or mix it with other sounds.

swish pan   A rapid sideways movement of a camera as it goes from one scene to another, causing the image to streak.

switched digital video or SDV   A technology for sending motion video through cable TV or phone lines in real time on request. VOD and VDT would use SDV.

switcher   A push-button device that selects one or another camera's picture to be viewed or recorded.

synchronous   Occurring at regular intervals. Most communication between computers and devices is asynchronous—it can occur at any time and at irregular intervals. Communication within a computer, however, usually is synchronous and is governed by the microprocessor clock.

telecine   A movie projector/TV camera combination designed for converting movie images to video. Also called a film chain.

teleprompter   A device that sits near the camera lens and allows the performer to read the text while his or her eyes appear to be looking at the camera lens (the viewer).

test (or production) monitor   A TV monitor designed to yield sharp, truthful images that accurately show flaws in a TV signal or picture.

test pattern   A chart used for measuring a camera or other video device's performance, such as resolution.

time-base corrector   An electronic device to remove jitter and other timing abnormalities from a video signal, usually the signal from a VCP.

time code   A way of measuring where (how far from the beginning of a tape) scenes are located. Usually a magnetic pulse recorded on the tape that can be converted into a listing of hours, minutes, seconds, and frames.

time lapse   A method of compressing time by taking a picture every few seconds (or minutes). Time-lapse VCRs can record many hours on the tape.

timeline   A graphic ruler stretching across a computer screen on which clips are placed during editing, indicating which scenes go where, what graphics and titles appear, what audio will be heard, and what transitions occur between scenes.

track A pathway along a tape set aside for a discrete (usually audio) signal. Several tracks allow you to indicate A/B rolls and effects.

tracking Adjustment on VTRs so that they play the video tracks from the tape following exactly the path that the recorder took. Good tracking results in a clear, stable picture.

transcoder An electronic device used to convert video signals.

transitions Ways of changing from one scene, title, or graphic to another.

TV standard A set of technical specifications describing how a TV picture is made. In the United States, the Federal Communications Commission (FCC) ordained the NTSC (National Television Standards Committee) standard. In Europe, a different, incompatible standard called Phase Alternate Line (PAL) is used. In Asia the standard is SECAM (Sequential Color and Memory).

UHF Ultrahigh frequency; TV channels 14 to 69.

uniplexer Device to couple a film projector to a TV camera, useful for making video copies of movies and so on.

vertical wipe A wipe in which a horizontal boundary line sweeps vertically through the screen, changing the picture as it goes.

VESA Video Electronics Standards Association; a consortium of video adapter and monitor manufacturers whose goal is to standardize video protocols, such as SuperVGA (SVGA).

VGA Video Graphics Array; a 1987 standard for graphics cards in IBM-compatible PCs determining sweep frequencies, colors, resolution, and wire connections in monitor plugs.

VHF Very high frequency; TV channels 2 to 13.

VHS Video home system (in videocassette format).

video Recording, manipulating, and displaying moving images, especially in a format that can be presented on a television or a computer monitor.

video adapter A board that plugs into a PC to give it display capabilities.

video capture card   A circuit installed in a computer to change video signals into data the computer can handle, and vice versa.

videocassette player or VCP   A machine that can play a videocassette but cannot record one.

videocassette recorder or VCR   A videotape recorder that uses cassettes rather than open reels of tape.

video distribution amplifier or VDA   An electronic device that splits one video signal into several (often four) and boosts each to make them as strong as the original signal.

video encoder   A device that makes a composite color video signal from component video signals.

video insert   Replacing a segment of old video with new video in the midst of prerecorded tape. Audio is not affected.

video on demand or VOD   Wide-bandwidth cable or phone network permitting users to download video (for example, a movie), playing it in real time on their TVs.

videotape player or VTP   A machine that can play a videotape but cannot record one.

videotape recorder or VTR   A machine that can record picture and sound on a tape. Nearly all also can play back a tape. Although a videocassette recorder is also a videotape recorder, a VTR usually implies that reel-to-reel tape is used rather than cassette.

VISCA   Sony Video System Control Architecture; a two-way protocol from Sony that permits computers, through their RS-232 or RS-422 ports, to communicate with VCRs and other control-M or LANC-enabled devices.

VITC or vertical interval time code   Time-code data recorded as part of the video signal in the sync pulse between pictures.

voiceover   Narration added to and louder than background sounds or music.

VU   Volume unit; a measure of loudness. A VU meter measures the strength of an audio signal. A 0 VU setting is considered optimal sound volume.

WAVE or .wav　A computer file of digitized sound.

waveform　A graphic representation of a video signal showing signal levels (whites and blacks), color, and timing (sync).

white balance　The mix of primary colors that results in pure white light. On color cameras, the controls that strengthen the blue or red colors so that none overpowers the other, allowing white objects to appear pure white, not tinted. Pressing one button and holding a white card in front of the camera will automatically adjust the camera's circuits to make pure white.

wild sound　A background sound without narration or performing going on. During editing, it can be mixed with the performer's sounds if he or she has to redo lines in a quiet studio.

window dub　A copy of a time-coded videotape with one change: Time-code numbers are visible on the TV screen, making it possible to log edit decisions while playing the tape on common VCRs not equipped with time-code readers.

wipe　Special effect that starts with one TV picture on the screen; then a boundary line moves across the screen (vertically, diagonally, or whatever), and where it passes, the first picture changes into a second picture.

working master　A carefully made copy of a master tape, which is in turn copied. The working master protects the master from damage and wear in the copying process because it is the working master that gets played many times while the master is archived.

Y　The luminance or black-and-white part of a video signal.

Y/C　A video signal separated into two parts: brightness (Y) and color (C). Such signals yield sharper, cleaner color than composite video signals (also another name for S connector).

zoom lens　A lens that can zoom in or zoom out to give a closer-looking picture or a wider angle of view.

What's on the CD-ROM

This appendix provides you with information on the contents of the CD that accompanies this book. For the latest and greatest information, please refer to the ReadMe file located at the root of the CD. Here is what you will find:

- System Requirements
- Using the CD with Windows, Linux, and Macintosh
- What's on the CD
- Troubleshooting

System Requirements

Make sure that your computer meets the minimum system requirements listed in this section. If your computer doesn't match up to most of these requirements, you may have a problem using the contents of the CD.

For Windows 9x, Windows 2000, Windows NT4 (with SP 4 or later), Windows Me, or Windows XP:

- A PC with a Pentium processor running at 400 Mhz or faster
- At least 128 MB of total RAM installed on your computer; for best performance, we recommend at least 256 MB

- Ethernet network interface card (NIC) or modem with a speed of at least 56,600 bps

- Hard drive available space of at least 5 MB

- A CD-ROM drive

For Linux:

- A PC with a Pentium processor running at 400 Mhz or faster

- At least 128 MB of total RAM installed on your computer; for best performance, we recommend at least 256 MB

- Ethernet network interface card (NIC) or modem with a speed of at least 28,800 bps

- Hard drive available space of at least 5 MB

- A CD-ROM drive

For Macintosh:

- A Mac computer with a 68040 or faster processor running OS 7.6 or later

- At least 128 MB of total RAM installed on your computer; for best performance, we recommend at least 256 MB

- Ethernet network interface card (NIC) or modem with a speed of at least 28,800 bps

- Hard drive available space of at least 5 MB

- A CD-ROM drive

Using the CD with Windows

To install the items from the CD to your hard drive, follow these steps:

1. Insert the CD into your computer's CD-ROM drive.

2. A window will appear with the following options: Install, Explore, Links, and Exit.

   - **Install:** Gives you the option to install the supplied software on the CD-ROM.

   - **Explore:** Allows you to view the contents of the CD-ROM in its directory structure.

- **Links:** Opens a hyperlinked page of Web sites.

- **Exit:** Closes the autorun window.

If you do not have autorun enabled or if the autorun window does not appear, follow the steps below to access the CD.

1. Click Start → Run.

2. In the dialog box that appears, type *d:***setup.exe**, where *d* is the letter of your CD-ROM drive. This will bring up the autorun window described above.

3. Choose the Install, Explore, Links, or Exit option from the menu. (See Step 2 in the preceding list for a description of these options.)

Using the CD with Linux

To install the items from the CD to your hard drive, follow these steps:

1. Log in as root.

2. Insert the CD into your computer's CD-ROM drive.

3. If your computer has Auto-Mount enabled, wait for the CD to mount. Otherwise, follow these steps:

   a. Command line instructions:

      At the command prompt type:

      ```
      mount /dev/cdrom /mnt/cdrom
      ```

      (This will mount the "cdrom" device to the mnt/cdrom directory. If your device has a different name, then exchange "cdrom" with that device name—for instance, "cdrom1")

   b. *Graphical:* Right-click on the CD-ROM icon on the desktop and choose "Mount CD-ROM" from the selections. This will mount your CD-ROM

4. Browse the CD and follow the individual installation instructions for the products listed below.

5. To remove the CD from your CD-ROM drive, follow these steps:

   a. Command line instructions:

      At the command prompt type:

      ```
      umount /mnt/cdrom
      ```

b. *Graphical:* Right click on the CD-ROM icon on the desktop and choose "UMount CD-ROM" from the selections. This will mount your CD-ROM.

Using the CD with the Mac OS

To install the items from the CD to your hard drive, follow these steps:

1. Insert the CD into your CD-ROM drive.
2. Double-click the icon for the CD after it appears on the desktop.
3. Most programs come with installers; for those, simply open the program's folder on the CD and double-click the Install or Installer icon. *Note:* To install some programs, just drag the program's folder from the CD window and drop it on your hard drive icon.

What's on the CD

The following sections provide a summary of the software and other materials you'll find on the CD.

Applications

The following sections describe the applications that are on the CD. Note that trial, demo, or evaluation versions are usually limited either by time or functionality. Note that if you alter your computer's date, these programs may "time out" and will no longer be functional.

Pathfinder (MaxVU, Inc.)

Pathfinder allows you to easily convert home videos to streaming files that can be posted to (and accessed from) the Internet. Specifically, Pathfinder converts AVI files to Microsoft's Windows Media formatted files. Although MaxVU promises that future versions of the software will be able to output to RealMedia and QuickTime files, these file formats are not yet supported in Pathfinder. Pathfinder is easy to use even if you're not an engineer, and allows remote transcoding and enables you to secure your content.

Rapid Response (MaxVU, Inc.)

RapidResponse enables you to convert streaming media files to a format that's suitable for broadcasting over television networks. Files can even be e-mailed or downloaded and then used in television broadcasts.

Screen Magic (MaxVU, Inc.)

Screen Magic is an add-in to Pathfinder that enhances the capabilities of distance learning services. With Screen Magic you can include screen captures and white board content in streaming media files that can then be posted to the Internet.

cleaner (Discreet Corp.)

cleaner is a professional video encoding program. Encoding is necessary when transferring files to streaming video format to keep file size to a minimum. cleaner works with other software, such as Adobe's Premiere and Apple's Final Cut Pro. cleaner allows for easy, fast encoding of streaming media and includes powerful features such as filters that let you tweak your video to ensure quality.

Adobe Premier (Adobe Systems, Inc.)

Premier is Adobe's software for digital video editing. Premier offers a nice feature set, including multi-layer editing capabilities, DVD authoring tools, MPEG-2 exporting, and extensive audio functionality.

Acrobat Reader (Adobe Systems, Inc.)

Acrobat Reader, which is the free viewer for PDF files, has a presence on the overwhelming majority of computers that connect to the Internet these days. The PDF format ensures that those who view your file will see it exactly as you intend them to see it.

Troubleshooting

If you have difficulty installing or using any of the materials on the companion CD, try the following solutions:

- **Turn off any anti-virus software that you may have running.** Installers sometimes mimic virus activity and can make your computer incorrectly believe that a virus is infecting it. (Be sure to turn the anti-virus software back on later.)

- **Close all running programs.** The more programs you're running, the less memory is available to other programs. Installers also typically update files and programs; if you keep other programs running, installation may not work properly.

- **Reference the ReadMe:** Please refer to the ReadMe file located at the root of the CD-ROM for the latest product information at the time of publication.

If you still have trouble with the CD, please call the Wiley Customer Care phone number: (800) 762-2974. Outside the United States, call 1 (317) 572-3994. You can also contact Wiley Customer Service by e-mail at techsupdum@wiley.com. Wiley will provide technical support only for installation and other general quality control items; for technical support on the applications themselves, consult the program's vendor or author.

Wiley Publishing, Inc.
End-User License Agreement

READ THIS. You should carefully read these terms and conditions before opening the software packet(s) included with this book "Book". This is a license agreement "Agreement" between you and Wiley Publishing, Inc."WPI". By opening the accompanying software packet(s), you acknowledge that you have read and accept the following terms and conditions. If you do not agree and do not want to be bound by such terms and conditions, promptly return the Book and the unopened software packet(s) to the place you obtained them for a full refund.

1. **License Grant.** WPI grants to you (either an individual or entity) a nonexclusive license to use one copy of the enclosed software program(s) (collectively, the "Software" solely for your own personal or business purposes on a single computer (whether a standard computer or a workstation component of a multi-user network). The Software is in use on a computer when it is loaded into temporary memory (RAM) or installed into permanent memory (hard disk, CD-ROM, or other storage device). WPI reserves all rights not expressly granted herein.

2. **Ownership.** WPI is the owner of all right, title, and interest, including copyright, in and to the compilation of the Software recorded on the disk(s) or CD-ROM "Software Media". Copyright to the individual programs recorded on the Software Media is owned by the author or other authorized copyright owner of each program. Ownership of the Software and all proprietary rights relating thereto remain with WPI and its licensers.

3. **Restrictions On Use and Transfer.**

   (a) You may only (i) make one copy of the Software for backup or archival purposes, or (ii) transfer the Software to a single hard disk, provided that you keep the original for backup or archival purposes. You may not (i) rent or lease the Software, (ii) copy or reproduce the Software through a LAN or other network system or through any computer subscriber system or bulletin- board system, or (iii) modify, adapt, or create derivative works based on the Software.

   (b) You may not reverse engineer, decompile, or disassemble the Software. You may transfer the Software and user documentation on a permanent basis, provided that the transferee agrees to accept the terms and conditions of this Agreement and you retain no copies. If the Software is an update or has been updated, any transfer must include the most recent update and all prior versions.

4. **Restrictions on Use of Individual Programs.** You must follow the individual requirements and restrictions detailed for each individual program in the About the CD-ROM appendix of this Book. These limitations are also contained in the individual license agreements recorded on the Software Media. These limitations may include a requirement that after using the program for a specified period of time, the user must pay a registration fee or discontinue use. By opening the Software packet(s), you will be agreeing to abide by the licenses and restrictions for these individual programs that are detailed in the About the CD-ROM appendix and on the Software Media. None of the material on this Software Media or listed in this Book may ever be redistributed, in original or modified form, for commercial purposes.

5. **Limited Warranty.**

   (a) WPI warrants that the Software and Software Media are free from defects in materials and workmanship under normal use for a period of sixty (60) days from the date of purchase of this Book. If WPI receives notification within the warranty period of defects in materials or workmanship, WPI will replace the defective Software Media.

(b) WPI AND THE AUTHOR OF THE BOOK DISCLAIM ALL OTHER WARRANTIES, EXPRESS OR IMPLIED, INCLUDING WITHOUT LIMITATION IMPLIED WARRANTIES OF MERCHANTABILITY AND FITNESS FOR A PARTICULAR PURPOSE, WITH RESPECT TO THE SOFTWARE, THE PROGRAMS, THE SOURCE CODE CONTAINED THEREIN, AND/OR THE TECHNIQUES DESCRIBED IN THIS BOOK. WPI DOES NOT WARRANT THAT THE FUNCTIONS CONTAINED IN THE SOFTWARE WILL MEET YOUR REQUIREMENTS OR THAT THE OPERATION OF THE SOFTWARE WILL BE ERROR FREE.

(c) This limited warranty gives you specific legal rights, and you may have other rights that vary from jurisdiction to jurisdiction.

6. **Remedies.**

(a) WPI's entire liability and your exclusive remedy for defects in materials and workmanship shall be limited to replacement of the Software Media, which may be returned to WPI with a copy of your receipt at the following address: Software Media Fulfillment Department, Attn.: *Streaming Media*, Wiley Publishing, Inc., 10475 Crosspoint Blvd., Indianapolis, IN 46256, or call 1-800-762-2974. Please allow four to six weeks for delivery. This Limited Warranty is void if failure of the Software Media has resulted from accident, abuse, or misapplication. Any replacement Software Media will be warranted for the remainder of the original warranty period or thirty (30) days, whichever is longer.

(b) In no event shall WPI or the author be liable for any damages whatsoever (including without limitation damages for loss of business profits, business interruption, loss of business information, or any other pecuniary loss) arising from the use of or inability to use the Book or the Software, even if WPI has been advised of the possibility of such damages.

(c) Because some jurisdictions do not allow the exclusion or limitation of liability for consequential or incidental damages, the above limitation or exclusion may not apply to you.

7. **U.S. Government Restricted Rights.** Use, duplication, or disclosure of the Software for or on behalf of the United States of America, its agencies and/or instrumentalities "U.S. Government" is subject to restrictions as stated in paragraph (c)(1)(ii) of the Rights in Technical Data and Computer Software clause of DFARS 252.227-7013, or subparagraphs (c) (1) and (2) of the Commercial Computer Software - Restricted Rights clause at FAR 52.227-19, and in similar clauses in the NASA FAR supplement, as applicable.

8. **General.** This Agreement constitutes the entire understanding of the parties and revokes and supersedes all prior agreements, oral or written, between them and may not be modified or amended except in a writing signed by both parties hereto that specifically refers to this Agreement. This Agreement shall take precedence over any other documents that may be in conflict herewith. If any one or more provisions contained in this Agreement are held by any court or tribunal to be invalid, illegal, or otherwise unenforceable, each and every other provision shall remain in full force and effect.